SOLARO
STUDY GUIDE

Mathematics 7

SOLARO Study Guide is designed to help students achieve success in school. The content in each study guide is 100% curriculum aligned and serves as an excellent source of material for review and practice. To create this book, teachers, curriculum specialists, and assessment experts have worked closely to develop the instructional pieces that explain each of the key concepts for the course. The practice questions and sample tests have detailed solutions that show problem-solving methods, highlight concepts that are likely to be tested, and point out potential sources of errors. **SOLARO Study Guide** is a complete guide to be used by students throughout the school year for reviewing and understanding course content, and to prepare for assessments.

Rao, Gautam, 1961 –
SOLARO STUDY GUIDE – Mathematics 7 (2013 Edition) Common Core State Standards

1. Mathematics – Juvenile Literature. I. Title

Castle Rock Research Corporation
2410 Manulife Place
10180 – 101 Street
Edmonton, AB T5J 3S4

1 2 3 MP 15 14 13

Printed in the United States of America

Publisher
Gautam Rao

Dedicated to the memory of Dr. V. S. Rao

THE *SOLARO STUDY GUIDE*

The *SOLARO Study Guide* is designed to help students achieve success in school and to provide teachers with a road map to understanding the concepts of the Common Core State Standards. The content in each study guide is 100% curriculum aligned and serves as an excellent source of material for review and practice. The *SOLARO Study Guide* introduces students to a process that incorporates the building blocks upon which strong academic performance is based. To create this resource, teachers, curriculum specialists, and assessment experts have worked closely to develop instructional pieces that explain key concepts. Every exercise question comes with a detailed solution that offers problem-solving methods, highlights concepts that are likely to be tested, and points out potential sources of errors.

The *SOLARO Study Guide* is intended to be used for reviewing and understanding course content, to prepare for assessments, and to assist each student in achieving their best performance in school.

The *SOLARO Study Guide* consists of the following sections:

TABLE OF CORRELATIONS

The Table of Correlations is a critical component of the *SOLARO Study Guide*.

Castle Rock Research has designed the *SOLARO Study Guide* by correlating each question and its solution to Common Core State Standards. Each unit begins with a Table of Correlations, which lists the standards and questions that correspond to those standards.

For students, the Table of Correlations provides information about how each question fits into a particular course and the standards to which each question is tied. Students can quickly access all relevant content associated with a particular standard.

For teachers, the Table of Correlations provides a road map for each standard, outlining the most granular and measurable concepts that are included in each standard. It assists teachers in understanding all the components involved in each standard and where students are excelling or require improvement. The Table of Correlations indicates the instructional focus for each content strand, serves as a standards checklist, and focuses on the standards and concepts that are most important in the unit and the particular course of study.

Some concepts may have a complete lesson aligned to them but cannot be assessed using a paper-and-pencil format. These concepts typically require ongoing classroom assessment through various other methods.

LESSONS

Following the Table of Correlations for each unit are lessons aligned to each concept within a standard. The lessons explain key concepts that students are expected to learn according to Common Core State Standards.

As each lesson is tied to state standards, students and teachers are assured that the information will be relevant to what is being covered in class.

EXERCISE QUESTIONS

Each set of lessons is followed by two sets of exercise questions that assess students on their understanding of the content. These exercise questions can be used by students to give them an idea of the type of questions they are likely to face in the future in terms of format, difficulty, and content coverage.

DETAILED SOLUTIONS

Some study guides only provide an answer key, which will identify the correct response but may not be helpful in determining what led to the incorrect answer. Every exercise question in the *SOLARO Study Guide* is accompanied by a detailed solution. Access to complete solutions greatly enhances a student's ability to work independently, and these solutions also serve as useful instructional tools for teachers. The level of information in each detailed solution is intended to help students better prepare for the future by learning from their mistakes and to help teachers discern individual areas of strengths and weaknesses.

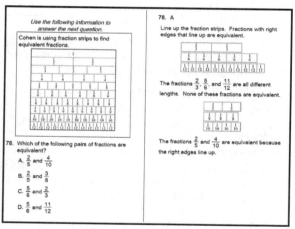

For the complete curriculum document, visit www.corestandards.org/the-standards.

SOLARO Study Guides are available for many courses. Check www.solaro.com/orders for a complete listing of books available for your area.

For more enhanced online resources, please visit www.SOLARO.com.

Student-Oriented Learning, Assessment, and Reporting Online

solaro

SOLARO is an online resource that provides students with regionally and age-appropriate lessons and practice questions. Students can be confident that SOLARO has the right materials to help them when they are having difficulties in class. SOLARO is 100% compliant with each region's core standards. Teachers can use SOLARO in the classroom as a supplemental resource to provide remediation and enrichment. Student performance is reported to the teacher through various reports, which provide insight into strengths and weaknesses.

TABLE OF CONTENTS

CREDITS

Every effort has been made to provide proper acknowledgement of the original source and to comply with copyright law. However, some attempts to establish original copyright ownership may have been unsuccessful. If copyright ownership can be identified, please notify Castle Rock Research Corp so that appropriate corrective action can be taken.

Some images in this document may be from www.clipart.com, copyright (c) 2013 Getty images.

Some images in this document may be from www.nasa.com.

Some images may be from National Atmospheric and Oceanic Administration http://www.noaa.gov/.

Some images may be from www.usgs.gov/.

NOTES

Key Tips for Being Successful at School

KEY TIPS FOR BEING SUCCESSFUL AT SCHOOL

KEY FACTORS CONTRIBUTING TO SCHOOL SUCCESS

In addition to learning the content of your courses, there are some other things that you can do to help you do your best at school. You can try some of the following strategies:

- **Keep a positive attitude:** Always reflect on what you can already do and what you already know.

- **Be prepared to learn:** Have the necessary pencils, pens, notebooks, and other required materials for participating in class ready.

- **Complete all of your assignments:** Do your best to finish all of your assignments. Even if you know the material well, practice will reinforce your knowledge. If an assignment or question is difficult for you, work through it as far as you can so that your teacher can see exactly where you are having difficulty.

- **Set small goals for yourself when you are learning new material:** For example, when learning the parts of speech, do not try to learn everything in one night. Work on only one part or section each study session. When you have memorized one particular part of speech and understand it, move on to another one. Continue this process until you have memorized and learned all the parts of speech.

- **Review your classroom work regularly at home:** Review to make sure you understand the material you learned in class.

- **Ask your teacher for help:** Your teacher will help you if you do not understand something or if you are having a difficult time completing your assignments.

- **Get plenty of rest and exercise:** Concentrating in class is hard work. It is important to be well-rested and have time to relax and socialize with your friends. This helps you keep a positive attitude about your schoolwork.

- **Eat healthy meals:** A balanced diet keeps you healthy and gives you the energy you need for studying at school and at home.

How to Find Your Learning Style

Every student learns differently. The manner in which you learn best is called your learning style. By knowing your learning style, you can increase your success at school. Most students use a combination of learning styles. Do you know what type of learner you are? Read the following descriptions. Which of these common learning styles do you use most often?

- **Linguistic Learner:** You may learn best by saying, hearing, and seeing words. You are probably really good at memorizing things such as dates, places, names, and facts. You may need to write down the steps in a process, a formula, or the actions that lead up to a significant event, and then say them out loud.

- **Spatial Learner:** You may learn best by looking at and working with pictures. You are probably really good at puzzles, imagining things, and reading maps and charts. You may need to use strategies like mind mapping and webbing to organize your information and study notes.

- **Kinesthetic Learner:** You may learn best by touching, moving, and figuring things out using manipulatives. You are probably really good at physical activities and learning through movement. You may need to draw your finger over a diagram to remember it, tap out the steps needed to solve a problem, or feel yourself writing or typing a formula.

SCHEDULING STUDY TIME

You should review your class notes regularly to ensure that you have a clear understanding of all the new material you learned. Reviewing your lessons on a regular basis helps you to learn and remember ideas and concepts. It also reduces the quantity of material that you need to study prior to a test. Establishing a study schedule will help you to make the best use of your time.

Regardless of the type of study schedule you use, you may want to consider the following suggestions to maximize your study time and effort:

- Organize your work so that you begin with the most challenging material first.

- Divide the subject's content into small, manageable chunks.

- Alternate regularly between your different subjects and types of study activities in order to maintain your interest and motivation.

- Make a daily list with headings like "Must Do," "Should Do," and "Could Do."

- Begin each study session by quickly reviewing what you studied the day before.

- Maintain your usual routine of eating, sleeping, and exercising to help you concentrate better for extended periods of time.

CREATING STUDY NOTES

MIND-MAPPING OR WEBBING

Use the key words, ideas, or concepts from your reading or class notes to create a mind map or web (a diagram or visual representation of the given information). A mind map or web is sometimes referred to as a knowledge map. Use the following steps to create a mind map or web:

1. Write the key word, concept, theory, or formula in the centre of your page.

2. Write down related facts, ideas, events, and information, and link them to the central concept with lines.

3. Use coloured markers, underlining, or symbols to emphasize things such as relationships, timelines, and important information.

The following examples of a Frayer Model illustrate how this technique can be used to study vocabulary.

Definition	**Notes**
• Perimeter is the distance around the outside of a polygon.	• Perimeter is measured in linear units (e.g., metres, centimetres, and so on).

Perimeter

Examples	**Non-Examples**
• The length of a fence around a yard	• The area of grass covering a lawn
• The distance around a circle (circumference)	• The size of a rug lying on a floor

Definition	**Notes**
• A cube is a solid 3-D object with six faces.	• A cube is different from other shapes because it has six equally-sized square faces, eight vertices, and twelve equal edges.

Cube

Examples	**Non-Examples**
	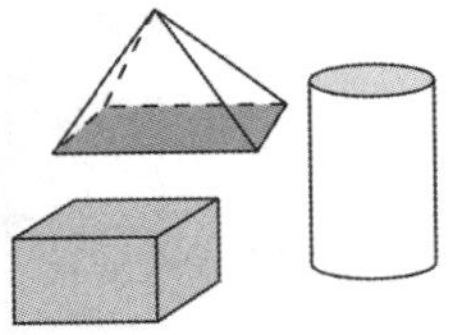

INDEX CARDS

To use index cards while studying, follow these steps:

1. Write a key word or question on one side of an index card.

2. On the reverse side, write the definition of the word, answer to the question, or any other important information that you want to remember.

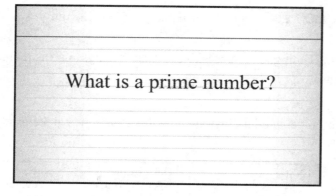

SYMBOLS AND STICKY NOTES—IDENTIFYING IMPORTANT INFORMATION

Use symbols to mark your class notes. The following are some examples:

- An exclamation mark (!) might be used to point out something that must be learned well because it is a very important idea.

- A question mark (?) may highlight something you are not certain about

- A diamond (◊) or asterisk (*) could highlight interesting information that you want to remember.

Sticky notes are useful in the following situations:

- Use sticky notes when you are not allowed to put marks in books.

- Use sticky notes to mark a page in a book that contains an important diagram, formula, explanation, or other information.

- Use sticky notes to mark important facts in research books.

MEMORIZATION TECHNIQUES

- **Association** relates new learning to something you already know. For example, to remember the spelling difference between dessert and desert, recall that the word *sand* has only one *s*. So, because there is sand in a desert, the word *desert* has only one *s*.

- **Mnemonic** devices are sentences that you create to remember a list or group of items. For example, the first letter of each word in the phrase "Every Good Boy Deserves Fudge" helps you to remember the names of the lines on the treble-clef staff (E, G, B, D, and F) in music.

- **Acronyms** are words that are formed from the first letters or parts of the words in a group. For example, RADAR is actually an acronym for Radio Detecting and Ranging, and MASH is an acronym for Mobile Army Surgical Hospital. HOMES helps you to remember the names of the five Great Lakes (Huron, Ontario, Michigan, Erie, and Superior).

- **Visualizing** requires you to use your mind's eye to "see" a chart, list, map, diagram, or sentence as it is in your textbook or notes, on the chalkboard or computer screen, or in a display.

- **Initialisms** are abbreviations that are formed from the first letters or parts of the words in a group. Unlike acronyms, an initialism cannot be pronounced as a word itself. For example, GCF is an initialism for **G**reatest **C**ommon **F**actor.

KEY STRATEGIES FOR REVIEWING

Reviewing textbook material, class notes, and handouts should be an ongoing activity. Spending time reviewing becomes more critical when you are preparing for a test. You may find some of the following review strategies useful when studying during your scheduled study time:

- Before reading a selection, preview it by noting the headings, charts, graphs, and chapter questions.

- Before reviewing a unit, note the headings, charts, graphs, and chapter questions.

- Highlight key concepts, vocabulary, definitions, and formulas.

- Skim the paragraph, and note the key words, phrases, and information.

- Carefully read over each step in a procedure.

- Draw a picture or diagram to help make the concept clearer.

KEY STRATEGIES FOR SUCCESS: A CHECKLIST

Reviewing is a huge part of doing well at school and preparing for tests. Here is a checklist for you to keep track of how many suggested strategies for success you are using. Read each question, and put a check mark (✓) in the correct column. Look at the questions where you have checked the "No" column. Think about how you might try using some of these strategies to help you do your best at school.

Key Strategies for Success	Yes	No
Do you attend school regularly?		
Do you know your personal learning style—how you learn best?		
Do you spend 15 to 30 minutes a day reviewing your notes?		
Do you study in a quiet place at home?		
Do you clearly mark the most important ideas in your study notes?		
Do you use sticky notes to mark texts and research books?		
Do you practise answering multiple-choice and written-response questions?		
Do you ask your teacher for help when you need it?		
Are you maintaining a healthy diet and sleep routine?		
Are you participating in regular physical activity?		

Ratios and Proportional Relationships

RATIOS AND PROPORTIONAL RELATIONSHIPS

Table of Correlations

Standard		Concepts	Exercise #1	Exercise #2
7.RP	Ratios and Proportional Relationships			
7.RP.1	*Compute unit rates associated with ratios of fractions, including ratios of lengths, areas and other quantities measured in like or different units.*	Dividing Fractions	1	25
		Calculating Unit Rates	2	26
		Identifying Equivalent Ratios	3	27
		Using a Ratio to Represent a Real-Life Situation	4	28
7.RP.2A	*Recognize and represent proportional relationships between quantities. Decide whether two quantities are in a proportional relationship.*	Identifying Equivalent Ratios	3	27
		Representing Proportional Relationships Using Tables	5	29
		Using a Table of Values to Graph a Linear Relation	6	30
		Determining if Two Ratios Are in Proportion	7	31
7.RP.2B	*Recognize and represent proportional relationships between quantities. Identify the constant of proportionality (unit rate) in tables, graphs, equations, diagrams, and verbal descriptions of proportional relationships.*	Calculating Unit Rates	2	26
7.RP.2C	*Recognize and represent proportional relationships between quantities. Represent proportional relationships by equations.*	Calculating Unit Rates	2	26
7.RP.2D	*Recognize and represent proportional relationships between quantities. Explain what a point (x, y) on the graph of a proportional relationship means in terms of the situation, with special attention to the points (0, 0) and (1, r) where r is the unit rate.*	Analyzing Graphs of Two-Variable Linear Relations	8	32
7.RP.3	*Use proportional relationships to solve multistep ratio and percent problems.*	Calculating Simple Interest	9	33
		Calculating Discounts	10	34
		Calculating Percentage Increase	11	35
		Converting Decimals to Percentages	12	36
		Converting Percentages to Decimals	13	37
		Converting Percentages to Decimals	13	37
		Comparing Rates	14	38
		Calculating Simple Commission	15	39
		Calculating Sales Tax	16	40
		Calculating Relative Error	17	41
		Calculating the Percentage of a Quantity	18	42
		Calculating the Whole Given a Part and a Percentage	19	43
		Calculating Percentages Given the Whole and a Part	20	44

		Setting up Proportions	21	48
		Using Proportions to Solve Problems	22	45
		Dividing a Quantity According to a Given Ratio	23	46
		Using Equivalent Fractions to Find a Missing Number	24	47

7.RP.1 Compute unit rates associated with ratios of fractions, including ratios of lengths, areas and other quantities measured in like or different units.

DIVIDING FRACTIONS

A strategy for dividing fractions is to use the multiplicative inverse.

If the product of two fractions is equal to one, we say that the two fractions are multiplicative inverses of one another.

For example, $\frac{2}{3} \times \frac{3}{2} = 1$, therefore $\frac{2}{3}$ and $\frac{3}{2}$ are multiplicative inverses.

Another word for multiplicative inverses is reciprocal.

In order to divide fractions, you must multiply the first fraction by the reciprocal of the second fraction. In other words, change the division sign into a multiplication sign and flip the second fraction upside down.

$$\frac{a}{b} \div \frac{c}{d} = \frac{a}{b} \times \frac{d}{c}$$

If necessary, reduce the resulting fraction to lowest terms and convert any improper fractions into mixed numbers.

Example

Simplify $\frac{1}{5} \div \frac{1}{4}$.

Solution

Step 1
Write the reciprocal of the second fraction.

The reciprocal of $\frac{1}{4}$ is $\frac{4}{1}$.

Step 2
Multiply the first fraction by the reciprocal of the second fraction.

Multiply numerator by numerator and denominator by denominator.

$$\frac{1}{5} \times \frac{4}{1} = \frac{1 \times 4}{5 \times 1} = \frac{4}{5}$$

Step 3
Reduce the fraction to lowest terms.

Since the only common factor shared by 4 and 5 is 1, the product is already in lowest terms.

The quotient of $\frac{1}{5}$ and $\frac{1}{4}$ is $\frac{4}{5}$.

In order to divide a fraction by a whole number, change the whole number into a fraction by giving it a denominator of 1.

Example

Simplify $\frac{4}{6} \div 4$.

Solution

Step 1
Write the reciprocal of the second fraction.

Change the whole number 4 into a fraction by giving it a denominator of 1: $\frac{4}{1}$.

The reciprocal of $\frac{4}{1}$ is $\frac{1}{4}$.

Step 2
Multiply the first fraction by the reciprocal of the second fraction.

Multiply numerator by numerator and denominator by denominator.

$$\frac{4}{6} \times \frac{1}{4} = \frac{4 \times 1}{6 \times 4} = \frac{4}{24}$$

Step 3
Reduce the fraction to lowest terms.

The greatest common factor of 4 and 24 is 4, so divide the numerator and denominator by 4.

$$\frac{4 \div 4}{24 \div 4} = \frac{1}{6}$$

Expressed in lowest terms, the quotient of $\frac{4}{6}$ and 4 is $\frac{1}{6}$.

When an improper fraction is the quotient, the reduced fraction should be changed to a mixed number.

Example

Simplify $\dfrac{5}{6} \div \dfrac{4}{6}$.

Solution

Step 1

Write the reciprocal of the second fraction.

The reciprocal of $\dfrac{4}{6}$ is $\dfrac{6}{4}$.

Step 2

Multiply the first fraction by the reciprocal. Multiply numerator by numerator and denominator by denominator.

$\dfrac{5}{6} \times \dfrac{6}{4} = \dfrac{5 \times 6}{6 \times 4} = \dfrac{30}{24}$

Step 3

Reduce the fraction to lowest terms.

Since the greatest common factor of 30 and 24 is 6, divide the numerator and denominator by 6.

$\dfrac{30 \div 6}{24 \div 6} = \dfrac{5}{4}$

Step 4

Change the reduced improper fraction to a mixed number.

Numerator of improper fraction ÷ Denominator

$= \text{Quotient} + \dfrac{\text{Remainder}}{\text{Denominator}}$.

$5 \div 4 = 1 + \dfrac{1}{4}$

$\qquad = 1\dfrac{1}{4}$

Expressed in lowest terms, the quotient of $\dfrac{5}{6}$ and $\dfrac{4}{6}$ is $1\dfrac{1}{4}$.

When you solve word problems, look for keywords that tell you what operation to perform. Some division keywords are *quotient*, *times greater*, *times less than*, and *groups*.

Example

Eric wants to split his hanging flower box into 5 equal sections.

If his flower box is $\dfrac{5}{8}$ m^2, how big will each section be?

Solution

Step 1

Identify information and the operation.

Flower box is split into 5 equal sections

The keyword *split* indicates division.

$\dfrac{5}{8} \div 5$

Step 2

Write the reciprocal of the second fraction.

The reciprocal of $\dfrac{5}{1}$ is $\dfrac{1}{5}$.

Step 3

Multiply the first fraction by the reciprocal. Multiply the numerator by the numerator and the denominator by the denominator.

$\dfrac{5}{8} \times \dfrac{1}{5} = \dfrac{5 \times 1}{8 \times 5} = \dfrac{5}{40}$

Step 4

Reduce the fraction to lowest terms.

5 and 40 share a common factor of 5.

$\dfrac{5 \div 5}{40 \div 5} = \dfrac{1}{8}$

Each section of the flower box will be $\dfrac{1}{8}$ m^2.

CALCULATING UNIT RATES

Total cost per number of units can also be described as **unit rate**.

Rate is a comparison of two items that are measured in different units. As one of the items change, it causes a change in the second item. The relationship between the two items can be used to solve problems.

Rate comparisons often involve money. A unit rate is a rate in which the second measure is 1.
For example, if 5 kg of potatoes cost $10.00, then 1 kg of potatoes costs $2.00.

To change a **rate** into a **unit rate**:

1. Divide the first term by the second term.
2. Write the units of measurement beside the result. The units should go after the unit rate, except for units in dollars.

Example

Allison charged $30.00 for babysitting for 5 h.

How much does she make per hour?

Solution

Step 1
Write the rate.

The rate is $\dfrac{\$30.00}{5\,h}$.

Step 2
Calculate the unit rate. The unit rate is Allison's hourly wage.
Divide the first term ($30.00) by the second term (5 h).
30 ÷ 5 = 6
Rates are written symbolically or in word form.

Symbolically, $\dfrac{\$30.00}{5\,h} = \dfrac{\$6.00}{h}$ or $6.00/h

In words, this rate can be written as "six dollars per hour."
The value of the denominator, 1, does not need to be written.
Allison makes $6.00 per hour.

Example

In a candy store, a sign says that chocolate fudge costs $2 per 100 g.

What is the cost of the chocolate fudge per gram?

Solution

Since 100 grams of fudge cost $2, divide $2 by 100 to get the cost of 1 gram.
$2.00 ÷ 100 = $0.02

A quick way to divide by 100 is to move the decimal point 2 places to the left. For this problem, you need to add a zero before the 2 to have 2 places.
2.00 → 0.02

The cost of 1 g of chocolate fudge is $0.02.

IDENTIFYING EQUIVALENT RATIOS

A ratio is a way to compare two or more quantities. It is possible to write the same ratio in different ways.

Example
Leon's lunch has a container with 12 grapes and 6 strawberries.

He says that the ratio of grapes to strawberries is 12:6.

His friend Nina says he can put the fruit into groups of 2. Then, there are 6 groups of grapes and 3 groups of strawberries, so the ratio is 6:3.

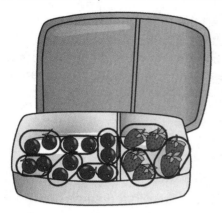

Sean says to make parts with 6 pieces of fruit in each part. Then, there will be 2 parts of grapes and 1 part of strawberries, so the ratio is 2:1.

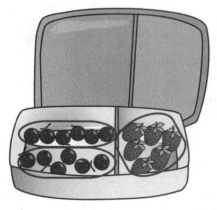

All of the children are correct. The ratios 12:6, 6:3, and 2:1 are all equal to each other.

Example
To find equivalent ratios, multiply or divide each term of a ratio by the same number.

One way to find a ratio that is equal to 6:8 is to multiply both sides of the ratio by 3.6:8 = 18:24

$$\times 3 \left(\begin{array}{c} 6:8 \\ 18:24 \end{array}\right) \times 3$$

Another way to find an equivalent ratio is to divide both sides of the ratio by 2.6:8 = 3:4

$$\div 2 \left(\begin{array}{c} 6:8 \\ 3:4 \end{array}\right) \div 2$$

This is very similar to finding equivalent fractions. If you find it easier to work with fractions than ratios, then you can convert the ratios to fractions as long as you remember to change them back to ratios.

$$\begin{array}{ll} 6:8 & 6:8 \\ = \dfrac{6}{8} & = \dfrac{6}{8} \\ = \dfrac{6 \times 3}{8 \times 3} & = \dfrac{6 \div 2}{8 \div 2} \\ = \dfrac{18}{24} & = \dfrac{3}{4} \\ = 18:24 & = 3:4 \end{array}$$

The two sides of a ratio should always be whole numbers. If you ever have a ratio with a fraction or a decimal in it, find an equivalent ratio with only whole numbers.

Example
Trudy and Michael each pull all their money out of their pockets. Trudy has $4.00, and Michael has $1.50.

What is the ratio of Trudy's money to Michael's money?

Solution
To write the ratio, the amount of money Trudy has comes first, followed by the amount of money Michael has. The ratio is 4:1.5.

A ratio should never have a decimal number in it. You need to find an equivalent ratio that has only whole numbers. If you multiply each side of the ratio by 2, that will get rid of the decimal.

$$\times 2 \left(\begin{array}{c} 4:1.5 \\ 8:3 \end{array}\right) \times 2$$

The ratio of Trudy's money to Michael's money is 8:3.

USING A RATIO TO REPRESENT A REAL-LIFE SITUATION

When working with ratios, the terms sometimes are given in different units. For example, the ratio of 2 m to 50 cm uses meters and centimeters. Ratios are written as a comparison of two numbers and do not include units. Therefore, before a ratio can be written, the numbers must have the same units.

It does not matter which units the numbers are changed to because once the ratio is simplified, it will always have the same value.

Example

The ratio of 2 m to 50 cm can be written in a ratio that has been simplified. To begin, the units need to be changed so that the terms are both expressed as either centimeters or meters.

If the numbers are both changed to cm, then the ratio would be 200:50. When this is simplified, the ratio is 4:1.

If the numbers are both changed to m, then the ratio would be 2:0.5. When simplified, this becomes 4:1.

Both units result in the same ratio. It is not important which unit is chosen. It is only important that all the terms have the same unit. In this case, it would have been easier to use the smaller unit, centimeters, because using meters resulted in working with a decimal number. This is often the case.

When you are writing a ratio that has terms expressed with different units, use the following steps:

1. Convert the terms to the same unit.
2. Write the ratio with the same unit.
3. Write the ratio in simplest terms.

Example

Write 240 min to 2 h to 1 day as a ratio in its simplest form.

Solution

Step 1

Convert the terms to the same unit.

The three different units given in the question are minutes, hours, and days. Hours will be the easiest unit to work with, so convert all three numbers to hours.

- 240 min = 4 h
- 2 h = 2 h
- 1 d = 24 h

Step 2

Write the ratio with the same units.

240 min to 4 h to 1 d = 4 h to 2 h to 24 h
$\qquad\qquad\qquad\qquad$ = 4:2:24

Step 3

Write the ratio in lowest terms

The greatest common factor of 4, 2, and 24 is 2. Divide each term in the ratio by 2.

$\qquad$ 4:2:24

4 ÷ 2:2 ÷ 2:24 ÷ 2

$\qquad$ 2:1:12

The ratio 240 min to 2 h to 1 day can be written as 2:1:12.

7.RP.2A Recognize and represent proportional relationships between quantities. Decide whether two quantities are in a proportional relationship.

REPRESENTING PROPORTIONAL RELATIONSHIPS USING TABLES

When two values have a proportional relationship, both of the values change according to a constant ratio. For example, if 1 yd is 3 ft, then 2 yd has to be 6 ft, and 3 yd is 9 ft. The number of feet increases by 3 every time the number of yards increases by 1. This relationship will stay the same no matter how many feet or yards there are, so the relationship is proportional.

You can show this relationship using a table of values. List the number of yards in one column and the number of feet in the other.

Yards	Feet
1	3
2	6
3	9
4	12
5	15

Follow these steps to create a table of values:

1. Create an outline for the table with headings.
2. Determine the pattern rule to find the values for the table.
3. Fill in the table with the values.

Example

Todd is learning about ladybugs at school. He finds out that ladybugs have six legs. His teacher asks him to create a table showing the relationship between the number of ladybugs and the total number of legs.

Draw a table that correctly illustrates the relationship between the number of ladybugs and the total number of legs.

Solution

Step 1

Create an outline for the table with headings.

The number of legs will depend on the number of ladybugs, so the first column heading should be "Number of Ladybugs," and the second column heading should be "Total Number of Legs."

Number of Ladybugs	Total Number of Legs

Step 2

Determine the pattern rule to find the values for the table.

Every ladybug has six legs. This means that every time you add a ladybug, you need to add another six legs.

Step 3

Place the correct values in the table.

Number of Ladybugs	Total Number of Legs
1	6
2	12
3	18
4	24

USING A TABLE OF VALUES TO GRAPH A LINEAR RELATION

A **linear relation** is a relationship between two variables. A table of values is used to display values that are true for each variable, given the relationship. The graph of a linear relation is always a straight line.

To graph a linear relation displayed in a table of values, follow these steps:

1. Write the ordered pairs from the table of values.
2. Label the axes of the graph.
3. Plot the ordered pairs on the Cartesian plane.
4. Use a straight edge, such as a ruler, to join the points.

Example

x	y
–2	5
–1	4
0	3
1	2
2	1

Graph the linear relation displayed in the given table of values.

Solution

Step 1
Write the ordered pairs from the table of values.

x	y	(x, y)
–2	5	(–2, 5)
–1	4	(–1, 4)
0	3	(0, 3)
1	2	(1, 2)
2	1	(2, 1)

Step 2
Label the axes of the graph.

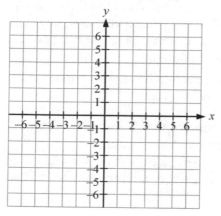

Step 3
Plot the ordered pairs on the Cartesian plane.

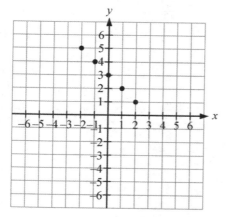

Step 4
Use a straight edge to join the points.

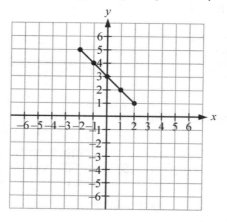

DETERMINING IF TWO RATIOS ARE IN PROPORTION

A proportion is another name for equivalent ratios or equivalent fractions. You can use cross products to test to see if two ratios are in proportion or if two fractions are equivalent.

Example

In order to find if $\frac{3}{4} = \frac{9}{12}$, multiply the numerator of the first fraction by the denominator of the second fraction. Then, multiply the denominator of the first fraction by the numerator of the second fraction. If the cross products are the same, then the two fractions are in proportion.

$$\frac{3}{4} = \frac{9}{12}$$
$$3 \times 12 = 4 \times 9$$
$$36 = 36$$

Both cross products are 36, so the fractions $\frac{3}{4}$ and $\frac{9}{12}$ are in proportion.

Ratios and Proportional Relationships
Castle Rock Research

Cross products can also be used when the proportion is given as ratios. The ratios can be changed into fractions in order to cross-multiply.

Example

Are the ratios 2:3 and 4:5 in proportion?

Solution

Step 1

Convert the ratios into fractions.

$2:3 = 4:5$

$$\frac{2}{3} = \frac{4}{5}$$

Step 2

Cross-multiply the fractions to determine if they are in proportion.

$$\frac{2}{3} = \frac{4}{5}$$

$2 \times 5 = 3 \times 4$

$10 \neq 12$

The ratios are not in proportion because the cross products are not equal.

Did You Know?

You can cross-multiply the ratios without changing them into fractions using the rule "the product of the extremes is equal to the product of the means." The means are the two middle numbers in the proportion. The extremes are the two numbers on the outside of the proportion.

For example, in the proportion 3:5 = 9:15, 5 and 9 are the means and 3 and 15 are the extremes.

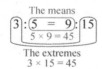

The means
$3 : (5 = 9) : 15$
$5 \times 9 = 45$
The extremes
$3 \times 15 = 45$

When cross-multiplying fractions, these terms are sometimes used as well.

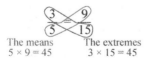

The means   The extremes
$5 \times 9 = 45$ $3 \times 15 = 45$

In both examples, the product of the means equals the product of the extremes, so the ratios are in proportion.

7.RP.2D Recognize and represent proportional relationships between quantities. Explain what a point (x, y) on the graph of a proportional relationship means in terms of the situation, with special attention to the points (0, 0) and (1, r) where r is the unit rate.

ANALYZING GRAPHS OF TWO-VARIABLE LINEAR RELATIONS

A graph is used to show the relationship between two variables. You can begin graphing with a table of values.

A table of values contains the independent variable (the variable that is purposely changed) and the dependent variable (the variable that changes as a result of changing the independent variable). An ordered pair is created by using an independent variable (the *x*-coordinate) and its corresponding dependent variable (the *y*-coordinate). The *x*- and *y*-coordinates are placed in parentheses separated by a comma to create ordered pairs in the form of (x, y).

To interpret any point (x, y) on a graph of linear relations, follow these steps:

1. Locate the known variable along one of the axes.
2. Find its corresponding variable on the other axis.
3. Determine the relationship, and draw conclusions.

Example

One day, Sandy decided to make a graph of the distance she walked in relation to the time it took. She plotted three points.

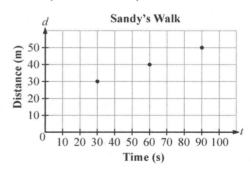

According to the graph, how long did it take Sandy to walk 40 m?

Solution

Step 1
Locate the known variable along one of the axes.

In this case the dependent variable, distance, is given.

Locate 40 m on the vertical axis. Draw a straight horizontal line until the point is reached.

Step 2
Find its corresponding variable on the other axis.

The independent variable is unknown. At this point, draw a straight line down to the time axis.

Step 3
Determine the relationship, and draw conclusions.

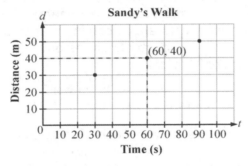

Read the number where the line intersects the time axis. The first number in the ordered pair represents the time and the second number represents the distance.

It takes Sandy 60 seconds to walk 40 m.

Example
According to the graph, how far had Sandy walked after 90 seconds?

Solution

Step 1
Locate the known variable along one of the axes.

In this case the independent variable, time, is given.

Locate 90 seconds on the time axis. Draw a straight line up until the point is reached.

Step 2
Find its corresponding variable on the other axis.

The dependent variable, distance, is unknown. At this point, draw a straight horizontal line to intersect the horizontal axis.

Step 3
Determine the relationship, and draw conclusions.

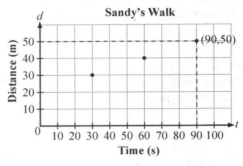

Read the number where the line intersects the distance axis. The first number in the ordered pair represents time, and the second number represents distance.

Sandy walked 50 m in 90 seconds.

7.RP.3 Use proportional relationships to solve multistep ratio and percent problems.

CALCULATING SIMPLE INTEREST

When dealing with financial institutions, interest is usually calculated on loans and deposits. If you borrow money from a bank, you are charged interest for using their money. If you deposit money into a bank, they pay you interest for using your money. The **interest rate** is stated as a percentage of the amount borrowed or deposited for a **period** of time (week, month, or year).

The amount of money borrowed or deposited is called the **principal**. **Simple interest** is calculated on the principal only. It is paid out at the end of the time the money is being invested.

To calculate the interest, use the formula:

interest =   principal (original amount) ×   interest rate (percentage converted to a decimal) ×   time (period)

OR

$i = p \times r \times t$ usually written $i = prt$.

Example

Sally puts $200 in a bank account. Each year, the account earns 8% simple interest.

How much interest will Sally earn in three years?

Solution

Step 1

Match the number with the corresponding part of the formula.

i = the amount of interest is the unknown.

p = she deposited $200.

r = the rate was 8%, which is equal to 0.08.

t = the period is one year, and she will be saving for 3 periods.

Step 2

Substitute the numbers into the formula, and solve for the unknown.

$i = prt$
$= \$200.00 \times 0.08 \times 3$
$= \$48.00$

Sally will earn $48.00 at the end of 3 years.

CALCULATING DISCOUNTS

Stores often put items on sale offering a discounted price. The discount can be stated as a sale price. For example, a shirt can have a regular price of $40.00 and a sale price of $30.00. The discount can also be stated as a percentage of a discount. For example, 20% off.

DETERMINING DISCOUNTED PRICE

To determine the discounted price when given a percentage of a discount, use one of the following methods:

1. Calculate the amount of the discount by multiplying the discount in decimal form by the regular price. Then, subtract this discount from the regular price.
2. Determine what percentage the sale price is of the original by subtracting the percentage of the discount from 100%. Then, convert this percentage to decimal form, and multiply by the regular price.

Example

A movie on DVD has a regular price of $24.95. The video store puts the movie on sale at 20% off.

Determine the sale price of the DVD.

Solution

Method 1

Determine the amount of the discount.

Convert 20% to its equivalent decimal form.

$20\% = \dfrac{20}{100}$, which is equivalent to 0.20.

Multiply this decimal numeral by the regular price.

$0.20 \times \$24.95 = \$4.99$

The discount is $4.99.

Determine the sale price.

Subtract the discount from the regular price.

$\$24.95 - \$4.99 = \$19.96$

The sale price is $19.96.

Method 2

Determine what percentage the sale price is of the regular price.

Subtract the percentage of the discount from 100%.

$100\% - 20\% = 80\%$

Determine the sale price.

Convert 80% to its equivalent decimal form.

$80\% = \dfrac{80}{100}$, which is equivalent to 0.80.

Multiply this decimal numeral by the regular price.

$0.80 \times \$24.95 = \$19.96$

The sale price is $19.96.

DETERMINING THE DISCOUNT AS A PERCENTAGE

To determine the discount as a percentage when given the discounted price, use one of the following methods:

1. Subtract the sale price from the original price to determine the amount of the discount. Then, convert this number to a percentage by dividing by the regular price and multiplying by 100.
2. Covert the sale price to a percentage by dividing by the regular price and multiplying by 100. Then, subtract this from 100%.

Example

A new car with a sticker price of $25,000 is put on sale for $21,500.

Determine the amount of the discount expressed to the nearest percentage.

Solution

Method 1

Determine the amount of the discount.
Subtract the sale price from the sticker price.
$25,000 – $21,500 = $3,500
The amount saved would be $3,500.
Determine the discount as a percentage.
Divide the amount of the discount by the sticker price, and multiply by 100.

$\dfrac{\$3,500}{\$25,000} \times 100 = 14\%$

The discount is 14% of the sticker price.

Method 2

Determine the ratio of the sale price to the sticker price expressed as a percentage.
Divide the sale price by the sticker price, and multiply by 100.

$\dfrac{\$21,500}{\$25,000} \times 100 = 86\%$

The sale price is 86% of the sticker price.
Determine the discount as a percentage.
Subtract the ratio of the sale price to the sticker price as percentages from 100%.
100% – 86% = 14%
The discount is 14% of the sticker price.

COMPARING DISCOUNTS

Sometimes, a shopper wants to compare two discounts. If one item has the discount stated as a reduced price and another item has the discount stated as a percentage, the reduced price must be converted to a percentage before the discounts can be compared.

Example

Two stores sell a dress that has a regular price of $105. One store puts the dress on sale with a discount of 15% off. The second store has a sale price of $86.10.

Determine which store has the better sale price.

Solution

For the second store, the discount needs to be calculated as a percentage.

Method 1

Determine the amount of money saved at the second store.
Subtract the sale price from the regular price.
$105.00 – $86.10 = $18.90
Convert the savings into a percentage.
Divide the amount saved by the regular price, and multiply by 100.

$\dfrac{\$18.90}{\$105.00} \times 100 = 18\%$

Compare the savings at the two stores.
The second store has the better deal because its price is 18% off compared to 15% off at the first store.

Method 2

Determine as a percentage the ratio of the sale price to the regular price.
Divide the sale price by the regular price, and multiply by 100.

$\dfrac{\$86.10}{\$105.00} \times 100 = 82\%$

The sale price is 82% of the regular price.
Determine the discount as a percentage.
Subtract the calculated percentage from 100%.
100% – 82% = 18%
Compare the savings at the two stores.
The second store has the better deal because its price is 18% off compared to 15% off at the first store.

CALCULATING PERCENTAGE INCREASE

To determine the percentage increase in a quantity, divide the amount of the increase by the original amount, and multiply by 100.

$$\text{percentage increase} = \frac{\text{amount of increase}}{\text{original amount}} \times 100$$

Example

Before being renovated, a movie theater had 150 seats. After the renovation, it had 225 seats.

Find the percentage increase in the seating capacity of the theater.

Solution

Step 1
Determine the amount of increase.
Subtract the original number of seats from the final number of seats to find out how many seats were added.
$225 - 150 = 75$

Step 2
Determine the percentage increase.
percentage increase
$= \dfrac{\text{amount of increase}}{\text{original amount}} \times 100$
$= \dfrac{75}{150} \times 100$
$= 50\%$
The seating capacity of the theater has increased by 50%.

CONVERTING DECIMALS TO PERCENTAGES

Decimals and percentages are related to one another. In mathematics, conversions between decimals and percentages are frequently done as a first step in solving problems.

There are two methods of changing a decimal to a percentage.

Method 1—Multiplication
Step 1: Multiply the decimal number by 100.
Step 2: Place a % sign behind the answer.

Example

Express 0.195 as a percentage.

Solution

Step 1
Multiply the decimal number by 100.
$0.195 \times 100 = 19.5$

Step 2
Place a % sign behind the answer.
19.5%
When 0.195 is expressed as a percentage, it is 19.5%.

Method 2—Moving the Decimal
Step 1: Move the decimal point two places to the right.
Step 2: Drop any zeros in front of the whole number.
Step 3: Place a % sign behind the answer.

Example

Express 0.425 as a percentage.

Solution

Step 1
Move the decimal point two places to the right.
$0.425 \rightarrow 42.5$

0.425

Step 2
Drop the zero in front of the whole number.
$42.5 \rightarrow 42.5$

Step 3
Place a % sign behind the answer.
42.5%

Example

Represent 0.7225 as a percentage.

Solution

Method 1

Multiply the decimal by 100. Add the percent sign behind the number.

$0.7225 = 0.7225 \times 100 = 72.25\%$

Method 2

Move the decimal two places to the right.

Delete the zero in front of the number.

Add the percent sign behind the number.

$0.7225 \rightarrow 72.25 \rightarrow 72.25\%$

When 0.7225 is expressed as a percentage, it is 72.25%.

CONVERTING PERCENTAGES TO DECIMALS

A percentage is a number out of 100. Two methods used to convert percentages to decimals are division and moving the decimal.

To convert a percentage to a decimal by dividing, follow these steps:

1. Write the percentage as a fraction.
2. Divide the numerator by the denominator (100).

Example

Use division to express 185% as a decimal number.

Solution

Step 1

Write the percentage as a fraction.

With a percent, the denominator is always 100.

$185\% = \dfrac{185}{100}$

Step 2

Divide the numerator by the denominator (100). Use a calculator, or do long division.

$185 \div 100 = 1.85$

Example

Use division to express 0.85% as a decimal number.

Solution

Step 1

Write the percentage as a fraction.

With a percentage, the denominator is always 100.

$0.85\% = \dfrac{0.85}{100}$

The numerator of a fraction cannot have a decimal number. Remove the decimal by multiplying the numerator and denominator by 100.

$\dfrac{0.85 \times 100}{100 \times 100} = \dfrac{85}{1,000}$

Step 2

Divide the numerator by the denominator (100). Use a calculator, or do long division.

$85 \div 10,000 = 0.0085$

To convert a percentage to a decimal by moving the decimal, follow these steps:

1. Locate the decimal point in the percentage, and remove the percent sign.
2. Move the decimal two places to the left.

Example

Move the decimal to express 185% as a decimal number.

Solution

Step 1

Locate the decimal point in the percentage, and remove the percent sign.

When there is no decimal, it is assumed to be after the last digit in the number.

185.

Step 2

185.

Move the decimal two places to the left.

Expressed as a decimal, 185% is 1.85.

Example
Move the decimal to express 0.85% as a decimal number.

Solution

Step 1
Locate the decimal point in the percentage, and remove the percent sign.
0.85

Step 2
00.85

Move the decimal two places to the left. Zeros are added to fill the places needed as a result of the move.
Expressed as a decimal, 0.85% is 0.0085.

CONVERTING PERCENTAGES TO DECIMALS
A percent is a number out of 100. Two methods used to convert percents to decimals are division and moving the decimal.

To convert a percent to a decimal by dividing, follow these steps:

1. Write the percent as a fraction.
2. Divide the numerator by the denominator 100.

Example
Use division to express 85% as a decimal number.

Solution

Step 1
Write the percentage as a fraction. With a percentage, the denominator is always 100.
$$85\% = \frac{85}{100}$$

Step 2
Divide the numerator by the denominator (100). Use a calculator, or do long division.
$85 \div 100 = 0.85$

To convert a percent to a decimal by moving the decimal, follow these steps:

1. Locate the decimal point in the percent.
2. Move the decimal two places to the left.

Example
Move the decimal to express 85% as a decimal number.

Solution

Step 1
Locate the decimal point in the percentage. When there is no decimal, it is assumed to be after the last digit in the number.
85.

Step 2
Move the decimal two places to the left.

.85

Expressed as a decimal, 85% is 0.85.

Example
Use two methods to express 5% as a decimal.

Solution
Method 1: Division.

Write the percentage as a fraction.
$$5\% = \frac{5}{100}$$

Divide the numerator by the denominator (100).
$5 \div 100 = 0.05$

Method 2: Move the decimal.

Locate the decimal point in the percentage.
5.

Move the decimal two places to the left.

.05

Expressed as a decimal, 5% is 0.05.

COMPARING RATES

A **rate** is a comparison of two items that are measured in different units. A **unit rate** compares two items, but the second item must have a unit of 1. The rate someone charges per hour is a common unit rate. The cost of fruit per kilogram is another common unit rate.

When comparing the cost of merchandise, a unit rate must be calculated before determining the better value. To calculate the better value, follow these steps:

1. From the given rate, calculate the unit rate of each item.
2. Compare the unit rates.

Example

In a local grocery store, tuna is sold in packs of 6 or in cases of 24. The pack of 6 costs $7.68 before tax. The case of 24 costs $26.88 before tax.

Which is the better value?

Solution

Step 1
From the given rate, calculate the unit rate of each item.
Divide the numerator by the denominator.

Rate	Unit Rate
$7.68 / 6 cans	7.68 ÷ 6 = $1.28 / can
$26.88 / 24 cans	26.88 ÷ 24 = $1.12 / can

Step 2
Compare the unit rates.
Since $1.28 per can is more than $1.12 per can, buying the tuna by the case is the better value.

CALCULATING SIMPLE COMMISSION

Many people working in sales do not earn a regular wage, but instead are paid commission as an incentive to sell more of the product.

Commission is money earned by the salesperson that is a percentage of the total amount of sales.

To determine the commission earned by a salesperson, the percentage is multiplied by the total amount of sales.

Example

Gary, a used-car salesman, receives 7.5% commission on all his sales.

If Gary sells a truck for $9,000, how much does he earn in commission?

Solution

Step 1
Convert the percentage to a decimal.
7.5% = 0.075

Step 2
Multiply the decimal by the amount of the sale.
0.075 × 9,000 = 675

Gary earns a commission of $675.00 for selling the truck.

To determine the commission rate as a percentage, divide the commission by the total sales and multiply by 100.

Example

In one month, a real estate agent earned $10,200.00 in simple commission on sales of $566,667.00.

Expressed to the nearest tenth of a percentage, determine the rate of commission paid to the real estate agent.

Solution

To determine the commission rate as a percentage, divide the commission by the total earnings and multiply by 100.

$$\frac{\$10,200}{\$566,667} \times 100 = 1.8\%$$

The real estate agent earns commission at a rate of 1.8% on the total sales.

CALCULATING SALES TAX

Calculating sales tax is calculating a percentage increase. There can be two percentages added to the price of goods: a local tax and a higher level of government tax. Because the percentages are applied to money, the resulting number is rounded to the hundredths place value.

To calculate the increase in price from sales tax, follow these steps:

1. Calculate the tax or taxes.
2. Add the tax or taxes to the original price.

Example

A CD costs $19.99.

Calculate the total cost after the state tax of 8.25% is added.

Solution

Step 1

Calculate the tax.

Multiply the price by the decimal equivalent of the tax. The decimal equivalent of 8.25% is 0.0825.

$19.99 × 0.0825
  = 1.649175
  ≈ $1.65

The state tax on a compact disc that costs $19.99 is approximately $1.65.

Step 2

Add the tax to the price of the CD.
$19.99 + $1.65 = $21.64
The total cost of the CD after tax is $21.64.

When two taxes are applied to the original price, calculate each of the taxes separately, then add both to the original price.

Example

A can of shaving cream costs $4.59.
The government tax is 5%, and the local tax is 6%.

What is the total cost of the shaving cream?

Solution

Step 1

Calculate the tax.

Calculate the government tax.

$$4.59 × 5\% = 4.59 × \frac{5}{100}$$
$$= 4.59 × 0.05$$
$$= \$0.23$$

Calculate the local.

$$4.59 × 6\% = 4.59 × \frac{6}{100}$$
$$= 4.59 × 0.06$$
$$= \$0.27$$

Add the two taxes together.
0.23 + 0.27 = $0.50

Step 2

Add the total tax to the original cost of the shaving cream.
4.59 + 0.50 = $4.99

The total cost including the taxes is $4.99.

CALCULATING RELATIVE ERROR

If you make a mistake when you are measuring something, the size of your error depends on the size of the thing that you are measuring.
For example, if your pencil is 6 in long but you say that it is 7 in long, that is quite a large error. If you say that the length of your classroom is 9 yd, but it is actually 1 in larger, the error is very small.

The size of your error compared to the size of the thing that you are measuring is called **relative error**. To calculate relative error, divide the size of the error by the correct measurement. You can multiply the number you get by 100 to express relative error as a percent.

Example

To calculate the relative errors of the mistaken measurements of the pencil and the classroom, use the formula relative error = $\dfrac{\text{size of error}}{\text{correct measure}}$.

PENCIL

In the case of the pencil, the size of the error is 1 in and the correct measurement is 6 in.

relative error = $\dfrac{\text{size of error}}{\text{correct measure}}$

relative error = $\dfrac{1 \text{ in}}{6 \text{ in}}$

relative error ≈ 0.167

To express this as a percent, multiply by 100.
0.167 × 100 ≈ 16.7%

CLASSROOM

In the case of the classroom, the size of the error is also 1 in. The actual length of the classroom is 1 in larger than 9 yd. Since 9 yd is equal to 324 in, the length of the classroom is 325 in.

relative error = $\dfrac{\text{size of error}}{\text{correct measure}}$

relative error = $\dfrac{1 \text{ in}}{325 \text{ in}}$

relative error ≈ 0.003

To express this as a percent, multiply by 100.
0.003 × 100 ≈ 0.3%

You can see that even though the size of the error is 1 in in both cases, the size of the relative error is much greater in the case of the pencil than in the case of the classroom.

If the size of the error stays the same, the size of the relative error will always be larger for measurements of smaller objects, such as the pencil, than it is for larger objects.

Example

In math class, students are practicing their estimation skills. They need to choose different objects in the classroom, estimate the mass of the objects, then measure the mass to see how close they are. Erin estimates that her pencil case has a mass of 150 g, but when she measures it, she finds that the mass is actually 213 g. Wahid estimates that the mass of his library book is 800 g, but the actual mass is 694 g.

Which student made the better estimate?

Solution

Step 1

Calculate the relative error of Erin's estimate.

She estimated that her pencil case had a mass of 150 g, but the actual mass is 213 g. The size of her error is 63 g. 213 – 150 = 63 g

relative error = $\dfrac{\text{size of error}}{\text{correct measure}}$

relative error = $\dfrac{63}{213}$

relative error ≈ 0.296

Step 2

Calculate the relative error of Wahid's estimate.

He estimated that his book had a mass of 800 g, but the actual mass is 694 g. The size of his error is 106 g. 800 – 694 = 106 g

relative error = $\dfrac{\text{size of error}}{\text{correct measure}}$

relative error = $\dfrac{106}{694}$

relative error ≈ 0.153

Step 3

Compare the size of the relative errors.

Erin's relative error is 0.296 and Wahid's is 0.153. Wahid has a smaller relative error, so his estimate is better.

CALCULATING THE PERCENTAGE OF A QUANTITY

A percentage can be represented as a fraction with a denominator of 100. The fraction can then be expressed as a decimal by dividing the numerator by the denominator.

To find the percentage of a quantity, you can either use equivalent fractions or multiply by the decimal representation of the percentage.

USING EQUIVALENT FRACTIONS

To find the percentage of a number using equivalent fractions, follow these steps:

1. Set up equivalent fractions.
2. Determine the number used to create the equivalent denominator.
3. Multiply or divide the numerator by the same factor.

Example

Using equivalent fractions, find 18% of 200.

Solution

Step 1

Set up equivalent fractions.

Write the percent as the first fraction and the part of the whole as the second fraction. The numerator is represented with a variable (a letter or symbol used to represent an unknown value). The denominator is the given number.

$$\frac{18}{100} = \frac{x}{200}$$

Step 2

Determine the number used to create the equivalent denominator.

The denominator is multiplied by 2 to get 200.

$$\frac{18}{100 \times 2} = \frac{x}{200}$$

Step 3

Multiply the numerator by the same factor.

$$\frac{18 \times 2}{100 \times 2} = \frac{36}{200}$$

18% of 200 is 36.

MULTIPLYING BY THE DECIMAL REPRESENTATION OF THE PERCENTAGE

To find the percentage of a quantity by multiplying by the decimal representation, follow these steps:

1. Convert the percentage to a decimal.
2. Multiply the decimal representation of the percentage by the given number or quantity.

Example

Using the decimal representation of the percentage, find 22% of 120 mm.

Solution

Step 1

Convert the percentage to a decimal. Place the percentage over 100, thereby converting it to a fraction.

$$22\% = \frac{22}{100}$$

Divide 22 by 100.

$$22 \div 100 = 0.22$$

Step 2

Multiply the decimal representation of the percentage by the given quantity.

$$0.22 \times 120 = 26.4$$

Therefore, 22% of 120 mm is 26.4 mm.

CALCULATING THE WHOLE GIVEN A PART AND A PERCENTAGE

There are times when you will be asked to calculate the whole given a number and a percentage. For example, 75 is 20% of what number?

When the percentage is less than 100, the whole number will be smaller than the given part. If the percentage is greater than 100, the whole number will be larger than the given part.

Two methods are used to find a whole given a part and a percentage: equivalent fractions and cross multiplication.

To solve a number given a part and a percentage by using equivalent fractions, follow these steps:

1. Set up equivalent fractions.
2. Determine the number used to create the equivalent fraction.
3. Multiply or divide the numerator or denominator by the same number.

Example

The number 60 is 10% of what number?

Solution

Step 1

Set up equivalent fractions.

Write the percentage as the first fraction and the part of the whole as the second fraction.

The numerator is the given number.

The denominator is represented as the variable x.

$$\frac{10}{100} = \frac{60}{x}$$

Step 2

Determine the number used to create the equivalent numerator.

$$\frac{10 \times 6}{100} = \frac{60}{x}$$

Step 3

Multiply the denominator by the same number to find the value of x.

$$\frac{10 \times 6}{100 \times 6} = \frac{60}{600}$$

The number 60 is 10% of 600.

Example

5 is 25% of what number?

Solution

Step 1

Set up equivalent fractions.

Write the percent as the first fraction and the part of the whole as the second fraction.

The numerator is the given number. Use a variable to represent the denominator.

$$\frac{25}{100} = \frac{5}{x}$$

Step 2

Determine the number used to create the equivalent numerator.

The numerator is divided by 5 to get 5.

$$\frac{25 \div 5}{100} = \frac{5}{x}$$

Step 3

Divide the denominator by the same divisor.

$$\frac{25 \div 5}{100 \div 5} = \frac{5}{20}$$

5 is 25% of 20.

To solve a number given a part and a percentage by using cross multiplication, follow these steps:

1. Set up equivalent fractions.
2. Cross-multiply to solve for the variable.

Example

The number 48 is 12% of what number?

Solution

Step 1

Set up equivalent fractions.

Write the percentage as the first fraction and the part of the whole as the second fraction.

The numerator is the given number.

The denominator is represented as the variable x.

$$\frac{12}{100} = \frac{48}{x}$$

Step 2

Cross-multiply to solve for the variable.

Multiply the numerator of the fraction on the left of the equal sign by the denominator of the fraction on the right of the equal sign. Place that product to the left of the equal sign. Multiply the denominator of the fraction on the left of the equal sign by the numerator of the fraction on the right side of the equal sign. Place that product to the right of the equal sign.

$$\frac{12}{100} = \frac{48}{x}$$

$$12 \times x = 48 \times 100$$

Simplify.

$$12 \times x = 48 \times 100$$
$$12x = 4{,}800$$

Divide both sides by 12.

$$\frac{12x}{12} = \frac{4{,}800}{12}$$
$$x = 400$$

The number 48 is 12% of 400.

CALCULATING PERCENTAGES GIVEN THE WHOLE AND A PART

Percent means "out of 100." The percent symbol (%) is another way to write a fraction with a denominator of 100. For example, 73 out of 100 is the same as $\frac{73}{100} = 73\%$.

If you want to know a percentage of a quantity, you need to write the amount as a fraction first.
Once you have a fraction, there are two ways to convert the fraction to a percentage:

1. Convert the fraction to a decimal.
2. Use equivalent fractions.

CONVERT TO A DECIMAL

You can convert a fraction to a decimal by dividing the numerator by the denominator. You can do this using a calculator or long division.

Example

Chen got 16 out of 22 questions correct on his math quiz.

What percentage, rounded to the nearest whole number, of the questions did he get correct?

Solution

Step 1
Determine the fraction.
The part is the numerator. The whole is the denominator.
The number of correct questions, 16, represents the part.
The total number of questions, 22, represents the whole.

The fraction is $\frac{16}{22}$.

Step 2
Calculate the decimal equivalent of the fraction.
Divide the numerator by the denominator.
$16 \div 22 = 0.7272\ldots$

Step 3
Write the percentage.
Multiply the result by 100, and place a percent sign after the answer.
$0.7272 \times 100 = 72.72\ldots = 72.\overline{72}\%$
Round up to the nearest whole number.
$72.\overline{72}\% \rightarrow 73\%$
Chen got 73% of the questions correct.

EQUIVALENT FRACTIONS

Percentage is another way to write a fraction with a denominator of 100. This means that if you can convert your fraction to become a fraction with a denominator of 100, you can change it to a percentage.

Example

At LollyPop Daycare, 20 children are under the age of five.

If there are 25 children registered at the daycare, what percentage of the children are under the age of five?

Solution

Step 1
Set up equivalent fractions.
Keep the part as the numerator and the whole as the denominator.
$\frac{20}{25} = \frac{x}{100}$

Step 2
Determine the factor used to create the equivalent denominator.
$\frac{20}{25 \times 4} = \frac{x}{100}$
Multiply the numerator by the same factor.
$\frac{20 \times 4}{25 \times 4} = \frac{80}{100}$
At the daycare, 80% of the children are under the age of five.

SETTING UP PROPORTIONS

A proportion is another name for an equivalent ratio. In a proportion, one quantity increases at the same rate as the other one increases.

Example
One week has 7 days. Two weeks have 14 days. These two relationships can be represented by the ratios 1:7 and 2:14. The ratios are equal because the relationship between days and weeks is proportional. You can show the proportional relationship with a pair of equivalent fractions.

$$\frac{1}{7} = \frac{2}{14}$$

Example
These triangles are proportional.

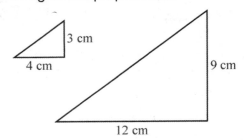

One way to set up a proportion showing the side lengths of the triangles is to have one fraction show the small triangle and the other fraction show the big triangle.

$$\overset{\text{Small triangle}}{}\quad\overset{\text{Big triangle}}{}$$
$$\frac{3}{4} = \frac{9}{12}$$

In both fractions, the numerator is the length of the short side and the denominator is the length of the longer side.

$$\begin{array}{c}\text{Short side}\\ \text{Long side}\end{array}\ \frac{3}{4} = \frac{9}{12}$$

You can tell that the triangles are proportional because both fractions are equal to $\frac{3}{4}$.

Another way to set up the proportion is to have one fraction show the short side length of both triangles and the other fraction show the longer side length of both triangles.

$$\overset{\text{Short side}}{}\quad\overset{\text{Long side}}{}$$
$$\frac{3}{9} = \frac{4}{12}$$

In both fractions, the numerator gives information for the small triangle and the denominator gives information for the big triangle.

$$\begin{array}{c}\text{Small triangle}\\ \text{Big triangle}\end{array}\ \frac{3}{9} = \frac{4}{12}$$

Because the proportion was set up differently, the fractions do not equal the fractions in the first proportion. This is not important as long as the fractions in this proportion are equal. Both fractions are equal to $\frac{1}{3}$.

It does not matter if you set up the fractions according to short side and long side or according to small triangle and big triangle. It is only important to choose a rule for each fraction and a rule for the tops and the bottoms of the fractions.

You can also set up proportions when only three of the values are given. To do this, you need to use a variable to represent the missing value.

Example

Tee Shirt Barn is having a sale on T-shirts, and all the shirts are the same price. Trish buys 2 t-shirts for $18.00. Jackson buys some T-shirts for $27.00.

Write a proportion to describe the relationship between the number of T-shirts purchased and the price paid.

Solution

Step 1

Decide how you will set up the proportion.

There is more than one way to set up this proportion. One way is to put Trish's information in one fraction and Jackson's information in the other. The numerator in both fractions can be the number of shirts purchased and the denominator can be the cost of the shirts.

Step 2

Write the information in the fraction on the left.

The fraction on the left has information about Trish. Trish bought 2 shirts, so the numerator is 2. She paid $18.00, so the denominator is 18.

	Trish
Number of shirts	2
Cost	18

Step 3

Write the information in the fraction on the right.

The fraction on the right has information about Jackson. The number of shirts that he bought is not given in the problem, so you need to use a variable to represent the number of shirts that he bought. The numerator can be the variable s. He paid $27.00, so the denominator is 27.

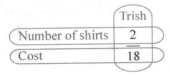

	Trish	Jackson
Number of shirts	2	s
Cost	18	27

USING PROPORTIONS TO SOLVE PROBLEMS

Proportions are equivalent ratios or equivalent fractions. If you are given a problem that involves a proportional relationship, you can use proportional reasoning to solve the problem using the following steps:

1. Identify the ratios given in the problem.
2. Write the ratios as a proportion.
3. Solve the proportion. There are two common ways of solving proportions: using equivalent fractions or using cross multiplication.

Example

Mrs. Hart is ordering 2 pizzas for every 5 students in her class for their year-end party. This works out to 12 pizzas in all.

How many students does Mrs. Hart have in her class?

Solution

Step 1

Identify the ratios.

The ratio of pizzas to students is 2:5.

The number of students in her class can be represented by the variable s. The ratio of the number of pizzas to the number of students is 12:s.

Step 2

Write the ratios as a proportion.

$2:5 = 12:s$

$$\frac{2}{5} = \frac{12}{s}$$

Step 3

Solve the proportion. There are two common ways of solving proportions: using equivalent fractions or using cross multiplication.

Method 1

Use equivalent fractions.

To go from a numerator of 2 to a numerator of 12, multiply by 6.

$$\frac{2}{5} = \frac{12}{s}$$

$$\frac{2 \times 6}{5 \times 6} = \frac{12}{s}$$

$$\frac{12}{30} = \frac{12}{s}$$

$$30 = s$$

Method 2

Use cross multiplication.

Multiply the numerator of each fraction by the denominator of the other fraction, and solve for s.

$$\frac{2}{5} = \frac{12}{s}$$
$$2 \times s = 5 \times 12$$
$$2s = 60$$
$$\frac{2s}{2} = \frac{60}{2}$$
$$s = 30$$

Mrs. Hart has 30 students in her class.

Example

Simone uses a total of 24 green and purple beads to make a bracelet. She makes a pattern that consists of two green beads, one purple bead, two green beads, and one purple bead.

If she follows the same pattern for the whole bracelet, how many purple beads will Simone use?

Solution

Step 1

Identify the ratios.

The number of purple beads that Simone needs can be represented by the variable p. The ratio of purple beads to total beads is $p{:}24$

The ratio of purple beads to green beads is 1:2. To solve the problem, you need to know the ratio of purple beads to total beads. There is 1 purple bead in every group of 3 beads.

The ratio of purple beads to total beads is 1:3.

Step 2

Write the ratios as a proportion.

$1{:}3 = p{:}24$
$$\frac{1}{3} = \frac{p}{24}$$

Step 3

Solve the proportion. There are two common ways of solving proportions: using equivalent fractions or using cross multiplication.

Method 1

Use equivalent fractions.

To go from a denominator of 3 to a denominator of 24, multiply by 8.

$$\frac{1}{3} = \frac{p}{24}$$
$$\frac{1 \times 8}{3 \times 8} = \frac{p}{24}$$
$$\frac{8}{24} = \frac{p}{24}$$
$$8 = p$$

Method 2

Use cross multiplication.

Multiply the numerator of each fraction by the denominator of the other fraction, and solve for p.

$$\frac{1}{3} = \frac{p}{24}$$
$$1 \times 24 = 3 \times p$$
$$24 = 3p$$
$$\frac{24}{3} = \frac{3p}{3}$$
$$8 = p$$

Simone will use 8 purple beads.

DIVIDING A QUANTITY ACCORDING TO A GIVEN RATIO

A ratio shows how different amounts of a quantity are related. When you divide an amount up according to a certain ratio, you take the total quantity, and divide it into two groups. Once the amount has been divided, the simplified ratio of those two groups will be equal to the ratio from the question.

To divide a quantity according to a given ratio, follow these steps:

1. Find the total number of parts in the ratio.
2. Find the quantity per part by dividing the quantity you want to split up by the total number of parts.
3. Find the answer by multiplying each section of the ratio by the quantity per part.

Example

Jamie and her younger brother get an allowance in a ratio of 3:2. That means for every $3 that Jamie gets, her brother gets $2. If Jamie's parents give them a combination of $20 each week, you can divide $20 into a ratio of 3:2 to find out how much they each get for allowance.

The first step is to find the total number of parts in the ratio. If Jamie gets 3 parts, and her brother gets 2 parts, then there are 5 parts in total.

The second step is to find out how much each part is worth. If the 5 parts are equal to $20, then divide 20 by 5 to find out how much each part is worth.
$20 \div 5 = 4$

Each part is worth $4.

- Jamie gets 3 parts, and each part is $4, so multiply 3 by $4 to find out how much she gets for her allowance.
  $3 \times 4 = 12$
- Jamie's brother gets 2 parts, so multiply 2 by $4 to find out how much he gets for his allowance.
  $2 \times 4 = 8$

Jamie will get $12, and her brother will get $8. If you reduce the ratio 12:8, you find that it is equal to 3:2. If you find the sum of $12 and $8, you get a total of $20.

Example

Nolan wants to spend more time studying for his math test than for his science test.
He decides to split his time up in a ratio of 5:3.

If Nolan has 80 min to study, how much time should he spend on each subject?

Solution

Step 1
Find the total number of parts in the ratio. The ratio is 5 parts to 3 parts. There are 8 parts in total because $5 + 3 = 8$.

Step 2
Divide the quantity you are splitting up by the total number of parts.
The quantity you need to split is the time that Nolan has to study. This is 80 min. Divide 80 by 8.
$80 \div 8 = 10$

Step 3
Multiply each section of the ratio by 10 to answer the question.

- Nolan will spend 5 parts of his time on math. Multiply 5 by 10.
  $5 \times 10 = 50$
- Nolan will spend 3 parts on science. Multiply 3 by 10.
  $3 \times 10 = 30$

Nolan will spend 50 min studying for math and 30 min studying for science.

USING EQUIVALENT FRACTIONS TO FIND A MISSING NUMBER

Equivalent fractions can be used to find the missing number in an equation with fractions.
The equivalent fraction strategy works if you have an equation with a fraction on either side of the equal sign and the numerator or denominator of one of the fractions is unknown.

Example

The equation $\frac{1}{2} = \frac{a}{6}$ has a fraction on both sides of the equal sign. To calculate the value of a, find a fraction that is equal to $\frac{1}{2}$ with a denominator of 6.

To go from a denominator of 2 to a denominator of 6, you need to multiply by 3. If you multiply both the numerator and the denominator of $\frac{1}{2}$ by 3, then you will get an equivalent fraction with a denominator of 6.

$$\frac{1}{2} = \frac{1 \times 3}{2 \times 3}$$
$$= \frac{3}{6}$$

If $\frac{1}{2} = \frac{a}{6}$ and $\frac{1}{2} = \frac{3}{6}$, then a must be equal to 3.

Example

What is the value of t in the equation $\dfrac{2}{t} = \dfrac{8}{12}$?

Solution

Step 1

Decide what you need to multiply or divide by to find the equivalent fraction you need.

To go from a numerator of 8 to a numerator of 2, you need to divide by 4.

Step 2

Solve for t.

Divide the numerator and denominator of $\dfrac{8}{12}$ by 4 to find an equivalent fraction with a numerator of 2.

$$\dfrac{2}{t} = \dfrac{8}{12}$$
$$\dfrac{2}{t} = \dfrac{8 \div 4}{12 \div 4}$$
$$\dfrac{2}{t} = \dfrac{2}{3}$$
$$t = 3$$

The value of t is 3.

Example

What is the value of y in the equation $\dfrac{6}{10} = \dfrac{y}{25}$?

Solution

There is no whole number that you can multiply or divide 10 by to get to 25. Try reducing $\dfrac{6}{10}$ to lowest terms.

Step 1

Reduce $\dfrac{6}{10}$ to lowest terms.

$$\dfrac{6}{10} = \dfrac{3}{5}$$

Step 2

Rewrite the equation.

$$\dfrac{6}{10} = \dfrac{y}{25}$$
$$\dfrac{3}{5} = \dfrac{y}{25}$$

Step 3

Decide what you need to multiply or divide by to find the equivalent fraction you need.

To go from a denominator of 5 to a denominator of 25, you need to multiply by 5.

Step 4

Solve for y.

Multiply the numerator and denominator of $\dfrac{3}{5}$ by 5 to find an equivalent fraction with a numerator of 25.

$$\dfrac{3}{5} = \dfrac{y}{25}$$
$$\dfrac{3 \times 5}{5 \times 5} = \dfrac{y}{25}$$
$$\dfrac{15}{25} = \dfrac{y}{25}$$
$$15 = y$$

The value of y is 15.

EXERCISE #1—RATIOS AND PROPORTIONAL RELATIONSHIPS

1. When $\frac{3}{4}$ is divided by $\frac{5}{6}$ the result is

   A. $\frac{3}{5}$ B. $\frac{4}{5}$

   C. $\frac{7}{10}$ D. $\frac{9}{10}$

Use the following information to answer the next question.

> Nicki earned $54 babysitting one night for six hours.

2. What is Nicki's hourly wage?

   A. $7.25   B. $8.50

   C. $9.00   D. $10.00

Use the following information to answer the next question.

> Jarren brings some milk candy bars and some white candy bars to school to share with his friends. At the end of the day, he has $\frac{1}{4}$ of a milk candy bar left and 2 white candy bars. Jarren says that the ratio of milk candy bars to white candy bars is $\frac{1}{4}$:2, but his friends say he cannot have a fraction in a ratio.

3. Which of the following whole number ratios is equivalent to $\frac{1}{4}$:2?

   A. 1:4   B. 1:8

   C. 4:2   D. 4:8

Use the following information to answer the next question.

> Isaac bought a candy bar for 90¢. He also bought a bag of chips for $1.20. The relationship of the cost of the candy bar to the cost of the bag of chips can be written as a ratio.

4. When the ratio is written in its simplest form, the first term of the ratio is _____.

5. The formula for finding the circumference of a circle is $C = \pi d$. If $\pi \approx 3.14$, which of the following tables represents the relationship between the diameter and the circumference of a circle?

   A.
Diameter	Circumference
1	3.14
2	6.28
3	9.42
4	12.56

   B.
Diameter	Circumference
3.14	1
6.28	2
9.42	3
12.56	4

   C.
Diameter	Circumference
1	3.14
2	6.28
3	12.56
4	15.70

   D.
Diameter	Circumference
3.14	1
6.28	2
12.56	3
15.70	4

Copyright Protected

*Use the following information to
answer the next question.*

A table of values for a particular linear relation is given.

x	y
−3	−3
−2	−1
−1	1
0	3
1	5

6. Which of the following graphs illustrates this linear relation?

A.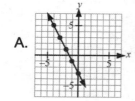

B.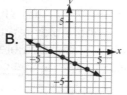

C.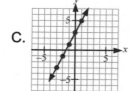

D.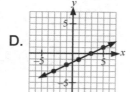

7. Which of the following pairs is in proportion?

A. $\frac{5}{15}$ and $\frac{2}{12}$

B. $\frac{7}{21}$ and $\frac{1}{4}$

C. 8:9 and 2:3

D. 3:12 and 1:4

*Use the following information to
answer the next question.*

The amount of snowfall in a city was monitored for 11 days and is shown on the given graph.

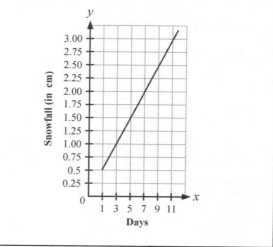

8. How much snow fell every day? _____cm

*Use the following information to
answer the next question.*

Anson borrows some money from a bank at a rate of 10% simple interest for 1 year. Jenny borrows $1,000 more than Anson from another bank at 8% simple interest for 6 months.

9. If the total interest paid by both Anson and Jenny is $740, what is the amount of money Anson borrowed?

A. $1,250   B. $3,750

C. $4,070   D. $5,000

Use the following information to answer the next question.

> A jacket is regularly priced at $149.95. It is on sale for 20% off with no sales tax.

10. How much will the jacket cost on sale? Show both possible methods.

Use the following information to answer the next question.

> Ted is choosing between regular and premium gas for his vehicle. The price of regular gas is 84.9¢/L, and the price of premium gas is 99.0¢/L.

11. Rounded to the nearest tenth, what is the percentage increase in price between the two types of gas?
    A. 2.5%   B. 14.2%
    C. 15.1%   D. 16.6%

12. When it is expressed as a percentage, the decimal number 45.31 is
    A. 4,531%   B. 453.1%
    C. 45.31%   D. 0.4531%

13. Use two methods to convert 8% to a decimal.

Use the following information to answer the next question.

> Tom, Diana, Enrique, and Ahmad tested the fuel efficiency of their vehicles. Tom drove 320 km on 40 L of fuel, Diana drove 390 km on 50 L of fuel, Enrique drove 222 km on 30 L of fuel, and Ahmad drove 152 km on 20 L of fuel.

14. Who has the **most fuel-efficient** vehicle?
    A. Tom   B. Diana
    C. Ahmad   D. Enrique

Use the following information to answer the next question.

> John works in a high-end clothing store and earns 7.5% commission on all his sales. In one particular month, he earned $3,600.

15. Which of the following amounts represents John's total sales for the given month?
    A. $27,000   B. $36,000
    C. $38,700   D. $48,000

Use the following information to answer the next question.

> Yana bought a camera case for $14.75 plus sales tax.

16. If the total bill was $15.49, how much money did Yana spend on sales tax?

Use the following information to answer the next question.

> George said that the driving distance from Seattle to Portland was about 160 mi. When he looked on the Internet, he discovered that it is actually 172 mi.

17. Rounded to the nearest hundredth, what was George's relative error? _____

Use the following information to answer the next question.

The given pie chart shows the percentage distribution of Robert's expenses in a month. His monthly income is $1,500.

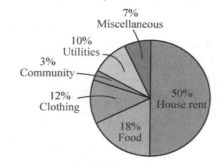

18. How much money does Robert donate to the community?
    A. $30
    B. $45
    C. $50
    D. $60

Use the following information to answer the next question.

Approximately 13.5 million people or 42% of the eligible population voted in the last state election in California.

19. Approximately how many voters were eligible to vote?

Use the following information to answer the next question.

There are 60 men on the official roster of a football team. Their average height is 192 cm, and 12 of the men are taller than average.

20. What is the percentage of men that are taller than 192 cm?
    A. 60%
    B. 48%
    C. 20%
    D. 12%

Use the following information to answer the next question.

Tony is drawing a map of his classroom on some centimeter grid paper. He decides that 1 cm on his map will represent 25 cm in real life. His desk is 75 cm long, so he makes it 3 cm long on the map.

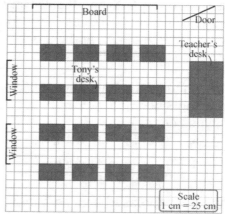

Tony then writes a proportion to show the relationship between the real desk and the desk on the map. He circles the denominators of the two fractions.

$$\frac{1}{3} = \frac{25}{75}$$

21. Both of the denominators give information about the lengths
    A. on the map
    B. of the desk
    C. in the classroom
    D. on the map scale

Manuela plays golf and consistently makes 8 out of 10 putts every time. During her last round of golf, she had to make 15 putts.

22. If she maintains the same consistency, how many of these putts can she expect to make?

    A. 10   B. 11

    C. 12   D. 13

Jamie has 16 lollipops. She wants to give some to her brother, some to her friend, and keep some for herself in a ratio of 1:3:4.

23. How many lollipops will Jamie keep for herself?_____ lollipops

Anton wants to use the equivalent fractions strategy to solve the proportion $\frac{2}{7} = \frac{b}{21}$. He decides to multiply the numerator and denominator of $\frac{2}{7}$ by 3 to find an equivalent fraction with a denominator of 21.

24. What is the value of b? _____

EXERCISE #1—RATIOS AND PROPORTIONAL RELATIONSHIPS   ANSWERS AND SOLUTIONS

1. D	7. D	13. See solution	19. See solution
2. C	8. 0.25	14. A	20. C
3. B	9. D	15. D	21. B
4. 3	10. See solution	16. 0.74	22. C
5. A	11. D	17. 0.07	23. 8
6. C	12. A	18. B	24. 6

1. D

Step 1

Write the reciprocal of the second fraction.

The reciprocal of $\frac{5}{6}$ is $\frac{6}{5}$.

Step 2

Multiply numerator by numerator and denominator by denominator.

$$\frac{3}{4} \times \frac{6}{5} = \frac{3 \times 6}{4 \times 5} = \frac{18}{20}$$

Step 3

Reduce the fraction to lowest terms.

The numbers 18 and 20 share a common factor of 2.

$$\frac{18 \div 2}{20 \div 2} = \frac{9}{10}$$

The quotient of $\frac{3}{4}$ and $\frac{5}{6}$ is $\frac{9}{10}$.

2. C

Step 1

Write the rate.

The rate is $\frac{\$54}{6\,h}$.

Step 2

Calculate the unit rate. The unit rate is Nicki's hourly wage.

Divide the first term, which is $54, by the second term, which is 6 h.

$54 \div 6 = 9$

Step 3

Rates are written symbolically or in word form.

Symbolically, the rate is $\frac{\$54}{6\,h} = \frac{\$9}{h}$, or $9.00/h.

In words, this rate can be written as nine dollars per hour.

3. B

To change to a ratio with no fraction, you need to find a number that multiplies by $\frac{1}{4}$ to equal a whole number. Four quarters is the same as one whole, so

$4 \times \frac{1}{4} = 1$.

Multiply both terms of the ratio by 4.

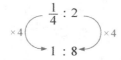

The whole number ratio that is equivalent to $\frac{1}{4}$:2 is 1:8.

4. 3

Step 1

Convert the terms to the same unit.

The dollar value has decimals, so express both values in cents to remove any decimals from the question.

90¢ = 90¢

$1.20 = 120¢

Step 2

Write the ratio with the same unit.

90¢ to $1.20 = 90¢ to 120¢

= 90:120

Step 3

Write the ratio in simplest terms.

The greatest common factor of 90 and 120 is 30.

Divide both terms by 30 to reduce the ratio.

90:120

90 ÷ 30:120 ÷ 30

3:4

The ratio of the cost of the candy bar to the cost of the chips is 3:4. The first term of the ratio is 3.

5. A

Step 1

Determine the pattern rule to find the values for the table.

The circumference of a circle is always π times larger than the diameter of the circle. This means that the circumference increases by π units every time the diameter increases by 1 unit.

Step 2

Place the correct values in the table.

The circumference of the circle will depend on the diameter. Therefore, diameter should go in the first column, and circumference should go in the second column.

Diameter	Circumference
1	3.14
2	6.28
3	9.42
4	12.56

6. C

Step 1

Write the ordered pairs that correspond to the values of x and y in each row of the table of values.

x	y	(x, y)
−3	−3	(−3, −3)
−2	−1	(−2, −1)
−1	1	(−1, 1)
0	3	(0, 3)
1	5	(1, 5)

Step 2

Look at the given graphs, and determine which line passes through the points (−3, −3), (−2, −1), (−1, 1), (0, 3), and (1, 5).

The line shown in graph C passes through the required points; therefore, graph C illustrates the linear relation defined by the given table of values.

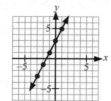

7. D

Cross-multiply each alternative to find if the cross products are equal. If they are equal, then the pair is in proportion.

Step 1

Cross-multiply $\frac{5}{15}$ and $\frac{2}{12}$.

$$\frac{5}{15} = \frac{2}{12}$$
$$5 \times 12 = 15 \times 2$$
$$60 \neq 30$$

The fractions $\frac{5}{15}$ and $\frac{2}{12}$ are not in proportion.

Step 2

Cross-multiply $\frac{7}{21}$ and $\frac{1}{4}$.

$$\frac{7}{21} = \frac{1}{4}$$
$$7 \times 4 = 21 \times 1$$
$$28 \neq 21$$

The fractions $\frac{7}{21}$ and $\frac{1}{4}$ are not in proportion.

Step 3

Write 8:9 and 2:3 as fractions, and then cross-multiply.

$$8:9 = 2:3$$
$$\frac{8}{9} = \frac{2}{3}$$
$$8 \times 3 = 9 \times 2$$
$$24 \neq 18$$

The ratios 8:9 and 2:3 are not in proportion.

Step 4

Write 3:12 and 1:4 as fractions, and then cross-multiply.

$$3:12 = 1:4$$
$$\frac{3}{12} = \frac{1}{4}$$
$$3 \times 4 = 12 \times 1$$
$$12 = 12$$

The ratios 3:12 and 1:4 are in proportion.

8. 0.25

The rate of snowfall increases in a linear pattern. This means that there was a regular increase in the amount of snowfall every day.

According to the graph, there was an additional 0.5 cm of snow every two days. This relationship indicates that 0.25 cm of snow fell every day.

9. D

Step 1

Determine the amount that Anson borrowed.

Anson borrowed money at a rate of 10% interest for 1 year.

Use the interest formula $i = prt$. Let p stand for the amount that Anson borrowed.

$$i = p \times 0.1 \times 1$$
$$= 0.1p$$

Step 2
Determine the amount that Jenny borrowed.
Jenny borrowed some money at a rate of 8% for half a year.
Recall that Jenny borrowed $1,000 more than Anson.
Use the formula $i = prt$. Let p stand for the amount that Anson borrowed.
$$i = (p + 1,000) \times 0.08 \times 0.5$$
$$= 0.04(p + 1,000)$$
$$= 0.04p + 40$$

Step 3
Add the two amounts together to determine the missing value.
The sum of the two interest amounts is $740.
Add both expressions together to determine the amount that Anson originally borrowed.
$$0.1p + (0.04p + 40) = 740$$
$$0.14p + 40 = 740$$
$$0.14p + 40 - 40 = 740 - 40$$
$$0.14p = 700$$
$$\frac{0.14p}{0.14} = \frac{700}{0.14}$$
$$p = 5,000$$
Anson originally borrowed $5,000.

10.

Method 1:
Subtract the discount from the original price.
Calculate the 20% discount by multiplying the original price by the percent, written as a decimal number.
Change the percent to a decimal by moving the decimal two places to the left.
$20\% = 0.20$
Multiply the original price by the decimal.
$149.95 \times 0.20 = 29.99$
The discount is $29.99.
Subtract the discount from the original price to obtain the sale price.
$149.95 - 29.99 = 119.96$
Therefore, the sale price of the jacket is $119.96

Method 2:
Multiply the original price by the percent of the original price.
Determine the percent of the original price.
20% off means the sale price is 80% of the original price.
Change the percent to a decimal by moving the decimal two places to the left.
$80\% = 0.80$
Multiply the original price by the decimal.
$149.95 \times 0.80 = 119.96$
Therefore, the sale price of the jacket is $119.96.

11. D

Step 1
Calculate the amount of increase.
The increase is the difference between 84.9 and 99.0.
$99.0 - 84.9 = 14.1$

Step 2
Calculate the percentage increase.
Divide the amount of increase by the price of regular gas, and multiply by 100.
$$\frac{14.1}{84.9} \times 100 \approx 16.608\%$$
The percentage increase in the price of gas from regular to premium is 16.6%.

12. A

Step 1
Multiply the decimal number by 100.
$45.31 \times 100 = 4,531$

Step 2
Place a percent sign behind the result.
$4,531\%$
Expressed as a percentage, the decimal number 45.31 is 4,531%.

13.

Step 1
Method 1: Division.
Write the percentage as a fraction over 100.
$$8\% = \frac{8}{100}$$
Divide the numerator by the denominator.
$8 \div 100 = 0.08$
Expressed as a decimal, 8% is 0.08.

Exercise #1 Answers and Solutions   44   Castle Rock Research

Step 2

Method 2: Move the decimal.

Locate the decimal point in the percentage.

If it is not written it is placed after the last digit.

8.

Move the decimal two places to the left.

.08

Expressed as a decimal, 8% is 0.08.

14. A

Step 1

Calculate the unit rate for each vehicle.

- Tom's fuel efficiency is $\dfrac{320\ km}{40\ L} = 8$ km/L.

- Diana's fuel efficiency is $\dfrac{390\ km}{50\ L} = 7.8$ km/L.

- Enrique's fuel efficiency is $\dfrac{222\ km}{30\ L} = 7.4$ km/L.

- Ahmad's fuel efficiency is $\dfrac{152\ km}{20\ L} = 7.6$ km/L.

Step 2

Compare the unit rates.

Since Tom can travel 8 km on 1 L of fuel, his vehicle is the most fuel efficient.

15. D

To calculate the total sales, divide John's earnings by the percentage of the commission he is paid. Convert the percentage to a decimal before performing the division.

$3{,}600 \div 7.5\%$
$= 3{,}600 \div 0.075$
$= 48{,}000$

John's total sales for the month were $48,000.

16. 0.74

Let x be the total amount Yana spent on tax.

To find the amount of the sales tax, subtract the price of the camera case from the total cost.

$x = 15.49 - 14.75$
$\quad = 0.74$

The total amount spent on tax is $0.74

17. 0.07

Step 1

Calculate the size of the error.

George's guess was 160 mi, and the actual distance was 172 mi.

$172 - 160 = 12$

Step 2

Calculate the relative error.

relative error $= \dfrac{\text{size of error}}{\text{actual measure}}$

relative error $= \dfrac{12}{172}$

relative error ≈ 0.0698

Rounded to the nearest hundredth, the relative error of George's guess is 0.07.

18. B

Step 1

Locate the percentage on the pie chart that represented the amount he gives to the community. The wedge that represents his donations to the community is equal to 3%.

Step 2

Convert the percentage to a decimal number. Drop the percent sign, and divide the percentage by 100.

$3 \div 100 = 0.03$

Step 3

Multiply Robert's monthly income by the decimal number.

Robert's monthly income is $1,500. The decimal number is 0.03.

$1{,}500 \times 0.03 = \$45$

The amount Robert donates to the community is $45.

19.

Step 1

Set up equivalent fractions.

Write the percent as a fraction over 100, and for the second fraction keep the part as the numerator and the whole as the denominator.

$\dfrac{42}{100} = \dfrac{13.5}{x}$

Step 2

Determine the number used to create the equivalent numerator.

Divide 42 by 13.5.

$42 \div 13.5 \approx 3.1$

Step 3

Divide the denominator by the same number.

$\dfrac{42 \div 3.1}{100 \div 3.1} \approx \dfrac{13.5}{32.3}$

Approximately, 32 million people were eligible to vote in the last state election.

20. C

Step 1

Write a fraction in lowest terms to represent the number of men taller than 192 cm.

The fraction that represents the number of men taller than 192 cm is $\frac{12}{60} = \frac{1}{5}$.

Step 2

Convert the fraction to a percentage.

Multiply the fraction that represents the number of men taller than 192 cm by 100 to obtain the percentage of men taller than 192 cm.

$\frac{1}{5} \times 100 = 20\%$

21. B

In the given proportion, the first fraction shows lengths on the map and the second fraction shows actual lengths in the classroom. The circled row has the numbers 3 and 75.

$$\frac{1}{3} = \frac{25}{75}$$

The number 3 is the length of the desk on the map, and 75 is the actual length of the desk.

	Map	Classroom
Scale	1	25
Desk	3	75

The denominators give information about the lengths of the desk.

22. C

Set up the ratio

$\frac{8}{10} = \frac{x}{15}$

$10x = 8 \times 15$

$10x = 120$

$\frac{10x}{10} = \frac{120}{10}$

$x = 12$

Manuela can expect to make 12 of the 15 putts.

23. 8

Step 1

Find the total number of parts in the ratio.

There are 8 parts in total because $1 + 3 + 4 = 8$.

Step 2

Find the number of lollipops per part.

The quantity that Jamie is dividing is 16 lollipops.

Divide this by 8 because there are 8 parts in the ratio.

$16 \div 8 = 2$

Each part in the ratio has 2 lollipops.

Step 3

Find the answer by multiplying.

Jamie keeps 4 parts to herself. Each part is equal to 2 lollipops. Multiply 2 by 4 to find how many lollipops Jamie will keep.

$2 \times 4 = 8$

Jamie will keep 8 lollipops for herself.

24. 6

Multiply the numerator and denominator of $\frac{2}{7}$ by 3.

$$\frac{2}{7} = \frac{b}{21}$$

$$\frac{2 \times 3}{7 \times 3} = \frac{b}{21}$$

$$\frac{6}{21} = \frac{b}{21}$$

$$6 = b$$

The value of b is 6.

EXERCISE #2—RATIOS AND PROPORTIONAL RELATIONSHIPS

25. If $\frac{36}{54}$ is divided by 19, then the quotient is

   A. $\frac{2}{27}$

   B. $\frac{2}{57}$

   C. $\frac{26,822}{27}$

   D. $\frac{27}{26,822}$

Use the following information to answer the next question.

Jackson spends $300 to purchase 15 cans of paint to finish painting the interior of his house.

26. What is the price for each can of paint?
   A. $10   B. $17
   C. $20   D. $23

Use the following information to answer the next question.

Deena needs to find a ratio that is equivalent to 2:5. She starts by multiplying the first term of the ratio by 8.

27. What is the second term of Deena's equivalent ratio?

28. Write three nickels, two dimes, and two quarters as a ratio in fraction form.

Use the following information to answer the next question.

Maddie travels 2 m for every three steps she takes.

29. Which of the following tables correctly represents the relationship between the number of steps Maddie takes and the distance she travels?

A.

Distance (m)	Number of Steps
3	2
5	5
7	8
9	11

B.

Distance (m)	Number of Steps
2	3
5	5
8	7
11	9

C.

Number of Steps	Distance (m)
3	2
6	4
9	6
12	8

D.

Number of Steps	Distance (m)
2	3
4	6
6	9
8	12

The given table of values represents the linear relation $y = 4x - 1$.

x	y
-2	-9
-1	-5
0	-1
1	3
2	7

30. Which of the following graphs represents this linear relation?

A.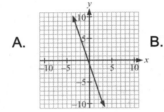

B.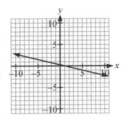

C.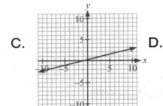

D.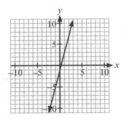

31. Which of the following pairs of ratios is **not** in proportion?

  A. 10:4 and 15:6

  B. 9:3 and 12:4

  C. 3:8 and 8:3

  D. 3:6 and 4:8

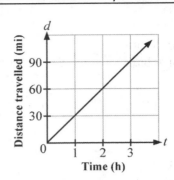

The given graph shows the distance traveled by a car over a period of time.

32. According to the graph, the car is traveling at _____ mph.

An investment of $7,600 earns an interest rate of 4.5% per year.

33. How long will it take for the investment to earn $1,368 in interest? _____ years

34. If a T-shirt that normally sells for $12.50 is sold at 12.5% off, what is the sale price of the T-shirt?

  A. $10.20   B. $10.35

  C. $10.65   D. $10.94

David is training for a marathon. He increases the distance of his daily run every week. During the first week, David ran 7.5 miles each day, and he ran 10.5 miles each day during the second week.

35. Calculate the percentage increase in the number of miles David ran each day during the second week compared to the first week.

3.5 ○ 350%

36. Write the decimal as a percent. Then, insert a >, <, or = sign to make the statement true.

37. Use two methods to convert 33% to a decimal.

Amanda is baking bread and needs to buy flour. She checks four grocery stores to see which offers the best price.

Grocery A	10 kg for $10.00
Grocery B	15 kg for $15.15
Grocery C	20 kg for $19.00
Grocery D	25 kg for $24.50

38. Which grocery store offers the **best** price for flour?
   A. Grocery A   B. Grocery B
   C. Grocery C   D. Grocery D

Harry works at a furniture store and earns 6% commission on all the sales he makes in a month.

39. If Harry sold $18,700 worth of furniture in November, how much commission did he earn that month?

40. Margaret wants to purchase a cooking set that costs $165. If the rate of the sales tax on the purchase is 10%, then the total retail price of the set is
   A. $148.50   B. $155.75
   C. $175.25   D. $181.50

Leslie's teacher asked her to raise her hand when she thought 1 min had passed. After 38 s, Leslie raised her hand.

41. Rounded to the nearest percentage, what is Leslie's relative error? _____%

On a mathematics test, Andrew attempted 70% of the questions. There was a total of 50 questions on the test.

42. How many questions did Andrew attempt?
   A. 35   B. 36
   C. 37   D. 38

The fraction $\frac{1}{5}$ is 8% of x.

43. Which of the following equivalent fractions can be used to solve for x?

A. $\dfrac{8 \times 20}{100 \times 20} = \dfrac{5}{x}$

B. $\dfrac{8 \div 20}{100 \div 20} = \dfrac{5}{x}$

C. $\dfrac{8 \div 20}{100 \div 20} = \dfrac{x}{5}$

D. $\dfrac{8 \times 20}{100 \times 20} = \dfrac{x}{5}$

44. If Sonya scored 36 out of 40 on her babysitting exam, what percentage of the questions did she get correct?

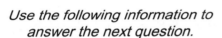

Troy traveled a distance of 50 km on this bike while pedalling at a speed of 30 km/h.

45. For how many hours did Troy ride his bike?

A. $\dfrac{2}{3}$ B. $1\dfrac{2}{3}$

C. $2\dfrac{1}{5}$ D. $3\dfrac{1}{5}$

George has two sunflower plants in his garden. The ratio of the height of one plant to the height of the other is 3:7.

46. If the sum of their heights is 160 cm, what are their respective heights?

A. 48 cm and 112 cm

B. 30 cm and 70 cm

C. 66 cm and 94 cm

D. 60 cm and 140 cm

Alyssa wants to use the equivalent fractions strategy to solve the proportion $\dfrac{2}{6} = \dfrac{5}{n}$.

47. Which of the following steps should Alyssa follow to find the value of n?

A. Multiply the numerator and denominator of $\dfrac{2}{6}$ by 5.

B. Multiply the numerator and denominator of $\dfrac{2}{6}$ by 6.

C. Reduce $\dfrac{2}{6}$ to $\dfrac{1}{3}$, and then multiply the numerator and denominator by 3.

D. Reduce $\dfrac{2}{6}$ to $\dfrac{1}{3}$, and then multiply the numerator and denominator by 5.

Use the following information to answer the next question.

Meena and Vickie are on the school track-and-field committee. They volunteer to make the signs for 12 events. Vickie has a piece of poster board that is 616 in^2, so she cuts it in half and uses it to make signs for 2 of the events.

Meena wants to buy poster board to make the signs for the other 10 events.

She decides to write a proportion to help her figure out the area of poster board that she will need. She uses the variable t to represent the total area of the poster board she will buy.

48. Which of the following proportions could Meena have written?

A. $\dfrac{t}{2} = \dfrac{10}{616}$

B. $\dfrac{10}{2} = \dfrac{616}{t}$

C. $\dfrac{2}{10} = \dfrac{616}{t}$

D. $\dfrac{t}{10} = \dfrac{2}{616}$

EXERCISE #2—RATIOS AND PROPORTIONAL RELATIONSHIPS ANSWERS AND SOLUTIONS

25. B	31. C	37. See solution	43. C
26. C	32. 30	38. C	44. See solution
27. 40	33. 4	39. See solution	45. B
28. See solution	34. D	40. D	46. A
29. C	35. 40	41. 37	47. D
30. D	36. See solution	42. A	48. C

25. B

Step 1

Write the reciprocal of the second fraction.

The reciprocal of 19 is $\frac{1}{19}$.

Step 2

Multiply the first fraction by the reciprocal of the second fraction.

$$\frac{36}{54} \div 19 = \frac{36}{54} \times \frac{1}{19}$$

Multiply numerator by numerator and denominator by denominator.

$$\frac{36}{54} \times \frac{1}{19} = \frac{36 \times 1}{54 \times 19}$$
$$= \frac{36}{1,026}$$

Step 3

Reduce the fraction to lowest terms.

Since the greatest common factor that 36 and 1,026 share is 18, divide the numerator and the denominator each by 18.

$$\frac{36 \div 18}{1,026 \div 18} = \frac{2}{57}$$

Therefore, $\frac{36}{54} \div 19 = \frac{2}{57}$.

26. C

Step 1

Write the rate.

The rate is $\frac{\$300}{15 \text{ cans}}$.

Step 2

Calculate the unit rate for the price of one paint can.

Divide the first term ($300) by the second term (15 cans).

$300 \div 15 = 20$

Step 3

Write the rate symbolically or in word form.

Symbolically, $\frac{\$300}{15 \text{ cans}} = \frac{\$20}{\text{can}}$, or $20 per can.

Each can of paint costs $20.

27. 40

To find equivalent ratios, you need to multiply or divide each term of the ratio by the same number. If Deena multiplies the first term of the ratio by 8, then she also needs to multiply the second term of the ratio by 8.

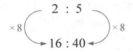

The second term of the ratio is 40.

28.

Step 1

Convert the terms to the same unit.

Cents is the easiest unit to work with.

   3 nickels = 15¢
    2 dimes = 20¢
2 quarters = 50¢

Step 2

Rewrite the ratio in lowest terms.

15:20:50

Reduce the ratio by dividing all the terms by their greatest common factor of 5.

3:4:10

Put in fraction form by dividing all terms by the smallest term in the ratio.

$$\frac{3}{3} : \frac{4}{3} : \frac{10}{3}$$

29. C

Step 1
Create an outline for the table with headings.

The distance Maddie travels depends on the number of steps she takes, so the first column heading should be "Number of Steps," and the second column heading should be "Distance in Meters."

Number of Steps	Distance (m)

Step 2
Determine the pattern rule to find the values for the table.

Every time Maddie takes three steps, she travels 2 m. This means that every time the number of steps Maddie takes increases by 3, the distance she travels increases by 2.

Step 3
Fill in the table with the values.

Number of Steps	Distance (m)
3	2
6	4
9	6
12	8

30. D

Step 1
Plot the ordered pairs on a graph.

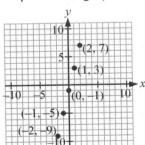

Step 2
Determine the graph that matches the ordered pairs by connecting the plotted coordinates.

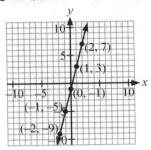

31. C

Write each of the alternatives as a pair of fractions. Cross-multiply them to find the cross products. If the cross products are the same, then the ratios are in proportion.

Step 1
Check if 10:4 and 15:6 are in proportion.

$$10:4 = 15:6$$
$$\frac{10}{4} = \frac{15}{6}$$
$$10 \times 6 = 4 \times 15$$
$$60 = 60$$

The ratios 10:4 and 15:6 are in proportion.

Step 2
Check if 9:3 and 12:4 are in proportion.

$$9:3 = 12:4$$
$$\frac{9}{3} = \frac{12}{4}$$
$$9 \times 4 = 3 \times 12$$
$$36 = 36$$

The ratios 9:3 and 12:4 are in proportion.

Step 3
Check if 3:6 and 4:8 are in proportion.

$$3:6 = 4:8$$
$$\frac{3}{6} = \frac{4}{8}$$
$$3 \times 8 = 6 \times 4$$
$$24 = 24$$

The ratios 3:6 and 4:8 are in proportion.

Step 4
Check if 3:8 and 8:3 are in proportion.

$$3:8 = 8:3$$
$$\frac{3}{8} = \frac{8}{3}$$
$$3 \times 3 = 8 \times 8$$
$$9 \neq 64$$

The ratios 3:8 and 8:3 are not in proportion.

32. 30

The graph is linear, which means that the car is traveling at a steady rate of speed.

According to the graph, for every hour the car travels, it covers a distance of 30 miles.

This means that the car is traveling at a speed of 30 miles per hour, written as 30 mph.

33. 4

Use the simple interest formula $i = prt$ to find the solution.

Step 1
Match the number with the corresponding part of the formula.

- The amount of interest, i, is $1,368.
- The original investment, p, is $7,600.
- The rate, r, is 4.5%, which is equal to 0.045.
- The period, t, is the unknown value.

Step 2
Substitute the numbers into the formula, and solve for the unknown.

$$i = prt$$
$$1,368 = 7,600 \times 0.045 \times t$$
$$1,368 = 342t$$
$$\frac{1,368}{342} = t$$
$$t = 4$$

It will take 4 years for the investment to earn the given amount of interest.

34. D

To determine the sale price, find the amount of the discount and subtract that amount from the original price.

Step 1
Calculate the amount of the discount.

The percentage taken off is given as 12.5%. To find the amount of the discount, d, change 12.5% into a decimal and multiply by the original price of $12.50.
$$d = 0.125 \times 12.50$$
$$d = 1.5625$$
$$d \approx 1.56$$
The amount of the discount is $1.56.

Step 2
Calculate the sale price.

To find the sale price, subtract the discount from the original price.
$$12.50 - 1.56 = 10.94$$
The actual sale price of the T-shirt is $10.94.

35. 40

Step 1
Determine the amount of increase.
Subtract the number of miles David ran each day in the first week from the number of miles he ran each day during the second week.
$$10.5 - 7.5 = 3.0$$

Step 2
Determine the percentage increase in the number of miles David ran.

$$\% \text{ increase} = \frac{\text{amount of increase}}{\text{original amount}} \times 100$$
$$= \frac{3.0}{7.5} \times 100$$
$$= 40$$

David increased the number of miles he ran in the second week by 40%.

36.

Method 1: Multiply by 100

Step 1
Multiply the decimal number by 100.
$$3.5 \times 100 = 350$$

Step 2
Place a percent sign behind the answer.
350%
The decimal 3.5 expressed as a percentage is 350%.

Step 3
Compare the two percentages and place the correct symbol in the given space.
$$3.5 = 350\%$$

Method 2: Moving the Decimal

Step 1
Move the decimal point two places to the right (add a zero if necessary).

3.50

Step 2
Place a percent sign behind the answer.
350%

Step 3
Compare the two percentages and place the correct symbol in the given space.
$$3.5 = 350\%$$

37.

Step 1

Method 1: Division.

Write the percentage as a fraction over 100.

$33\% = \dfrac{33}{100}$

Divide the numerator by the denominator.

$33 \div 100 = 0.3333...$

Round to two decimal places.

Therefore, the decimal is 0.33.

Step 2

Method 2: Move the decimal.

Locate the decimal point in the percentage. If it is not written it is placed after the last digit.

33.

Move the decimal two places to the left.

Expressed as a decimal, 33% is 0.33.

38. C

Step 1

Calculate the unit rate for each rate.

- Grocery A: 10 kg for $10.00

  $\dfrac{\$10.00}{10kg} = \$1.00/kg$

- Grocery B: 15 kg for $15.15

  $\dfrac{\$15.15}{15kg} = \$1.01/kg$

- Grocery C: 20 kg for $19.00

  $\dfrac{\$19.00}{20kg} = \$0.95/kg$

- Grocery D: 25 kg for $24.50

  $\dfrac{\$24.50}{25kg} = \$0.98/kg$

Step 2

Compare the unit rates.

Grocery C has the lowest unit rate where flour costs $0.95/kg.

39.

Step 1

Change the percentage to its decimal equivalent.

$6 \div 100 = 0.06$

The decimal equivalent of 6% is 0.06.

Step 2

Multiply Harry's total sales by the decimal equivalent of the commission percentage.

$18,700 \times 0.06 = 1,122$

Harry's commission is $1,122.

40. D

Step 1

Calculate the tax.

Multiply the price by the decimal equivalent of the tax rate. The decimal equivalent of 10% is 0.1.

$165 \times 0.1 = 16.50$

The sales tax is $16.50.

Step 2

Add the sales tax to the original price.

$165 + 16.50 = 181.50$

The total retail price is $181.50.

41. 37

Step 1

Calculate the size of Leslie's error.

Leslie's estimate was 38 s, and the time was 1 min, which is equal to 60 s.

$60 - 38 = 22$

Step 2

Calculate Leslie's relative error.

$\text{relative error} = \dfrac{\text{size of error}}{\text{actual measure}}$

$\text{relative error} = \dfrac{22}{60}$

$\text{relative error} \approx 0.3666$

Step 3

Express the relative error as a percentage.

$0.3666 \times 100 \approx 36.66\%$

Rounded to the nearest percentage, Leslie's relative error is 37%.

42. A

Step 1

Convert the percentage to a decimal.

$70 \div 100 = 0.70$

Step 2

Multiply the given number by the percentage as a decimal number.

$50 \times 0.7 = 35$

Andrew attempted 35 questions on the test.

43. C

Step 1

Set up the equivalent fractions.

Write the percentage as the first fraction and the part of the whole as the second fraction. Because the given number is a fraction, 1 is the numerator and 5 is the denominator. The variable, x, will be multiplied by the numerator of this fraction.

$\dfrac{8}{100} = \dfrac{1x}{5}$

Step 2

Determine the number used to create the equivalent fraction.

You need to divide 100 by 20 to get 5.

Step 3

Divide the numerator by the same divisor to find the value of *x*.

$$\frac{8 \div 20}{100 \div 20} = \frac{x}{5}$$

44.

Step 1

Write as a fraction.

The fraction that represents 36 questions correct out of 40 questions is $\frac{36}{40}$.

Step 2

Determine the equivalent fraction that has 100 as a denominator.

First, reduce $\frac{36}{40}$ to a fraction that has a denominator that is a factor of 100.

$$\frac{36 \div 4}{40 \div 4} = \frac{9}{10}$$

Then, multiply both the numerator and denominator by 10.

$$\frac{9 \times 10}{10 \times 10} = \frac{90}{100}$$

Step 3

Write as a percentage.

Since a percentage is a number out of 100,

$$\frac{90}{100} = 90\%.$$

Sonya got 90% of the questions correct.

45. B

Step 1

Set up a proportion.

$$\frac{30 \text{ km}}{1 \text{ h}} = \frac{50 \text{ km}}{x}$$

Step 2

Solve for *x* using cross products.

$$\frac{30 \text{ km}}{1 \text{ h}} = \frac{50 \text{ km}}{x}$$
$$(30)(x) = (50)(1)$$
$$30x = 50$$
$$\frac{30x}{30} = \frac{50}{30}$$
$$x = \frac{5}{3}$$

Step 3

Convert the improper fraction into a mixed number.

$$\frac{5}{3} = 1\frac{2}{3}$$

Troy rode his bike for $1\frac{2}{3}$ hours.

46. A

Step 1

Find the total number of parts in the ratio.

There are 10 parts in the ratio because 3 + 7 = 10.

Step 2

Find the height per part.

The sum of the heights is 160 cm. Divide 160 by the number of parts, 10.

160 ÷ 10 = 16

The height per part is 16 cm.

Step 3

Find the answers by multiplying.

The shorter plant has 3 parts, so multiply 3 by 16 cm to find its height.

3 × 16 = 48

The taller plant has 7 parts, so multiply 7 by 16 cm to find its height.

7 × 16 = 112

The shorter plant is 48 cm tall, and the taller plant is 112 cm tall.

47. D

There is no whole number that you can multiply or divide 2 by to get to 5. Start by reducing $\frac{2}{6}$ to lowest terms.

Step 1

Reduce $\frac{2}{6}$ to lowest terms.

$$\frac{2}{6} = \frac{1}{3}$$

Step 2

Rewrite the equation.

$$\frac{2}{6} = \frac{5}{n}$$
$$\frac{1}{3} = \frac{5}{n}$$

Step 3

Decide what you need to multiply or divide by to find the equivalent fraction you need.

To go from a numerator of 1 to a numerator of 5, you need to multiply by 5.

$$\frac{1}{3} = \frac{5}{n}$$

$$\frac{1 \times 5}{3 \times 5} = \frac{5}{n}$$

$$\frac{5}{15} = \frac{5}{n}$$

Alyssa needs to reduce $\frac{2}{6}$ to $\frac{1}{3}$ and then multiply the numerator and denominator by 5.

48. C

Look at each proportion. Decide what kind of information is given in the numerator and denominator of each fraction.

Step 1

Look at $\frac{t}{2} = \frac{10}{616}$.

The fraction on the left has the total area for 10 posters and the number of events for 2 posters. The fraction on the right has the number of events for 10 posters and the area for 2 posters.

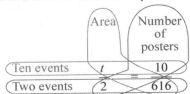

This is not a correct proportion.

Step 2

Look at $\frac{10}{2} = \frac{616}{t}$.

The numerators have the number of events for 10 posters and the area for 2 posters.
The denominators have the number of events for 2 posters and the area of 10 posters.

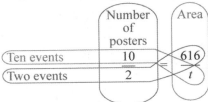

This is not a correct proportion.

Step 3

Look at $\frac{t}{10} = \frac{2}{616}$.

The numerators have the area for 10 posters and the number of events for 2 posters. The denominators have the number of events for 10 posters and the area of 2 posters.

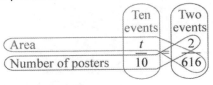

This is not a correct proportion.

Step 4

Look at $\frac{2}{10} = \frac{616}{t}$.

The fraction on the left has the number of posters needed, and the fraction on the right has the total area needed. The numerators show the amount needed for 2 events, and the denominators show the amount needed for 10 events.

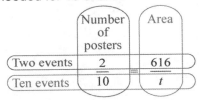

This is a correct proportion. The only proportion that Meena could have written is $\frac{2}{10} = \frac{616}{t}$.

NOTES

The Number System

THE NUMBER SYSTEM

	Table of Correlations			
Standard		**Concepts**	**Exercise #1**	**Exercise #2**
7.NS	The Number System			
7.NS. 1A	*Apply and extend previous understandings of addition and subtraction to add and subtract rational numbers; represent addition and subtraction on a horizontal or vertical number line diagram. Describe situations in which opposite quantities combine to make 0.*	Understanding Integers	49	74
7.NS. 1B	*Apply and extend previous understandings of addition and subtraction to add and subtract rational numbers; represent addition and subtraction on a horizontal or vertical number line diagram.*	Zero Principle	50	75
		Adding Integers with Manipulatives	51	76
		Solving Problems Involving the Addition & Subtraction of Integers	53	78
		Adding Integers	55	80
7.NS. 1C	*Apply and extend previous understandings of addition and subtraction to add and subtract rational numbers; represent addition and subtraction on a horizontal or vertical number line diagram. Understand subtraction of rational numbers as adding the additive inverse, p – q = p + (–q). Show that the distance between two rational numbers on the number line is the absolute value of their difference, and apply this principle in real-world contexts.*	Subtracting Integers	52	77
		Solving Problems Involving the Addition & Subtraction of Integers	53	78
		Subtracting Integers with Manipulatives	52, 54	79
7.NS. 1D	*Apply and extend previous understandings of addition and subtraction to add and subtract rational numbers; represent addition and subtraction on a horizontal or vertical number line diagram. Apply properties of operations as strategies to add and subtract rational numbers.*	Subtracting Integers	52	77
		Adding Integers	55	80
		Understanding Negative Fractions and Decimals		
7.NS. 2A	*Apply and extend previous understandings of multiplication and division and of fractions to multiply and divide rational numbers. Understand that multiplication is extended from fractions to rational numbers by requiring that operations continue to satisfy the properties of operations, particularly the distributive property, leading to products such as (–1)(–1) = 1 and the rules for multiplying signed numbers. Interpret products of rational numbers by describing real-world contexts.*	Multiplying Integers Algebraically	56	81
		Solving Problems Involving the Multiplication & Division of Integers	57	82

7.NS. 2B	Apply and extend previous understandings of multiplication and division and of fractions to multiply and divide rational numbers. Understand that integers can be divided, provided that the divisor is not zero, and every quotient of integers (with non-zero divisor) is a rational number. If p and q are integers, then –(p/q) = (–p)/q = p/(–q). Interpret quotients of rational numbers by describing realworld contexts.	Solving Problems Involving the Multiplication & Division of Integers	57	82
		Dividing Integers Algebraically	58	83
7.NS. 2C	Apply and extend previous understandings of multiplication and division and of fractions to multiply and divide rational numbers. Apply properties of operations as strategies to multiply and divide rational numbers.	Dividing Fractions	1	25
		Understanding Negative Fractions and Decimals		
		Multiplying Integers Algebraically	56	81
		Dividing Integers Algebraically	58	83
		Adding Decimal Numbers	59	84
		Subtracting Decimal Numbers	60	85
		Multiplying Fractions	61	86
		Adding Fractions with Unlike Denominators	62	87
		Multiplying Decimals by Decimals	63	88
		Dividing Decimals by Decimals	64	89
7.NS. 2D	Apply and extend previous understandings of multiplication and division and of fractions to multiply and divide rational numbers. Convert a rational number to a decimal using long division; know that the decimal form of a rational number terminates in 0s or eventually repeats.	Converting Fractions to Terminating Decimals	65	90
		Converting Fractions to Repeating Decimals	66	91
7.NS.3	Solve real–world and mathematical problems involving the four operations with rational numbers.	Solving Addition Problems	67	92
		Solving Problems by Subtracting Decimals	68	93
		Solving Problems by Multiplying Decimals	73	94
		Solving Problems by Adding and Subtracting Fractions	72	95
		Solving Problems Involving the Simple Multiplication of Fractions	70	96
		Solving Problems Involving the Simple Division of Fractions	71	97
		Solving Problems by Dividing Decimals	69	98
		Solving Problems by Adding Decimals	67	92

7.NS.1A Apply and extend previous understandings of addition and subtraction to add and subtract rational numbers; represent addition and subtraction on a horizontal or vertical number line diagram. Describe situations in which opposite quantities combine to make 0.

UNDERSTANDING INTEGERS

Every whole number other than 0 has a number that is its negative opposite. For example, –2 is the opposite of 2. Whole numbers and their opposites are always the same distance away from 0 on a number line.

All the numbers on this number line are called integers. **Integers** include all whole numbers and their negative opposites. Negative numbers are used in many everyday situations.

Example

If you have some money, you can show that using a positive number.

If you have $5, that is a positive number (5). If you borrow $5, that is a negative number (–5). If you have $–20, this means that you have $20 less than 0.

Example

The elevation of an object is its height above sea level. Objects that are below sea level have a negative elevation.

The castle has an elevation of 60 m, and the shipwreck has an elevation of –15 m.

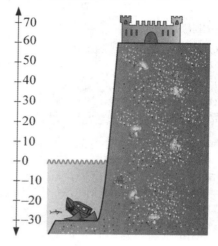

Example

The music group The Screaming Criers went from number 4 to number 1 on the top 10 hits list. This is a movement of +3. Trixie went from number 1 down to 6. This is a movement of –5.

7.NS.1B Apply and extend previous understandings of addition and subtraction to add and subtract rational numbers; represent addition and subtraction on a horizontal or vertical number line diagram.

ZERO PRINCIPLE

For every integer, there is always an opposite (negative or positive) integer. Zero pairs are opposite integers. The **zero principle** states that when zero pairs are added, their sum is 0.
For example, $(-4) + (+4) = 0$ and $(+4) + (-4) = 0$.

Number lines can be used to model the zero principle. When using number lines, modeling a positive value means moving to the right. Modeling a negative value means moving to the left.

Example

Use a number line to show that $(-4) + (+4) = 0$.

Solution

Step 1
Starting above the zero on a number line, draw an arrow to the value of the first integer in the question.
The first integer is −4. Draw an arrow moving 4 steps left.

Step 2
Starting above the tip of the arrow drawn, draw another arrow that moves to the left or right the number of places indicated by the value of the second integer.
The second integer is +4. Draw an arrow moving 4 steps right.

A move in one direction with an equal move in the opposite direction results in an answer of 0 because there is no change in position.
Since the arrow ends exactly where it started, the sum of opposites is zero.

Integer tiles can also be used to model the zero principle. A shaded tile paired with an unshaded tile will cancel each other out.  These are called **zero pairs**.

Example

Use integer tiles to show that $(-4) + (+4) = 0$.

Solution

Step 1
Draw the correct number of tiles representing the first integer in the expression.
The first integer is −4. Draw four unshaded tiles.
The integer tiles are placed side by side or one tile on top of the other. It does not matter which way they are displayed. Shaded are positive tiles. Unshaded are negative tiles.

☐ ☐☐☐☐
☐
☐
☐

Step 2
Draw the correct number of tiles representing the second integer in the expression opposite the first row of tiles.
The second integer is +4. Draw four shaded tiles opposite the first row of tiles.

☐■ ☐☐☐☐
☐■ ■■■■
☐■
☐■

There is one negative tile for every positive tile or four zero pairs. The tiles cancel each other out. There are no leftover tiles, meaning the sum is zero.

Using zero pairs allows you to represent integers in many ways.

Example

Using integer tiles, express –3 in three different ways.

Solution

Step 1

Draw the correct number of tiles representing the integer.

Three negative tiles equal –3.

Step 2

Draw the correct number of tiles representing the integer after adding any number of zero pairs to the integer.

The zero pairs cancel each other out and do not change the value of the integer.

Three negative tiles are left over equaling –3.

Step 3

Repeat step 2 with a different number of zero pairs.

Three negative tiles are left over equaling –3.

ADDING INTEGERS WITH MANIPULATIVES

Manipulatives can be used to demonstrate the addition process of integers.

Use the following steps to add integers using a number line:

1. Starting from zero, draw an arrow to the value of the first integer in the expression.
2. Starting from above the tip of the arrow drawn, draw another arrow that moves the number of places indicated by the value of the second integer.
3. Determine the sum.

Example

Use a number line to evaluate the expression $(+4) + (–3)$.

Solution

Step 1

Starting from above the zero, draw an arrow to the value of the first integer in the question.

The first integer is +4. Start at zero and draw an arrow four places to the right.

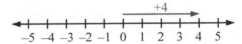

Step 2

Starting above the tip of the arrow drawn, draw another arrow that moves the number of places indicated by the value of the second integer.

Draw an arrow three places to the left of $(+4)$.

Step 3

Determine the sum.

The position of the second arrow is the sum.

The arrow stops at $(+1)$.

$(+4) + (–3) = (+1)$

Use the following steps to add integers using integer tiles:

1. Draw the number of tiles representing the first integer in the expression.
2. Draw the number of tiles representing the second integer in the expression opposite the first row of tiles.
3. Cancel the zero pairs.
4. Determine the sum.

Example

Use integer tiles to evaluate the expression $(+4) + (–3)$.

Solution

Step 1

Draw the number of tiles representing the first integer in the expression.

The first term is $(+4)$. Draw four shaded tiles.

Step 2

Draw the number of tiles representing the second integer in the expression opposite the first row of tiles.

The second term is (-3). Draw three unshaded tiles lined up below the first term tiles.

Step 3

Cancel the zero pairs.

Step 4

Determine the sum.

The color and the number of the remaining tiles represents the sum.

One positive tile remains, the sum is $+1$.
$(+4) + (-3) = (+1)$

7.NS.1C Apply and extend previous understandings of addition and subtraction to add and subtract rational numbers; represent addition and subtraction on a horizontal or vertical number line diagram. Understand subtraction of rational numbers as adding the additive inverse, $p - q = p + (-q)$. Show that the distance between two rational numbers on the number line is the absolute value of their difference, and apply this principle in real-world contexts.

SUBTRACTING INTEGERS

When subtracting integers using paper and pencil, follow these steps:

1. Change the integer following the subtraction sign to the additive inverse.
2. Follow the same rules that apply for adding integers.

Example

Simplify the expression $(+4) - (+3)$.

Solution

Step 1

Change the integer following the subtraction sign to the additive inverse.

The additive inverse of $- (+3)$ is $+(-3)$.
$(+4) - (+3) = (+4) + (-3)$

Step 2

Follow the same rules that apply for adding integers.

The signs are different, so subtract the positive values and take the sign of the larger value.
$$4 - 3 = 1$$
$(+4) - (+3) = (+1)$

Example

Simplify the expression $(-4) - (-3)$.

Solution

Step 1

Change the integer following the subtraction sign to the additive inverse.

The additive inverse of $- (-3)$ is $+(+3)$.
$(-4) - (-3) = (-4) + (+3)$

Step 2

Follow the same rules that apply for adding integers.

The signs are different, so subtract the positive values and take the sign of the larger value.
$$4 - 3 = 1$$
$(-4) - (-3) = (-1)$

Example

Simplify the expression $(-4) - (+3)$.

Solution

Step 1

Change the integer following the subtraction sign to the additive inverse.

The additive inverse of $- (+3)$ is $+(-3)$.
$(-4) - (+3) = (-4) + (-3)$

Step 2
Follow the same rules that apply for adding integers.
The signs are the same, so add the positive values and keep the same sign.
$$4 + 3 = 7$$
$$(-4) - (+3) = (-7)$$

Example
Simplify the expression $(+4) - (-3)$.

Solution
Step 1
Change the integer following the subtraction sign to the additive inverse.
The additive inverse of $-(-3)$ is $+(+3)$.
$$(+4) - (-3) = (+4) + (+3)$$

Step 2
Follow the same rules that apply for adding integers.
The signs are the same, so add the positive values and keep the same sign.
$$4 + 3 = 7$$
$$(+4) - (-3) = (+7)$$

SOLVING PROBLEMS INVOLVING THE ADDITION & SUBTRACTION OF INTEGERS

When working with integer problems, translate the words into a mathematical expression. Look for keywords indicating the value of all integers.

A few examples of positive (+) keywords include *above, increased, gain, higher, rise, up, over, much, more,* and *profit.*

A few examples of negative (−) keywords include *below, lower, decreased, diminished, down, under, less,* and *loss.*

The last sentence of the problem usually indicates the operation to solve the problem.
Some examples of addition keywords include *sum, altogether, total, equal, plus, increased by, combined, add,* and *in all.*

A few examples of subtraction keywords include the following: *difference, reduced by, left over, less than, fall, subtracted from, minus,* and *decreased by.*

To solve an integer problem, follow these steps:

1. Identify integer and operation keywords.
2. Write an expression representing the problem.
3. Solve.

Example
Lyla received $20.00 for mowing the lawn but owes her mom $11.00.

How much does she have after she pays her mom back?

Solution
Step 1
Identify integer and operation keywords.
Integer keywords: *received* indicates positive, and *owed* indicates negative.
Received $20.00 → (+$20.00)
Owed $11.00 → (−$11.00)
Operation keyword: *much* indicates addition.

Step 2
Write an expression representing the problem.
$$(+\$20.00) + (-\$11.00)$$

Step 3
Solve.
$$(+\$20.00) + (-\$11.00) = (+\$9.00)$$
Lyla has $9.00.

Example
A submarine was at a depth of 65 m when it was brought up to a depth of 21 m.

What was the change in depth of the submarine?

Solution
Step 1
Identify integer and operation keywords.
Integer keyword: *depth* indicates negative.
Depth of 65 m→(−65)
Operation keyword: *up* indicates addition.

Step 2
Write an expression representing the problem.
$$(-65) + (21)$$

Step 3

Solve.

$(-65) + (21) = (-44)$

The submarine is now at a depth of –44 m, which means 44 m below the surface of the water.

SUBTRACTING INTEGERS WITH MANIPULATIVES

When subtracting integers it is easier to use the additive inverse. **Inverse** means the opposite. For example, zipping up a jacket is the inverse of unzipping a jacket. The inverse of a number is its opposite. For example, the inverse of +5 is –5. The inverse of –9 is +9.

To rewrite an expression using the **additive inverse**, change the operation and value of the integer to its opposite. The additive inverse of $(+2) - (+6)$ is $(+2) + (-6)$.

When subtracting integers using a number line, use the following steps:

1. Rewrite the expression using the additive inverse.
2. Starting from above the zero, draw an arrow to the value of the first integer in the expression.
3. Starting above the tip of the arrow drawn, draw another arrow that moves the number of places indicated by the value of the second integer.
4. Determine the sum.

Example

Use a number line to solve the expression $(+4) - (+3)$.

Solution

Step 1

Rewrite the expression using the additive inverse.

$(+4) + (-3)$

Step 2

Starting from above the zero, draw an arrow to the value of the first integer in the expression.

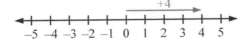

Step 3

Starting above the tip of the arrow drawn, draw another arrow that moves the number of places indicated by the value of the second integer.

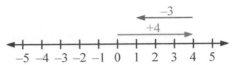

Step 4

Determine the sum.

The second arrow landed on (+1).

$(+4) - (+3) = (+1)$

The difference for the subtraction of integers is the same as the sum for the additive inverse.

Example

Use a number line to solve the expression $(-4) - (-3)$.

Solution

Step 1

Rewrite the expression using the additive inverse.

$(-4) + (+3)$

Step 2

Starting from above the zero, draw an arrow to the value of the first integer in the expression.

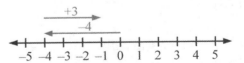

Step 3

Starting above the tip of the arrow drawn, draw another arrow that moves the number of places indicated by the value of the second integer.

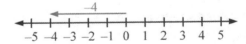

Step 4

Determine the sum.

The arrow landed on (–1).

$(-4) - (-3) = (-1)$

Example

Use a number line to solve the expression $(-4) - (+3)$.

Solution

Step 1

Rewrite the expression using the additive inverse.

$(-4) + (-3)$

Step 2

Starting from above the zero, draw an arrow to the value of the first integer in the expression.

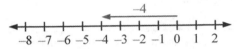

Step 3

Starting above the tip of the arrow drawn, draw another arrow that moves the number of places indicated by the value of the second integer.

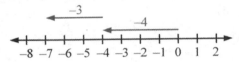

Step 4

Determine the sum.

The arrow landed on (-7).

$(-4) - (+3) = (-7)$

Example

Use a number line to solve the expression $(+3) - (-4)$.

Solution

Step 1

Rewrite the expression using the additive inverse.

$(+3) + (+4)$

Step 2

Starting from above the zero, draw an arrow to the value of the first integer in the expression.

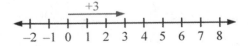

Step 3

Starting above the tip of the arrow drawn, draw another arrow that moves the number of places indicated by the value of the second integer.

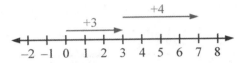

Step 4

Determine the sum.

The arrow stopped at $(+7)$.

$(+3) - (-4) = (+7)$

When subtracting integers using integer tiles, follow these steps:

1. Rewrite the expression using the additive inverse.
2. Draw integer tiles to represent the first integer.
3. Draw integer tiles to represent the second integer.
4. Cancel the zero pairs.
5. Determine the sum.

Example

Use integer tiles to solve the expression $(+4) - (+3)$.

Solution

Step 1

Rewrite the question using the additive inverse.

$(+4) + (-3)$

Step 2

Draw integer tiles to represent the first integer.

Draw four shaded tiles to represent the first integer $(+4)$.

■ ■ ■ ■

Step 3

Draw integer tiles to represent the second integer.

Draw three unshaded tiles to represent the second integer (-3).

☐ ☐ ☐

Step 4

Cancel the zero pairs.

▨ ▨ ▨ ■ + ▨ ▨ ▨

Step 5
Determine the sum.
One shaded tile is left. The sum is +1.
(+4) – (+3) becomes (+4) + (–3) = (+1)

Example
Use integer tiles to solve the expression
(–4) – (–3).

Solution

Step 1
Rewrite the question using the additive inverse.
(–4) + (+3)

Step 2
Draw integer tiles to represent the first integer.
Draw four unshaded tiles to represent the first integer (–4).

□ □ □ □

Step 3
Draw integer tiles to represent the second integer.
Draw three shaded tiles to represent the second integer (+3).

■ ■ ■

Step 4
Cancel the zero pairs.

▨ ▨ ▨ □ + ▨ ▨ ▨

Step 5
Determine the sum.
One unshaded tile is left. The sum is –1.
(–4) – (–3) becomes (–4) + (+3) = (–1)

Example
Use integer tiles to solve the expression
(+4) – (–3).

Solution

Step 1
Rewrite the question using the additive inverse.
(+4) + (+3)

Step 2
Draw integer tiles to represent the first integer.
Draw four shaded tiles to represent the first integer (+4).

 ■ ■ ■ ■

Step 3
Draw three integer tiles to represent the second integer.
Draw three shaded tiles to represent the second integer (+3).

■ ■ ■

Step 4
Cancel the zero pairs.
All the tiles are positive. There are no zero pairs to cancel.

■ ■ ■ ■ + ■ ■ ■

Step 5
Determine the sum.
There are seven shaded tiles left. The sum is +7.
(+4) – (–3) becomes (+4) + (+3) = (+7)

7.NS.1D Apply and extend previous understandings of addition and subtraction to add and subtract rational numbers; represent addition and subtraction on a horizontal or vertical number line diagram. Apply properties of operations as strategies to add and subtract rational numbers.

ADDING INTEGERS

When adding integers using paper and pencil, there are two rules to follow.

Rule 1
If the signs are the same on all the integers, add the positive values and keep the sign.

Rule 2
If the signs are different on the integers, subtract the smaller value from the larger value. Then, take the sign of the larger value.

The following examples use rule 1 to add the integers.

Example
    Solve the expression $(+3) + (+5)$.

Solution
    ### Step 1
    The signs are the same, so add the positive values.
    The positive values are 3 and 5.
    $3 + 5 = 8$
    ### Step 2
    Place the integer sign in front of the sum.
    The integer sign was positive (+).
    $(+3) + (+5) = (+8)$

Example
    Solve the expression $(-3) + (-5)$.

Solution
    ### Step 1
    The signs are the same, so add the positive values.
    The positive values are 3 and 5.
    $3 + 5 = 8$

Step 2
Place the integer sign in front of the sum.
The integer sign was negative (–).
$(-3) + (-5) = (-8)$

The following examples use rule 2 to add the integers.

Example
    Solve the expression $(-8) + (+3)$.

Solution
    ### Step 1
    The signs are different, so subtract the smaller positive value from the larger positive value.
    The positive values are 8 and 3.
    $8 - 3 = 5$
    ### Step 2
    Take the sign of the larger value.
    Since 8 is the larger value and had a negative integer sign, apply it to the answer.
    $(-8) + (+3) = (-5)$

Example
    Solve the expression $(+4) + (-6)$.

Solution
    ### Step 1
    The signs are different, so subtract the smaller positive value from the larger positive value.
    The positive values are 4 and 6.
    $6 - 4 = 2$
    ### Step 2
    Take the sign of the larger value.
    Since 6 is the larger value and had a negative integer sign, apply it to the answer.
    $(+4) + (-6) = (-2)$

UNDERSTANDING NEGATIVE FRACTIONS AND DECIMALS

Like all numbers other than zero, fractions and decimals can be positive or negative. Working with negative fractions and decimals is exactly the same as working with other negative numbers. This means that if you know how to compare negative numbers and you know how to compare fractions, you also know how to compare negative fractions. If you need to subtract with negative decimals, you can use what you know about subtracting negative numbers and subtracting decimals.

COMPARING AND ORDERING

With negative numbers, the number that is farthest to the left on the number line is always the smaller number. For example, the number –5 is less than –2, even though the digit 5 seems bigger than the digit 2. This is because –5 is farther to the left on a number line.

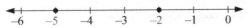

This is also true with negative fractions and decimals. For example, the number –0.8 is smaller than –0.3.

OPERATIONS

When you are adding, subtracting, multiplying, or dividing with negative fractions or decimals, follow the same rules as you do with other negative numbers.

When you subtract a negative number, you need to add its inverse. This means that if you need to solve $\frac{3}{8} - \left(-\frac{2}{8}\right)$, you can change it to $\frac{3}{8} + \left(+\frac{2}{8}\right)$.

$$\frac{3}{8} - \left(-\frac{2}{8}\right) = \frac{3}{8} + \left(+\frac{2}{8}\right)$$
$$= \frac{5}{8}$$

When you multiply a negative number by a positive number, the answer is always negative.
For example, the answer to $1.2 \times (-0.6)$ will be negative.

$$\begin{array}{r} \overset{1}{1.2} \\ \times\ -0.6 \\ \hline -0.72 \end{array}$$

PROPERTIES

Any properties of negative numbers apply to negative fractions and decimals.

The zero principle says that any number plus its inverse equals zero. Inverse numbers are pairs of numbers with the same digits but opposite signs.

For example, $-2\frac{1}{3}$ and $2\frac{1}{3}$ are inverses.

According to the zero principle, $-2\frac{1}{3} + 2\frac{1}{3} = 0$.

The absolute value of a negative number is the number with the same digits, but without a negative sign. This means that the absolute value of –4.125 is 4.125.

7.NS.2A Apply and extend previous understandings of multiplication and division and of fractions to multiply and divide rational numbers. Understand that multiplication is extended from fractions to rational numbers by requiring that operations continue to satisfy the properties of operations, particularly the distributive property, leading to products such as (–1)(–1) = 1 and the rules for multiplying signed numbers. Interpret products of rational numbers by describing real-world contexts.

MULTIPLYING INTEGERS ALGEBRAICALLY

To multiply integers, follow these steps:

1. Multiply the positive values of the numbers.
2. Count the number of negative signs: If there is an even number of negative signs, the quotient is positive; if there is an odd number of negative signs, the quotient is negative.

Example
Find the product of (+4) and (+6).

Solution
Step 1
Multiply the positive values.
The positive values are 4 and 6.
$4 \times 6 = 24$

Step 2

Count the number of negative signs.

Since there are no negative signs in the question, the answer must be positive.

$(+4) \times (+6) = (+24)$

Example

Find the product of (-4) and (-6).

Solution

Step 1

Multiply the positive values.

The positive values are 4 and 6.

$4 \times 6 = 24$

Step 2

Count the number of negative signs.

Two negative signs in the question result in a positive sign in the answer.

$(-4) \times (-6) = (+24)$

Example

Find the product of $(+4)$ and (-6).

Solution

Step 1

Multiply the positive values.

The positive values are 4 and 6.

$4 \times 6 = 24$

Step 2

Count the number of negative signs.

One negative sign in the question results in a negative sign in the answer.

$(+4) \times (-6) = (-24)$

Example

Simplify the expression $(-4)(+3)(-8)$.

Solution

Step 1

Multiply the positive values.

The positive values are 4, 3, and 8.

$4 \times 3 \times 8 = 96$

Step 2

Count the number of negative signs.

Two negative signs in the question result in a positive sign in the answer.

$(-4)(+3)(-8) = (+96)$

Example

Simplify the expression $(-2)(+3)(-4)(-5)$.

Solution

Step 1

Multiply the positive values.

The positive values are 2, 3, 4, and 5.

$2 \times 3 \times 4 \times 5 = 120$

Step 2

Count the number of negative signs.

Three negative signs in the question result in a negative sign in the answer.

$(-2)(+3)(-4)(-5) = (-120)$

SOLVING PROBLEMS INVOLVING THE MULTIPLICATION & DIVISION OF INTEGERS

When working with integer problems, translate the words into a mathematical expression. Look for keywords indicating the value of all integers.

A few examples of positive (+) keywords include *above*, *increased*, *gain*, *higher*, *rise*, *up*, *over*, *more*, and *profit*.

A few examples of negative (−) keywords include *below*, *lower*, *decreased*, *diminished*, *down*, *under*, *less*, and *loss*.

The last sentence of the problem usually indicates the operation to solve the problem.

Keywords for multiplication include *product*, *multiply*, *double*, *triple*, *times*, *percent*, and *how much*.

Keywords for division include *quotient*, *per*, *each*, *divide*, and *average*.

To solve an integer problem, follow these steps:

1. Identify integer and operation keywords.
2. Write an expression representing the problem.
3. Solve.

Example

A sports card shop has a two-for-one special on their sets of hockey cards. During the special, they sold 63 sets of cards.

If the shop lost $3.00 on each set of cards sold during the sale, how much did they lose in total?

Solution

Step 1

Identify integer and operation keywords.

Integer keywords: *lost* indicates negative.

Lost $3.00 → (−3)

Operation keywords: *sold 63 sets* and *much*. When larger amounts are involved, multiplication is indicated.

Step 2

Write an expression representing the problem.

63 × (−3)

Step 3

Solve.

63 × (−3) = (−189)

During the two-for-one sale, the shop lost $189.00.

Example

Over 9 days, the temperature steadily dropped 45 degrees Celsius. The drop in temperature was the same each day.

How much did it drop daily?

Solution

Step 1

Identify integer and operation keywords.

Integer keywords: *dropped* indicates negative.

Dropped 45 degrees Celsius→ (−45)

Operation keyword: *how much* and *daily*.

Step 2

Write an expression representing the problem.

(−45) ÷ 9

Step 3

Solve.

(−45) ÷ 9 = (−5)

The daily drop in temperature was −5°C.

7.NS.2B Apply and extend previous understandings of multiplication and division and of fractions to multiply and divide rational numbers. Understand that integers can be divided, provided that the divisor is not zero, and every quotient of integers (with non-zero divisor) is a rational number. If p and q are integers, then −(p/q) = (−p)/q = p/(−q). Interpret quotients of rational numbers by describing realworld contexts.

DIVIDING INTEGERS ALGEBRAICALLY

To divide integers, follow these steps:

1. Divide the positive values of the numbers.
2. Count the number of negative signs: If there is an even number of negative signs, the quotient is positive; if there is an odd number of negative signs, the quotient is negative.

Example

Find the quotient of (+24) divided by (+6).

Solution

Step 1

Divide the positive values.

The positive values are 24 and 6.

24 ÷ 6 = 4

Step 2

Count the number of negative signs.

Since there are no negative signs in the question, the answer must be positive.

(+24) ÷ (+6) = (+4)

Example

Find the quotient of (−24) divided by (−6).

Solution

Step 1

Divide the positive values.

The positive values are 24 and 6.

24 ÷ 6 = 4

Step 2

Count the negative signs.

Two negative signs in the question result in a positive sign in the answer.

(−24) ÷ (−6) = (+4)

Example

Find the quotient of $(+24)$ divided by (-6).

Solution

Step 1

Divide the positive values.

The positive values are 24 and 6.

$24 \div 6 = 4$

Step 2

Count the negative signs.

One negative sign in the question results in a negative sign in the answer.

$(+24) \div (-6) = (-4)$

Example

Simplify the expression $(-208) \div (+4) \div (-2)$.

Solution

Step 1

Divide the positive values.

The positive values are 208, 4, and 2.

$208 \div 4 \div 2 = 26$

Step 2

Count the number of negative signs.

Two negative signs in the question result in a positive sign in the answer.

$(-208) \div (+4) \div (-2) = (+26)$

Example

Simplify the expression $\dfrac{(-24)}{(-4)} \div (-6) \div (+1)$.

Solution

Step 1

Divide the positive values.

The positive values are 24, 4, 6, and 1.

$\dfrac{24}{4} \div 6 \div 1 = 1$

Step 2

Count the number of negative signs.

Three negative signs in the question results in a negative sign in the answer.

$\dfrac{(-24)}{(-4)} \div (-6) \div (+1) = (-1)$.

7.NS.2C Apply and extend previous understandings of multiplication and division and of fractions to multiply and divide rational numbers. Apply properties of operations as strategies to multiply and divide rational numbers.

ADDING DECIMAL NUMBERS

Adding decimal numbers is similar to adding whole numbers. Place value is important because only the digits in the same place value position can be added together. In both cases, you work from right to left.

When adding decimals, it is important to line up the decimal points. Also, remember to place the decimal point in the correct position in the answer.

Example

$3.780 + 2.134 = ?$

Follow these steps when adding two decimal numbers:

1. Write the numbers below each other, lining up the decimal points and the same place value digits.

    $\begin{array}{r} 3.780 \\ +2.134 \\ \hline \end{array}$

2. Work from right to left, regrouping where necessary. Remember to place the decimal point in the answer, lining it up with the other decimal points.

    $\begin{array}{r} {}^{1} \\ 3.780 \\ +2.134 \\ \hline 5.914 \end{array}$

If the numbers that you are working with do not have the same number of digits to the right of the decimal point, you still line the numbers up according to the decimal points.

Remember that you can add zeroes to the ends of the decimal numbers without changing their values. For example, 0.4 can be written as 0.40 or 0.400. Keeping the same number of digits after the decimal point makes it easier to keep the numbers in line.

Example

Add 1.12 + 3.2 + 4.325.

Write the numbers below each other, lining up the decimal points and the same place value digits.

```
 1.120
 3.200
+4.325
```

Work from right to left, regrouping where necessary. Remember to place the decimal point in the answer, lining it up with the other decimal points.

```
 1.120
 3.200
+4.325
 8.645
```

Example

Harry added the numbers 4.754 and 5.324.

What is the sum of the two numbers rounded to the nearest hundredth?

Solution

Step 1

Write the numbers below each other, lining up the decimal points. Start at the right, and add the numbers in the same place value positions, working to the left: thousandths, then hundredths, then tenths, and then ones. Regroup where necessary (from the tenths to the ones).

```
  4.754
+5.324
 10.078
```

Step 2

Since you are rounding 10.078 to the nearest hundredth, look at the digit in the thousandth place.

Since 8 > 5, 7 rounds up to 8 and the 8 in the thousandths place is dropped.

10.078 → 10.08

SUBTRACTING DECIMAL NUMBERS

Subtracting decimal numbers is similar to subtracting whole numbers. Place value is important because only the digits in the same place value position can be subtracted from one another. Also, you work from right to left in both cases, regrouping where necessary.

When subtracting decimals, it is important to line up the decimal points. Remember to place the decimal point in the correct position in the answer.

Example

3.780 − 2.134 = ?

Write the numbers below each other, lining up the decimal points and the place values.

Follow these steps when subtracting 2.134 from 3.780:

1. Start on the right side. In order to subtract 4 thousandths from 0 thousandths, you need to regroup. Borrow 1 hundredth from 8 hundredths. You now have 7 hundredths and 10 thousandths.
    Subtract the thousandths.
    10 − 4 = 6
    Write the 6 below the line in the thousandths position.

    $$\begin{array}{r} 7\,10 \\ 3.78\cancel{0} \\ -2.134 \\ \hline 6 \end{array}$$

2. Subtract the hundredths.
    7 − 3 = 4
    Write the 4 below the line in the hundredths position.

    $$\begin{array}{r} 7\,10 \\ 3.7\cancel{8}\cancel{0} \\ -2.134 \\ \hline 46 \end{array}$$

3. Subtract the tenths.
    7 − 1 = 6
    Write the 6 below the line, in the tenths position.

    $$\begin{array}{r} 7\,10 \\ 3.78\cancel{0} \\ -2.134 \\ \hline 646 \end{array}$$

4. Place the decimal point to the left of the tenths position in line with the other decimals.
    Subtract the ones.
    3 − 2 = 1
    Write the 1 below the line in the ones position.

    $$\begin{array}{r} 7\,10 \\ 3.78\cancel{0} \\ -2.134 \\ \hline 1.646 \end{array}$$

3.780 − 2.134 = 1.646

Example

Jenny ran the first half of a race in 24.35 s and the second half in 34.657 s.

How much longer did it take Jenny to run the second half of the race?

Solution

Step 1

Write the numbers in a vertical position, with the number with the smaller value (24.35) at the bottom. Remember to line up the decimal points. It may be helpful to add a zero to the end of 24.35 so that you have the same number of digits after the decimal point. This will not change the value of the number.

$$\begin{array}{r} 34.657 \\ -\ 24.350 \\ \hline \end{array}$$

Step 2

Start with the thousandths, and work to the left. Be sure to place the decimal in the correct position, which is between the ones and the tenths. This subtraction problem does not need any regrouping.

$$\begin{array}{r} 34.657 \\ -\ 24.350 \\ \hline 10.307 \end{array}$$

It took Jenny 10.307 s longer to run the second half of the race than the first half of the race.

MULTIPLYING FRACTIONS

A common denominator is not needed in order to multiply fractions.

To multiply fractions, follow these steps:

1. Multiply numerator by numerator and denominator by denominator.
2. Reduce the resulting fraction to lowest terms.

Example

Simplify $\dfrac{1}{2} \times \dfrac{3}{4}$.

Solution

Step 1

Multiply numerator by numerator and denominator by denominator.

$$\frac{1}{2} \times \frac{3}{4} = \frac{1 \times 3}{2 \times 4} = \frac{3}{8}$$

Step 2
Reduce the resulting fraction to lowest terms.
Since the only common factor of 3 and 8 is 1, the product is already in lowest terms.

The product of $\frac{1}{2}$ and $\frac{3}{4}$ is $\frac{3}{8}$.

Example

Calculate $\frac{3}{4} \times \frac{4}{5}$ and express the answer in lowest terms.

Solution

Step 1
Multiply the numerator by the numerator and the denominator by the denominator.

$$\frac{3}{4} \times \frac{4}{5} = \frac{3 \times 4}{4 \times 5}$$
$$= \frac{12}{20}$$

Step 2
Reduce the fraction to lowest terms.
Since the greatest common factor (GCF) of 12 and 20 is 4, divide the numerator and the denominator by 4.

$$\frac{12 \div 4}{20 \div 4} = \frac{3}{5}$$

$\frac{3}{4} \times \frac{4}{5}$ expressed in lowest terms is $\frac{3}{5}$.

When an improper fraction is the product, the reduced fraction should be changed to a mixed number. **Mixed numbers** are a combination of a whole number and a proper fraction.

Example

Simplify $\frac{2}{4} \times 7$.

Solution

Step 1
Multiply numerator by numerator and denominator by denominator.
Change the whole number 7 to a fraction by giving it a denominator of 1: $\frac{7}{1}$.

$$\frac{2}{4} \times \frac{7}{1} = \frac{2 \times 7}{4 \times 1} = \frac{14}{4}$$

Step 2
Reduce the fraction to lowest terms.
The greatest common factor of 14 and 4 is 2.

$$\frac{14 \div 2}{4 \div 2} = \frac{7}{2}$$

Step 3
Change the reduced improper fraction to a mixed number.
numerator of improper fraction ÷ denominator

$$= \text{quotient} + \frac{\text{remainder}}{\text{denominator}}.$$

$7 \div 2 = 3$, with a remainder of 1

The product of $\frac{2}{4}$ and 7 is $3\frac{1}{2}$.

When solving word problems, look for keywords that tell you what operation to perform. Some multiplication keywords are *of*, *times*, *product*, *double*, and *triple*.

Example

Mandy is at the beach making sand castles.

Each tower of the castle requires $\frac{2}{3}$ of a bucket of sand.

How many buckets of sand will Mandy need to make four towers?

Solution

Step 1
Identify the operation.
The keyword **of** indicates multiplication.
The amount of sand for each tower is multiplied by the number of towers.

$$\frac{2}{3} \times 4$$

Step 2
Multiply the numerator by the numerator and the denominator by the denominator.
Change the whole number to a fraction by writing it as a fraction with the whole number as the numerator and 1 as the denominator.

$$4 = \frac{4}{1}$$
$$\frac{2}{3} \times \frac{4}{1} = \frac{2 \times 4}{3 \times 1}$$
$$= \frac{8}{3}$$

Step 3

Change the improper fraction to a mixed number by dividing the numerator by the denominator.

numerator ÷ denominator

$= \text{quotient} + \dfrac{\text{remainder}}{\text{denominator}}$

$8 \div 3 = 2 + \dfrac{2}{3}$

$\qquad = 2\dfrac{2}{3}$

Mandy needs $2\dfrac{2}{3}$ buckets of sand to make the 4 towers.

ADDING FRACTIONS WITH UNLIKE DENOMINATORS

To add fractions with different denominators, follow these steps:

1. Write the fractions with the lowest common denominator (LCD).
2. Add the numerators of the fractions while keeping the denominators the same.
3. Reduce the resulting fraction to lowest terms.

Example

Add $\dfrac{1}{4}$ and $\dfrac{2}{3}$.

Solution

Step 1

Write the fractions with the lowest common denominator (LCD).

Write the multiples of each denominator until a common one appears.

- Multiples of 3: 3, 6, 9, 12, 15
- Multiples of 4: 4, 8, 12, 16, 20

The lowest common denominator for 3 and 4 is 12.

Use the LCD to create new equivalent fractions with a denominator of 12.

Multiply the numerator and the denominator by the same factor.

$\dfrac{1 \times 3}{4 \times 3} = \dfrac{3}{12}, \dfrac{2 \times 4}{3 \times 4} = \dfrac{8}{12}$

Step 2

Add the numerators of the fractions while keeping the denominators the same.

$\dfrac{3 + 8}{12} = \dfrac{11}{12}$

Step 3

Reduce the resulting fraction to lowest terms.

The fraction is in lowest terms.

$\dfrac{1}{4} + \dfrac{2}{3} = \dfrac{11}{12}$

MULTIPLYING DECIMALS BY DECIMALS

To multiply decimal numbers by thousandths, follow these steps:

1. Remove the decimal points.
2. Line up the numbers based on place value.
3. Multiply the two whole numbers together.
4. Add the products together. (Only if you are multiplying by a hundred or thousandth).
5. Place the decimal back into the product.

To replace the decimal in the product, count the number of digits to the right of each of the original decimals. Add the totals together. This will tell you how many digits should be after the decimal point. If there are not enough digits in the product, add zeros right after the decimal point.

Example

What is the product of 0.134 × 0.2?

Solution

Step 1

Remove the decimal point.

The zeros before the decimal point can be removed as well because having a zero in front does not change the value of the number.

134 × 2 =

Step 2

Line up the numbers based on place value.

```
  134
×   2
```

Step 3

Multiply the two whole numbers together.

```
  134
×   2
  268
```

Step 4

Replace the decimal into the product.

Count the number of digits to the right of each of the original decimals. The first decimal number has 3 digits to the right of the decimal point. The second decimal has 1 digit to the right of the decimal point. Added together, the new decimal should have 4 digits after the decimal point.

Because there are only 3 digits in the product, place a 0 in front of the 2 so that there will be 4 digits.

$0.134 \times 0.2 = 0.0268$

Example

What is the product of $0.123 \times 0.311 = \square$?

Solution

Step 1

Remove the decimal point.

The zeros before the decimal point can be removed as well because having a zero in front does not change the value of the number.

$123 \times 311 =$

Step 2

Line up the numbers based on place value.

$$\begin{array}{r} 123 \\ \times\ 311 \\ \hline \end{array}$$

Step 3

Multiply the two whole numbers together.

Start by multiplying 1 by the top number.

$$\begin{array}{r} 123 \\ \times\ 1 \\ \hline 123 \end{array}$$

Multiply 10 by the top number. Remember to add a zero on the right side before multiplying to hold the place value of the tens. Continue multiplying the top number by 1.

$$\begin{array}{r} 123 \\ \times\ 10 \\ \hline 1{,}230 \end{array}$$

Multiply 300 by the top number. Remember to add two zeros on the right side before multiplying to hold the place value of the hundreds. Continue multiplying the top number by 3.

$$\begin{array}{r} 123 \\ \times\ 300 \\ \hline 36{,}900 \end{array}$$

Step 4

Add the products together.

$$\begin{array}{r} 123 \\ {}^{1}1{,}230 \\ +36{,}900 \\ \hline 38{,}253 \end{array}$$

Step 5

Replace the decimal into the product.

Count the number of digits to the right of each of the original decimals. Both decimal numbers have 3 digits to the right of the decimal point. Added together, the new decimal should have 6 digits after the decimal point.

Because there are only 5 digits in the product, you need to place a 0 in front of the 3 so that there will be 6 digits.

$0.123 \times 0.311 = 0.038253$

DIVIDING DECIMALS BY DECIMALS

Dividing decimals by decimals is similar to dividing whole numbers. Follow these steps to divide decimals by decimals:

1. Convert the divisor to a whole number by moving the decimal point. What is done to the divisor must also be done to the dividend. For example, if you move the decimal point two places to the right in the divisor, you must also move the decimal point two places to the right in the dividend.
2. Set up the division equation. Remember to place the decimal point into the quotient by lining up the decimal points above and below the division sign.
3. Perform the division.

Example

Solve the expression 14.64 ÷ 2.4.

Solution

Step 1

Since the diviser is not a whole number, make it a whole number by moving the decimal point one place to the right.

The divisor is 2.4. Move the decimal point one place to the right, and it becomes 24. Because you moved the decimal point one place to the right in the divisor, you must do the same thing to the dividend. The dividend is 14.64. After you move the decimal point one place to the right, the dividend becomes 146.4.

Step 2

Set up the division equation, and line up the decimal points above and below the division sign.

$$24\overline{)146.4}$$

Step 3

Divide the two decimals normally, as if they were two whole numbers.

$$
\begin{array}{r}
6.1 \\
24\overline{)146.4} \\
-144 \downarrow \\
\hline
24 \\
-24 \\
\hline
0
\end{array}
$$

14.64 ÷ 2.4 = 6.1

Example

What is the quotient of 2.592 ÷ 0.54?

Solution

Step 1

Rewrite the divisor as a whole number.

The divisor is 0.54. Move the decimal point two places to the right.

0.54 → 54

Move the decimal point two places to the right in the dividend as well.

2.592 → 259.2

Step 2

Set up the division equation. Line up the decimal points above and below the division sign.

$$54\overline{)259.2}$$

Step 3

Perform the division.

$$
\begin{array}{r}
4.8 \\
54\overline{)259.2} \\
-216 \downarrow \\
\hline
432 \\
-432 \\
\hline
0
\end{array}
$$

The quotient is 4.8.

7.NS.2D Apply and extend previous understandings of multiplication and division and of fractions to multiply and divide rational numbers. Convert a rational number to a decimal using long division; know that the decimal form of a rational number terminates in 0s or eventually repeats.

CONVERTING FRACTIONS TO TERMINATING DECIMALS

Fractions are parts of a whole. A fraction can also indicate an operation. The line between the numerator and denominator is a division operator.

To represent a fraction as a decimal, divide the numerator (dividend) by the denominator (divisor).

Sometimes, a fraction can be represented as a terminating decimal. **Terminating decimals** are decimal numbers that come to an end. All the digits can be written down. Some examples include 0.4, 0.174, 3.24, and 9.81902.

Example

Write the fraction $\frac{5}{8}$ as a decimal.

Solution

Divide the numerator by the denominator. You can do this in two different ways.

Method 1
Use long division to divide the fraction.

$\frac{5}{8} = 5 \div 8$

$$
\begin{array}{r}
0.625 \\
8\overline{)5.000} \\
48\downarrow\downarrow \\
\overline{20\downarrow} \\
16\downarrow \\
\overline{40} \\
40 \\
\overline{0}
\end{array}
$$

The fraction $\frac{5}{8}$ is equal to 0.625.

Method 2
Use a calculator to divide the fraction.

$\frac{5}{8} = 5 \div 8$

Type in $\boxed{5}\ \boxed{\div}\ \boxed{8}\ \boxed{=}$.

The fraction $\frac{5}{8}$ is equal to 0.625.

Looking at the denominator of a fraction can help you see if it represents a terminating decimal.

The decimal form of a fraction will always terminate if the denominator is a power of 2, 5, or 10.

Example

Is the fraction $\frac{7}{25}$ equivalent to a terminating decimal?

Solution

Step 1
Use the divisibility rules to determine if 5 is a factor of 25.

- 25 ends in 5.
- 25 is divisible by 5.

Because 5 is a factor of 25, $\frac{7}{25}$ is equivalent to a terminating decimal.

Step 2
Verify.

$\frac{7}{25} = 7 \div 25$

$\phantom{\frac{7}{25}} = 0.28$

A reduced fraction cannot be written as a terminating decimal if the denominator is a prime number other than 2 or 5.

CONVERTING FRACTIONS TO REPEATING DECIMALS

Fractions are parts of a whole. A fractions is also an operation. The line between the numerator and the denominator is a division operator.

To represent a fraction as a decimal, divide the numerator (dividend) by the denominator (divisor).

Example

Write the fraction $\frac{2}{9}$ as a decimal.

Solution

Divide the numerator by the denominator.

There are two methods for doing the division.

Method 1: Pencil and paper

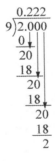

Method 2: Calculator

Type in $\boxed{2}\ \boxed{\div}\ \boxed{9}\ \boxed{=}$.

The answer in the screen is 0.2222222222.

Repeating decimals are decimal numbers where the numbers following the decimal continue on forever, with one or more digits repeating. If one digit after the decimal repeats, it is referred to as a single-digit repeating decimal. Some examples include 0.999…, 0.63422222… and 7.254444….

If more than one digit repeats, it is referred to as a multi-digit repeating decimal. Some examples include 0.125125... and 17.080808....

Since writing the same number or numbers over and over again is not practical or efficient, a bar is placed over top of the repeating digits. This is referred to as bar notation. The number 0.63422222 is written as $0.634\overline{2}$ and 17.080808... is written as $17.\overline{8}$.

The equivalent decimal repeats in these cases:

- The denominator is a prime number other than 2 or 5.
- The denominator is divisible by 3.

Example

Is the fraction $\dfrac{14}{24}$ equivalent to a repeating decimal?

Solution

Step 1
Use the divisibility rules to determine if 3 is a factor of 24.
$2 + 4 = 6$
24 is divisible by 3.

Because 3 is a factor of 24, $\dfrac{14}{24}$ is equivalent to a repeating decimal.

Step 2
Verify.
$\dfrac{7}{24} = 7 \div 24$
$= 0.58333...$
$= 0.58\overline{3}$

Example

Is the fraction $\dfrac{8}{11}$ equivalent to a repeating decimal?

Solution

Step 1
Determine whether the denominator is a prime number.
The denominator is a prime number; only 1 and 11 are factors of 11.
Because the denominator is a prime number other than 2 or 5, $\dfrac{8}{11}$ is equivalent to a repeating decimal.

Step 2
Verify.
$\dfrac{8}{11} = 8 \div 11$
$= 0.727,272...$
$= 0.\overline{72}$

7.NS.3 Solve real–world and mathematical problems involving the four operations with rational numbers.

Solving Addition Problems

When solving decimal problems involving addition, look for keywords such as *add, sum, in addition to, change, increased by, more than, plus, altogether, in total, in all,* and *more than.*

Use these problem-solving steps to work through decimal problems involving addition:

1. Determine what the problem is asking.
2. Identify the information that is given.
3. Decide on the strategy or operation to use.
4. Apply the strategy or operation.
5. Check the answer.

Example

Mindy goes to a store that is having a "Get Ready" for winter sale. There is no no sales tax on any of the products. The items are priced as follows:

- Scarf—$7.49
- Gloves—$14.99
- Knitted hat —$12.49

If Mindy chooses to buy a knitted hat and a scarf, how much will she spend altogether?

Solution

Step 1

Determine what the problem is asking.
The problem is asking how much it will cost for the knitted hat and scarf.

Step 2

Identify the information that is given.

-
- The price of the scarf is $7.49.
- There is no sales tax.

Keyword: altogether

Step 3

Decide on the strategy or operation to use.
The keyword *altogether* implies addition.

Step 4

Apply the strategy or operation.
Write the decimal numbers in a vertical column, lining up the decimal points and place values. Starting at the far right and working left, add the digits in each vertical column.

$$
\begin{array}{r}
\overset{1}{1}2.49 \\
+\ 7.49 \\
\hline
19.98
\end{array}
$$

Step 5

Check by estimating.

$$
\begin{array}{r}
12.49 \rightarrow 12 \\
+7.49 \rightarrow \ \underline{7} \\
19
\end{array}
$$

The scarf and toque will cost $19.98.

SOLVING PROBLEMS BY SUBTRACTING DECIMALS

When solving problems that involve subtraction, look for keywords such as *difference*, *left over*, *change*, *decreased by*, *less than*, *minus*, *how much more*, *take away*, *how much less*, *taken from*, and *diminished*.

Use these problem-solving steps to work through the question:

1. Determine what the problem is asking.
2. Identify the information that is given.
3. Decide on the strategy or operation to use.
4. Apply the strategy or operation.
5. Check the answer.

Example

John bought a computer for $2,346.79. Three years later, he sold it for $725.

How much money did John lose?

Solution

Step 1

Determine what the problem is asking.
How much money did John lose?

Step 2

Identify the information that is given.
Original price: $2,346.79
Selling price: $725
Keyword: lose

Step 3

Decide on the strategy or operation to use.
The keyword *lose* implies subtraction.

Step 4

Apply the strategy or operation.
Write the minuend above the subtrahend in a vertical column, lining up the decimal points and place values. Starting at the far right and working left, subtract the bottom number from the top number.

$$
\begin{array}{r}
\overset{1\ 1}{2}346.79 \\
-\ 725.00 \\
\hline
1{,}621.79
\end{array}
$$

Step 5

Check the answer.

Add the bottom two rows of numbers.

$9 + 0 = 9$
$7 + 0 = 7$
$1 + 5 = 6$
$2 + 2 = 4$
$6 + 7 = 13$
$1 + 0 = 1$

John lost $1,621.79 from the original purchase price.

SOLVING PROBLEMS BY MULTIPLYING DECIMALS

When solving problems involving the multiplication of decimals, look for keywords such as *times*, *product*, *by*, *of*, *doubled*, *tripled*, *factor of*, and *multiple of*.

Use these problem-solving steps to work through the question:

1. Determine what the problem is asking.
2. Identify the information that is given.
3. Decide on the strategy or operation to use.
4. Apply the strategy or operation.
5. Check the answer.

Example

Eman is asked to buy 3.5 kg of grapes, which cost $2.80/kg.

How much will the grapes cost?

Solution

Step 1
Determine what the problem is asking.

Eman has to determine the total cost of the grapes.

Step 2
Identify the information that is given.

Price of grapes: $2.80/kg.
He needs to purchase 3.5 kg.

Keyword: of

Step 3
Decide on the strategy or operation to use.

The keyword *of* implies multiplication.

Step 4
Apply the strategy or operation.

Place the multiplicand over the multiplier with the digits lined up in vertical columns. Multiply the decimal numbers following the same process as multiplying whole numbers.
Place the decimal point into the answer.

$$
\begin{array}{r}
280\,(2 \text{ decimal places}) \\
\times \quad\underline{35}\,(1 \text{ decimal place}) \\
1,400 \\
+ \quad\underline{8,400} \\
9,800
\end{array}
$$

There are three digits behind the decimal places in the factors being multiplied. There will be three digits after the decimal place in the product. The zero place holders can be dropped.

$9,800 \rightarrow 9.800$

Step 5
Check by doing the inverse operation.
$9.8 \div 3.5 = 2.8$
$9.8 \div 2.8 = 3.5$
It will cost $9.80 to buy 3.5 kg of grapes.

SOLVING PROBLEMS BY ADDING AND SUBTRACTING FRACTIONS

When solving questions involving more than one operation $(+, -, \times, \div)$, an order is followed to get the correct answer. Use the acronym BEDMAS to help remember the order of operations.

Brackets	Start by performing the operations inside the brackets, and then carry out all the operations outside the brackets.
Exponents	Carry out exponents within brackets before other operations.
Division	Carry out operations in the order they appear from left to right (reading order).
Multiplication	
Addition	Carry out operations in the order they appear from left to right (reading order).
Subtraction	

To solve word problems involving fractions, carefully read the question. Then, translate the words into a mathematical expression. Look for keywords that indicate what operation to use to solve the problem. Underline or highlight the keywords if necessary.

The following are some keywords to focus on when you are adding and subtracting:

- Adding—sum, total, altogether, more than
- Subtracting—difference, less than, take away, taken from, have left

To solve a problem involving fractions, follow these steps:

1. Identify the fractions and the operational keywords.
2. Write an expression representing the problem.
3. Solve. Reduce the answer to lowest terms if possible.

Example

James owns $2\frac{3}{5}$ acres of land and his brother Art owns $3\frac{1}{5}$ acres of land that they farm together. One day, Sheila offers to buy $1\frac{2}{5}$ acres of the brothers' combined land.

If the brothers decide to sell the land to Sheila, how much land will they still own?

Solution

Step 1
Identify the fractions and the operational keywords.

- James owns $2\frac{3}{5}$ acres of land.

- Art owns $3\frac{1}{5}$ acres of land.

Sheila wants to buy $1\frac{2}{5}$ acres of land.

The keyword *together* means addition. The keywords *how much land will they still own* means subtraction.

Step 2
Write an expression representing the problem.
$\left(2\frac{3}{5} + 3\frac{1}{5}\right) - 1\frac{2}{5}$

Step 3
Solve.

Follow the order of operations.

Change the mixed numbers into improper fractions.

$2 \times 5 + 3 = \dfrac{15}{3}$

$3 \times 5 + 1 = \dfrac{16}{5}$

$1 \times 5 + 2 = \dfrac{7}{5}$

$\left(\dfrac{15}{5} + \dfrac{16}{5}\right) - \dfrac{7}{5}$

Calculate the brackets first.

$\left(\dfrac{13}{5} + \dfrac{16}{5}\right) - \dfrac{7}{5}$

$= \dfrac{29}{5} - \dfrac{7}{5}$

Complete the subtraction.

$\dfrac{29 - 7}{5} = \dfrac{22}{5}$

Convert to a mixed number.
$22 \div 5 = 4$, with a remainder of 2.

$\dfrac{22}{5} = 4\frac{2}{5}$

The brothers will have $4\frac{2}{5}$ acres of land left if they decide to sell some of it to Sheila.

Example

Everyone should drink $8\frac{1}{4}$ cups of water and $2\frac{2}{5}$ cups of milk every day.

How much fluid should everyone drink in total on a daily basis?

Solution

Step 1
Identify the fractions and the operational keywords

- $8\frac{1}{4}$ cups of water

- $2\frac{2}{5}$ cups of milk

The keywords *in total* means addition.

Step 2

Write an expression representing the problem.

$8\frac{1}{4} + 2\frac{2}{5}$

Step 3

Solve.

Change the mixed numbers into improper fractions.

$8 \times 4 + 1 = \frac{33}{4}$

$2 \times 5 + 2 = \frac{12}{5}$

$\frac{33}{4} + \frac{12}{5}$

Rewrite the improper fractions with a common denominator.

$= \frac{33 \times 5}{4 \times 5} + \frac{12 \times 4}{5 \times 4}$

$= \frac{165}{20} + \frac{48}{20}$

Add the numerators while keeping the same denominator.

$= \frac{165 + 48}{20}$

$= \frac{213}{20}$

Convert to a mixed number.

$213 \div 20 = 10$, with a remainder of 13.

$\frac{213}{20} = 10\frac{13}{20}$

Everyone should drink $10\frac{13}{20}$ cups of fluid a day.

SOLVING PROBLEMS INVOLVING THE SIMPLE MULTIPLICATION OF FRACTIONS

When solving word problems, look for keywords that tell you what operation to perform.

Some multiplication keywords are *of*, *times*, *product*, *double*, and *triple*.

Example

Mandy is at the beach making sand castles.

Each tower of the castle requires $\frac{2}{3}$ of a bucket of sand.

How many buckets of sand will Mandy need to make four towers?

Solution

Step 1

Identify the operation.

The keyword **of** indicates multiplication.

The amount of sand for each tower is multiplied by the number of towers.

$\frac{2}{3} \times 4$

Step 2

Multiply the numerator by the numerator and the denominator by the denominator.

Change the whole number to a fraction by writing it as a fraction with the whole number as the numerator and 1 as the denominator.

$4 = \frac{4}{1}$

$\frac{2}{3} \times \frac{4}{1} = \frac{2 \times 4}{3 \times 1}$

$= \frac{8}{3}$

Step 3

Change the improper fraction to a mixed number by dividing the numerator by the denominator.

$$\text{numerator} \div \text{denominator}$$
$$= \text{quotient} + \frac{\text{remainder}}{\text{denominator}}$$
$$8 \div 3 = 2 + \frac{2}{3}$$
$$= 2\frac{2}{3}$$

Mandy needs $2\frac{2}{3}$ buckets of sand to make the 4 towers.

SOLVING PROBLEMS INVOLVING THE SIMPLE DIVISION OF FRACTIONS

When you solve word problems, look for keywords that tell you what operation to perform.
Some division keywords are: *quotient*, *times greater*, *times less than*, and *groups*.

Example

Eric wants to split his hanging flower box into 5 equal sections.

If his flower box is $\frac{5}{8}$ m², how big will each section be?

Solution

Step 1

Identify information and the operation.
Flower box is split into 5 equal sections
The keyword *split* indicates division.

$$\frac{5}{8} \div 5$$

Step 2

Write the reciprocal of the second fraction.

The reciprocal of $\frac{5}{1}$ is $\frac{1}{5}$.

Step 3

Multiply the first fraction by the reciprocal.
Multiply the numerator by the numerator and the denominator by the denominator.

$$\frac{5}{8} \times \frac{1}{5} = \frac{5 \times 1}{8 \times 5} = \frac{5}{40}$$

Step 4

Reduce the fraction to lowest terms.

5 and 40 share a common factor of 5.

$$\frac{5 \div 5}{40 \div 5} = \frac{1}{8}$$

Each section of the flower box will be $\frac{1}{8}$ m².

SOLVING PROBLEMS BY DIVIDING DECIMALS

Dividing decimals by decimals is similar to dividing whole numbers. To divide decimals by decimals, use the following steps:

1. Convert the divisor to a whole number by moving the decimal. What is done to the divisor must also be done to the dividend.
   For example, if the decimal is moved two places to the right in the divisor, the decimal must be moved two places to the right in the dividend.
2. Set up the division equation. Remember to place the decimal into the quotient by moving it directly above its place in the dividend.
3. Perform the division.

Example

Andy correctly solved the expression $14.64 \div 2.4$.

$$
\begin{array}{r}
6.1 \\
24 \overline{)146.4} \\
-144 \downarrow \\
\hline
24 \\
-24 \\
\hline
0
\end{array}
$$

You can use your knowledge about dividing decimals to solve a wide variety of real-world problems. Whenever you have a problem you need to solve, use the following steps:

1. Read the question carefully and understand the problem.
2. Make a plan. Decide which operations you need to use and in which order.
3. Solve the problem. Carry out your plan.
4. Decide if your answer is reasonable.

When you are trying to understand the problem, pay special attention to the numbers and values that are given, and look for keywords. Sometimes you may want to draw a picture or diagram to help you understand the problem more clearly.

Decide what kind of answer you will give. Is it a money amount? A volume? A quantity? Decide if your answer will be a big number or a small one.

When solving problems involving the division of decimals, look for keywords such as *quotient*, *split*, *share*, *divide*, *per*, *average*, *each*, and *group*.

To decide if your answer is reasonable, you can use estimation or the context of the problem. You can also think about the operation that you are using. For example, if you are dividing, you know that the answer will be smaller than the dividend. If the answer is larger, then it is not reasonable. Once you have made sure your answer is reasonable you should write your answer as a sentence.

Example

Marge won $112.80 that she split evenly between her grandchildren.

If each grandchild receives $7.52, how many grandchildren does Marge have?

Solution

Step 1

Understand the problem.

The question is asking for the number of grandchildren Marge split her winnings between. Therefore, the answer will be a whole number. The following information is important to the question:

• Marge won $112.80.
• Each grandchild received $7.52.

Step 2

Make a plan. Decide which operations to use and in which order.

Marge split her winnings, so the operation to use is division.

Step 3

Solve the problem by carrying out the plan. Since the divisor is not a whole number, make it a whole number by moving the decimal two places to the right. What is done to the divisor must also be done to the dividend.

The decimal in the divisor, 7.52, will move two places to the right to create 752, and the decimal in the dividend, 112.80, will move two places to the right to create 11,280.

Divide the numbers.

$$
\begin{array}{r}
15. \\
752 \overline{)11{,}280.} \\
-752\downarrow \\
\hline
3{,}760 \\
-3{,}760 \\
\hline
0
\end{array}
$$

Step 4

Decide if your answer is reasonable.

As predicted, the answer is a whole number. Using estimation, 7.52 can be rounded to 8 and 112.80 can be rounded to the compatible number 112.

$112 \div 8 = 14$

This is close to what was calculated, so the answer is reasonable.

Marge has 15 grandchildren.

Solving Problems by Adding Decimals

Use the following problem-solving steps to work through decimal problems involving addition:

1. Determine what the problem is asking.
2. Identify the information that is given.
3. Decide on the strategy or operation to use.
4. Apply the strategy or operation.

A good way to determine what the problem is asking is by looking for these keywords:

- Add
- Sum
- In addition to
- Change
- Increased by
- More than
- Plus
- Altogether
- In total
- In all

Example

Mindy goes to a store that is having a spring sale. There is no tax on any of the products. The items are priced as follows:

- Scarves—$7.49
- Skirts—$14.99
- T-shirts—$12.49

If Mindy chooses to buy a T-shirt and a scarf, how much will she spend altogether?

Solution

Step 1

Determine what the problem is asking.

The problem is asking how much it will cost for a T-shirt and scarf.

Step 2

Identify the information that is given.

The following information is needed to solve the problem:

- The price of a T-shirt is $12.49.
- The price of a scarf is $7.49.
- There is no tax.
- The keyword *altogether* is used.

Step 3

Decide on the strategy or operation to use.

The keyword *altogether* means you should use addition to solve the problem.

Step 4

Add the numbers together.

Write the decimal numbers in a vertical column, lining up the decimal points and place values. Starting at the far right and working left, add the digits in each vertical column.

$$\begin{array}{r} \overset{1}{12.49} \\ +7.49 \\ \hline 19.98 \end{array}$$

Mindy will spend $19.98.

EXERCISE #1—THE NUMBER SYSTEM

49. Which of the following situations can be represented by the integer –9?

   A. A temperature of 9°C

   B. A weight gain of 9 kg

   C. A kite flying 9 m above ground

   D. A diver swimming 9 m below sea level

Use the following information to answer the next question.

A number line representing an expression is shown.

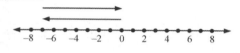

50. The expression that is represented by the given number line is

   A. $(+7) \times (-7)$

   B. $(+7) + (-7)$

   C. $(-7) \div (+7)$

   D. $(-7) + (+7)$

51. Use integer tiles to evaluate the expression $(-2) + (+4)$.

Use the following information to answer the next question.

☐ Negative 1
■ Positive 1

52. Which of the following sets of algebra tiles represents the expression 2 – 5 and its solution?

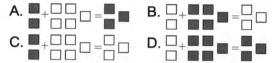

Use the following information to answer the next question.

During a football game, Jessie caught three passes. One was for a touchdown and went for 39 yards. The second was for a loss of 12 yards. The third was for a gain of 24 yards.

53. What was the total yardage gained by Jessie for the three plays?

   A. 75 yards   B. 55 yards

   C. 51 yards   D. 3 yards

Use the following information to answer the next question.

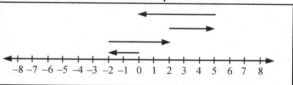

54. Which of the following expressions represents the series of operations shown on the number line?

   A. $(-2) - 4 + 3 - 5$

   B. $(-2) + 4 - 3 - 5$

   C. $(-2) + 4 + 3 - 5$

   D. $(-2) + (-4) + (-3) - 5$

55. Solve the expression $(+61) + (-21)$.

56. What is the product of 3, 2, and –1? _____

Use the following information to answer the next question.

Nicole's watch is losing 3 minutes each hour. She resets her watch to the correct time each morning at 8 o'clock.

57. How many minutes will her watch have lost after 24 hours?

58. What is the result when the expression $(-64) \div (-4) \div (-2) \div 4 \div 1$ is simplified?
A. 6   B. 2
C. –2   D. –4

Use the following information to answer the next question.

Brent added the numbers 82.437 + 31.293.

59. Rounded to the nearest tenth, what is the sum of the two numbers?

60. What is the difference between 52.4 and 5.935?

61. When $\frac{5}{8}$ is multiplied by $\frac{4}{15}$, the answer is
A. $\frac{9}{120}$ B. $\frac{9}{13}$
C. $\frac{1}{8}$ D. $\frac{1}{6}$

62. Solve $\frac{5}{7} + \frac{4}{5}$.

63. What is the product of 0.221×0.411?

64. When the number 578.042 is divided by 0.01, the decimal moves
    A. two places to the left
    B. five places to the left
    C. two places to the right
    D. five places to the right

65. Write the fraction $\frac{23}{25}$ as a decimal.

Use the following information to answer the next question.

Jasmine is the assistant coach for the community soccer team. The team consists of 11 boys and 7 girls, of which 12 must be on the field at all times. Jasmine's responsibility is to make sure that there are at least 7 boys and 5 girls on the field at all times.

66. Expressed as a decimal, the number of boys that must be playing on the field at all times is
    A. 0.583   B. 0.58$\bar{3}$
    C. 0.58$\overline{3}$ D. 0.$\overline{583}$

Use the following information to answer the next question.

Jason spent 23.2% of his salary on entertainment, 21.4% on clothing, 36.17% on food and rent, and 8.73% on charitable donations. He also put 10.5% of his salary into savings.

67. What percent of Jason's total salary was spent on entertainment, clothing, and charitable donations?

Use the following information to answer the next question.

John has $20, and he buys a CD on sale for $14.87.

68. How much change will he get back?

69. A garden club planted 14 fir trees in a local park. If the total cost of the trees was $598.50, how much did each tree cost?
    A. $42.25   B. $42.65
    C. $42.75   D. $42.85

Phillipa has $\frac{3}{4}$ of a regular deck of 52 cards. One-third of these are red.

70. How many black cards does she have?
    A. 39   B. 26
    C. 18   D. 13

Thomas brings over $\frac{1}{2}$ of his marble collection. He divides these marbles equally among 3 friends.

71. What fraction of Thomas's entire marble collection did each friend get?
    A. $\frac{6}{1}$ B. $\frac{1}{6}$
    C. $\frac{1}{5}$ D. $\frac{5}{1}$

Kane and Kaia are saving money to buy a Mother's Day gift. Kane has saved $\frac{1}{2}$ of the money they need. Kaia has saved another $\frac{1}{6}$ of the money.

72. What fraction of the money have Kane and Kaia already saved?
    A. $\frac{2}{4}$ B. $\frac{2}{3}$
    C. $\frac{2}{6}$ D. $\frac{2}{8}$

Ruby's family was on their way to Jasper when her dad decided to fill up the vehicle. The price of gas was $4.024/gal at the pumps.

73. How much did Ruby's dad pay, to the nearest cent, if he needed 13.9 gal of gas?
    A. $52.31   B. $55.88
    C. $55.93   D. $58.94

EXERCISE #1—THE NUMBER SYSTEM ANSWERS AND SOLUTIONS

49. D	56. -6	63. 0.090831	70. B
50. D	57. See solution	64. C	71. B
51. See solution	58. C	65. See solution	72. B
52. C	59. See solution	66. B	73. C
53. C	60. See solution	67. See solution	
54. C	61. D	68. See solution	
55. See solution	62. See solution	69. C	

49. D

Sea level would be represented by 0 on a number line. Any heights above sea level would be represented by positive integers. Any distances below sea level would be represented by negative integers.

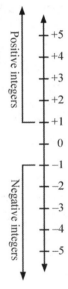

Since the diver is 9 m deep into the water, the diver is 9 m below sea level. Therefore, this situation can be represented by the integer – 9.

50. D

Step 1
Determine the integer represented by the first arrow. The first arrow shows 7 units left from 0, so it represents the integer –7.

Step 2
Determine the integer represented by the second arrow.

The second arrow is moved 7 units to the right of –7. Therefore, the second arrow represents the integer +7.

Therefore, the number line shows the expression $(-7) + (+7)$.

51.

Step 1
Draw the number of tiles representing the first integer in the expression.

The first term is (-2). Draw two unshaded tiles.
□ □

Step 2
Draw the number of tiles representing the second integer in the expression opposite the first row of tiles.

The second term is $(+4)$. Draw four shaded tiles lined up below the first term tiles.
□ □
■ ■ ■ ■

Step 3
Cancel the zero pairs.

▨ ▨
▨ ▨ ■ ■

Step 4
Determine the sum.

The color and the number of the remaining tiles represent the sum.

Two positive tiles remain, so the sum is $(+2)$.
$(-2) + (+4) = (+2)$

52. C

Step 1
Rewrite the expression using the additive inverse.
$(+2) + (-5)$

Step 2
Draw integer tiles to represent the first integer.
Draw two shaded tiles to represent (+2).

Step 3
Draw integer tiles to represent the second integer.
Draw five unshaded tiles to represent (−5).

Step 4
Cancel the zero pairs.

Step 5
Complete the solution.
Count the remaining squares.
Three unshaded squares are left, so the answer is −3.
The set of algebra tiles that represents the equation 2 − 5 = −3 is as follows:

53. C
Step 1
Identify integer and operation keywords.
Integer keywords: *gain* indicates positive, and *loss* indicates negative.
Operation keyword: *total*

Step 2
Write an expression representing the problem.
Touchdown of 39 yards → +39
Loss of 12 yards → −12
Gain of 24 yards → +24
The total yardage can be calculated by adding the three numbers.
(+39) + (−12) + (+24)

Step 3
Solve.
$(+39) + (−12) + (+24) = (+27) + (+24)$
$= +51$
Therefore, Jessie gained 51 yards.

54. C
Step 1
Determine the first and second integers in the expression.
The first movement is 2 units to the left. Moving to the left is equivalent to moving in the negative direction.
The first integer is (−2).
The second movement is 4 units to the right. Moving to the right is equivalent to adding 4. (−2) + 4

Step 2
Determine the third and fourth operations on the number line.
The third movement is 3 units to the right. Moving to the right is equivalent to adding 3. (−2) + 4 + 3
The fourth movement is 5 units to the left. Moving to the left is equivalent to subtracting 5.
(−2) + 4 + 3 − 5

Step 3
Write the expression.
(−2) + 4 + 3 − 5

55.
Step 1
The signs are different, so subtract the smaller positive value from the larger positive value.
The positive value of +61 is 61. The positive value of −21 is 21.
61 − 21 = 40

Step 2
Take the sign of the larger value.
Since 61 has a larger value and a positive sign, apply it to the answer.
(+61) + (−21) = +40

56. -6
Step 1
Remove the negative signs, and multiply the numbers.
The values are 3, 2, and 1.
3 × 2 × 1 = 6

Step 2
Count the number of negative signs.
There is one negative sign in the question. An odd number of negative signs indicates that the answer will be negative.
This means that 3 × 2 × (−1) = −6.

57.

Step 1
Identify integer and operation keywords.
Integer keywords: *losing* indicates negative.
Losing 3 minutes→ (−3)
Operation keyword: *How many*—when larger amounts are involved, multiplication is indicated.

Step 2
Write an expression representing the problem.
Multiply the number of minutes lost each hour by the number of hours in one day.
$24 × (−3)$

Step 3
Simplify.
$24 × (−3) = (−72)$
During the day, Nicole's watch loses 72 minutes.

58. C

Step 1
Divide the absolute values.
$64 ÷ 4 ÷ 2 ÷ 4 ÷ 1$
$16 ÷ 2 ÷ 4 ÷ 1$
$8 ÷ 4 ÷ 1$
$2 ÷ 1$
2

Step 2
Count the number of negative signs.
Three negative signs in the question result in a negative sign in the answer.
$(−64) ÷ (−4) ÷ (−2) ÷ 4 ÷ 1 = (−2)$

59.

Step 1
To add the numbers vertically, line up the decimal points and the digits in the same place values. Beginning with the thousandths, add the numbers vertically from right to left. Regroup where necessary.
Be sure to place the decimal point in the correct position in the answer, between the ones and the tenths.

$$\begin{array}{r} {}^{11} \\ 82.437 \\ +31.293 \\ \hline 113.730 \end{array}$$

Step 2
Round the sum to the nearest tenth.
Since $3 < 7$, $113.730 → 113.7$.
Rounded to the nearest tenth, the sum of the two numbers is 113.7.

60.

To determine the difference between the two numbers, subtract the lesser amount from the greater amount.

Since $5.935 < 52.4$, the lesser amount is 5.935 and the greater amount is 52.4.

When writing the numbers vertically, line up the decimal points and the place values. It might be helpful to add two zeros to the end of 52.4 so that the place values line up. Adding the zeros will not change the value of the number.
$52.4 → 52.400$

Regroup where necessary.

$$\begin{array}{r} {}^{4\ 11\ \ 13\,\overset{9}{1\!0}\,10} \\ \cancel{52.400} \\ -5.935 \\ \hline 46.465 \end{array}$$

The difference between 52.4 and 5.935 is 46.465.

61. D

Step 1
Multiply numerator by numerator and denominator by denominator.
$$\frac{5}{8} × \frac{4}{15} = \frac{5 × 4}{8 × 15} = \frac{20}{120}$$

Step 2
Reduce the fraction to lowest terms.
Since the greatest common factor that 20 and 120 share is 20, divide both the numerator and the denominator by 20.
$$\frac{20 ÷ 20}{120 ÷ 20} = \frac{1}{6}$$
Therefore, $\frac{5}{8} × \frac{4}{15} = \frac{1}{6}$.

62.

Step 1
Find the lowest common denominator.
Write multiples of each denominator until a common one appears.

- Multiples of 7 are 7, 14, 21, 28, and 35.
- Multiples of 5 are 5, 10, 15, 20, 25, 30, and 35.

The lowest common denominator (LCD) of 7 and 5 is 35.

Step 2

Use the LCD to create new equivalent fractions with a denominator of 35.

Multiply the numerator and denominator of each fraction by the same factor.

$$\frac{5 \times 5}{7 \times 5} = \frac{25}{35}$$

$$\frac{4 \times 7}{5 \times 7} = \frac{28}{35}$$

Step 3

Add the numerators of the fractions while keeping the denominator the same.

$$\frac{25}{35} + \frac{28}{35} = \frac{53}{35}$$

Step 4

Convert the improper fraction to a mixed fraction, and reduce to lowest terms.

$$\frac{53}{35} = 1\frac{18}{35}$$

The mixed fraction $1\frac{18}{35}$ is in lowest terms.

Therefore, $\frac{5}{7} + \frac{4}{5} = 1\frac{18}{35}$.

63. 0.090831

Step 1

Remove the decimal point.

The zeros before the decimal point can be removed as well because having a zero in front does not change the value of the number.

221 × 411

Step 2

Line the numbers up based on place value.

$$\begin{array}{r} 221 \\ \times\ 411 \\ \hline \end{array}$$

Step 3

Multiply the two whole numbers together.

Multiply 1 by 221.

$$\begin{array}{r} 221 \\ \times\ 1 \\ \hline 221 \end{array}$$

Multiply 10 by 221.

Remember to add a zero on the right side before multiplying to hold the place value of the tens.

Continue multiplying the top number by 1.

$$\begin{array}{r} 221 \\ \times\ 10 \\ \hline 2,210 \end{array}$$

Multiply 400 by 221.

Remember to add two zeros on the right side before multiplying to hold the place value of the hundreds.

Continue multiplying the top number by 4.

$$\begin{array}{r} 221 \\ \times\ 400 \\ \hline 88,400 \end{array}$$

Step 4

Add the products together.

$$\begin{array}{r} 221 \\ 2,210 \\ 1 \\ +\ 88,400 \\ \hline 90,831 \end{array}$$

Step 5

Put the decimal back into the product.

Count the number of digits to the right of each of the original decimals. Both decimal numbers have three digits to the right of the decimal point. Added together, the new decimal should have six digits after the decimal point.

Because the product has only five digits in it, you need to place a zero in front of the 9 so that there are six digits after the decimal point.

0.221 × 0.411 = 0.090831

64. C

A decimal number that is used as a divisor needs to be made into a whole number first. This is done by multiplying the decimal divisor by a power of ten for each place value to the right of the decimal point.

To remove the decimal, 0.01 must be multiplied by 100 because the last digit, 1, is in the hundredths place.

0.01 × 100 = 1

This means that the decimal moved two places to the right.

65.

Divide the numerator by the denominator.

23 ÷ 25 = 0.92

66. B

Before the answer can be expressed as a decimal, it must be put into fraction form.

Since at least 7 boys need to be on the field at all times, 7 becomes the numerator. The denominator is 12, which is the total number of players on the field at any given time.

$$\frac{7}{12}$$

To express $\frac{7}{12}$ as a decimal, divide the numerator by the denominator.

$7 \div 12 = 0.58333...$

The number of boys on the field at all times is $0.58333...$, which can also be written as $0.58\overline{3}$.

67.

Step 1
Determine what the problem is asking.
The problem is to determine what percent of Jason's salary was spent on entertainment, clothing, and charitable donations.

Step 2
Identify the information that is given.
Jason spent 23.2% of his salary on entertainment, 21.4% on clothing, and 8.73% on donations.
The keyword is *in total*.

Step 3
Decide on the strategy or operation to use.
The keyword *in total* implies addition.

Step 4
Apply the strategy or operation.
Write the percentages in a vertical column, lining up the decimal points and place values. Starting at the far right and working left, add the digits in each vertical column.

$$\begin{array}{r} {}^{1\,1} \\ 23.20 \\ 21.40 \\ +8.73 \\ \hline 53.33 \end{array}$$

Step 5
Check by estimating.

$$\begin{array}{r} 23.20 \rightarrow \ 23 \\ 21.40 \rightarrow \ 21 \\ 8.73 \rightarrow \ \ 9 \\ \hline 53 \end{array}$$

Therefore, 53.33% of Jason's salary went to entertainment, clothing, and charitable donations.

68.

Step 1
Identify the information that is given.
John has $20, and the price of the CD is $14.87.

Step 2
Decide on the strategy or operation to use.
Subtract the selling price of the CD from the amount John has to determine the change he will receive.

Step 3
Apply the strategy or operation.
Write the minuend above the subtrahend in a vertical column, lining up the decimal points and place values. Starting at the far right and working left, subtract the bottom number from the top number.

$$\begin{array}{r} {}^{1\,9}\ {}^{9\,1} \\ 20.00 \\ -14.87 \\ \hline 5.13 \end{array}$$

Step 5
Verify the result.
Add the bottom two rows of numbers, and check that the minuend is obtained.

$$\begin{array}{r} {}^{1\,1}\ {}^{1} \\ 14.87 \\ +5.13 \\ \hline 20.00 \end{array}$$

John will get back $5.13 in change.

69. C

Divide the total cost of the trees ($598.50) by the number of trees (14).

When dividing, be sure to line up the decimal points in the quotient and dividend.

$$\begin{array}{r} 42.75 \\ 14\overline{)598.50} \\ 56 \\ \hline 38 \\ 28 \\ \hline 105 \\ 98 \\ \hline 70 \\ 70 \\ \hline 0 \end{array}$$

The cost of each tree was $42.75.

70. B

Step 1
Determine the number of cards Phillipa has.

Since Phillipa has $\frac{3}{4}$ of 52 cards, multiply $\frac{3}{4}$ by 52.

Multiply numerator by numerator and denominator by denominator, and reduce the fraction to its lowest terms.

$$\frac{3}{4} \times \frac{52}{1} = \frac{3 \times 52}{4 \times 1} = \frac{156}{4} = 39$$

Phillipa has 39 cards.

Step 2
Determine the number of red cards she has.

Since $\frac{1}{3}$ of 39 cards are red, multiply $\frac{1}{3}$ by 39.

$$\frac{1}{3} \times \frac{39}{1} = \frac{1 \times 39}{3 \times 1} = \frac{39}{3} = 13$$

There are 13 red cards.

Step 4
Calculate how many black cards she has.

To calculate the number of black cards, subtract the number of red cards (13) from the total number of cards (39).

$39 - 13 = 26$

71. B

Step 1
Write a division sentence.

$$\frac{1}{2} \div 3$$

Step 2
Write the division as a multiplication sentence.

Change the whole number 3 into a fraction by giving it a denominator of 1.

$$\frac{3}{1}$$

The reciprocal of $\frac{3}{1}$ is $\frac{1}{3}$.

$$\frac{1}{2} \div 3 = \frac{1}{2} \div \frac{3}{1}$$
$$= \frac{1}{2} \times \frac{1}{3}$$

Step 3
Multiply numerator by numerator and denominator by denominator.

$$\frac{1}{2} \times \frac{1}{3} = \frac{1 \times 1}{2 \times 3}$$
$$= \frac{1}{6}$$

Each friend gets $\frac{1}{6}$ of the marble collection.

72. B

Step 1
Identify the important information.

Kane has saved $\frac{1}{2}$ of the money.

Kaia has saved $\frac{1}{6}$ of the money.

The question is asking how much they have saved in total, so you need to add the two fractions together.

Step 2
Create equivalent fractions.

Only fractions with the same denominator can be added together. To create equivalent fractions, you must find the lowest common multiple of the two denominators and use it to create new fractions.

• Multiples of 2 are 2, 4, 6, and 8.
• Multiples of 6 are 6, 12, and 18.

The lowest common multiple is 6. Use 6 as the denominator for the new fractions. Remember that the operations performed on the denominator must also be done to the numerator.

$$\frac{1}{2} = \frac{1 \times 3}{2 \times 3} = \frac{3}{6}$$

Since $\frac{1}{6}$ already has a denominator of 6, it remains the same.

Step 3
Add the fractions.

The denominator remains the same while you add the numerators.

$$\frac{3}{6} + \frac{1}{6} = \frac{4}{6}$$

Simplify the fraction.

$$\frac{4}{6} = \frac{4 \div 2}{6 \div 2} = \frac{2}{3}$$

Altogether, Kane and Kaia have saved $\frac{2}{3}$ of the money.

73. C

To multiply a decimal number by another decimal number, multiply as for whole numbers.

```
   4.024
 × 13.9
  36,216
 120,720
 402,400
 559,336
```

Then, place the decimal in the answer. Since there are four digits after the decimal places in the question, count four places from the right in the answer, and place the decimal there as follows: 559,336 → 55.9336

Rounded to the nearest cent, $55.9336 is $55.93.

EXERCISE #2—THE NUMBER SYSTEM

74. Which of the following examples **cannot** be represented by the integer −5?

A. A loss of $5.00

B. A temperature of minus 5°

C. A road 5 km above sea level

D. A parkade 5 floors below ground level

75. Which of the following set of calculator sequences will result in an answer of +2?

A. +2 + −2 + −2 + −2 + +2 + +2 + −2

B. −2 + −2 + −2 + +2 + +2 + +2 + −2

C. +2 + −2 + −2 + +2 + +2 + +2 + −2

D. −2 + +2 + +2 + +2 + −2 + −2 + −2

76. Add (+3) + (−6) using a number line.

77. Which of the following values is the result of 11 − (−6) − (−12) − 13 − 14?

A. −34

B. −22

C. 2

D. 28

78. Theo is riding in a hot-air balloon. Presently, it is 89 m above the ground. If the balloon rises 32 m, descends 44 m, descends another 27 m, and finally rises 18 m, how high will the balloon be above the ground?

A. 21 m

B. 68 m

C. 157 m

D. 210 m

79. When a negative integer is subtracted from a positive integer, the difference is

A. zero

B. lower

C. positive

D. negative

80. Solve the expression (+12) + (−30).

Use the following information to answer the next question.

Rhonda won $100 worth of groceries in a contest at her local grocery store. To receive her reward, Rhonda must answer this skill-testing question correctly: −3 × 2 × −1 × −1 × −4 × 2.

81. If Rhonda received her prize, what answer did she give for the skill-testing question?

A. 64

B. 48

C. −48

D. −64

Over 13 days, there was a total decrease in temperature of 39 degrees Celsius.

82. What was the average daily change in temperature?

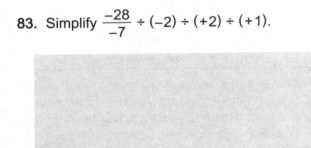

83. Simplify $\dfrac{-28}{-7} \div (-2) \div (+2) \div (+1)$.

Christine traveled by bus to visit her grandparents. On the way, the bus stopped at three different towns.

- At the first town, the bus had traveled 107 km.
- At the second town, the bus had traveled 223.56 km from the first town.
- At the last town, the bus had traveled 584.062 km from the second town.

84. What was the total distance the bus traveled?

85. When 2.73 is subtracted from 6.491, what is the difference?

86. When $\dfrac{2}{3}$ is multiplied by $\dfrac{3}{7}$, the result is

A. $\dfrac{1}{4}$　　　　　B. $\dfrac{2}{7}$

C. $\dfrac{5}{21}$　　　　　D. $\dfrac{6}{10}$

87. Solve $\frac{1}{5} + \frac{3}{4}$.

88. What is the product of the equation
0.341 × 0.637 = □ ? _____

89. The solution to the expression
22.223 ÷ 3.13 is
   A. 7.0   B. 7.1
   C. 7.4   D. 7.7

Use the following information to answer the next question.

Mrs.Mackenzie conducted a survey on favorite colors in her Art 7 class of 32 students. Results from the survey were that 8 students liked blue, 11 liked red, 7 liked green, and the rest liked yellow.

90. Which of the following decimals, rounded to the nearest thousandths, represents the number of students that liked yellow?
   A. 0.188   B. 0.219
   C. 0.250   D. 0.343

91. Is the fraction $\frac{2}{13}$ equivalent to a repeating decimal?

Use the following information to answer the next question.

A hot-air balloon is 33.5 m above the ground.

92. If it rises 2.8 m and then another 1.22 m, how far above the ground will it be?

Use the following information to answer the next question.

A hot air balloon is 47.2 m above the ground. It falls 3.26 m and then another 8.6 m.

93. How far above the ground will the balloon be after the two falls?

94. Mrs. Singh used 0.78 kg of rice to make Rice Pulao. If the price of rice is $2 / kg, how much did Mrs. Singh spend on rice for this recipe?

Use the following information to answer the next question.

Jasdeep and Marco are taking turns reading to each other from a book. Jasdeep reads $\frac{3}{8}$ of the book, and Marco reads $\frac{1}{4}$ of the book.

95. What fraction of the book did the two students read to each other in total?

   A. $\frac{4}{8}$ B. $\frac{5}{8}$

   C. $\frac{4}{12}$ D. $\frac{5}{12}$

96. The length of a pole is 180 cm. Three-fifths of the pole is colored blue. The length of the pole that is blue is

   A. 72 cm   B. 100 cm

   C. 108 cm   D. 300 cm

Use the following information to answer the next question.

Alton buys a wooden board $3\frac{3}{5}$ m long and cuts it in half.

97. What is the length of each piece?

   A. $1\frac{3}{5}$ m   B. $1\frac{4}{5}$ m

   C. 2 m   D. $2\frac{1}{5}$ m

Use the following information to answer the next question.

In June, ABC Lake Resort received a 117.5 kg shipment of sugar for their general store. The sugar came in equal-sized bags weighing 2.5 kg each.

98. How many bags of sugar did the general store receive in this shipment? _____

EXERCISE #2—THE NUMBER SYSTEM ANSWERS AND SOLUTIONS

74. C	81. B	88. 0.217217	95. B
75. C	82. See solution	89. B	96. C
76. See solution	83. See solution	90. A	97. B
77. C	84. See solution	91. See solution	98. 47
78. B	85. See solution	92. See solution	
79. C	86. B	93. See solution	
80. See solution	87. See solution	94. 1.56	

74. C

The integer −5 is a negative integer. Negative integers are used to represent things such as temperatures below the 0° mark on a thermometer, the spending of money, distances below sea level, and floors below ground level.

The example that cannot be represented by a negative integer is a road 5 km above sea level because it is a positive value.

75. C

Step 1
Determine the sum of each sequence using the zero principle.

The zero principle states that the sum of a number and its opposite number is 0. These are referred to as *zero pairs*.

Cross out the zero pairs. In other words, match up a +2 and a − 2 and cross them out, since their sum is 0.

$\boxed{+2} + \boxed{-2} + \boxed{-2} + \boxed{-2} + \boxed{+2} + \boxed{+2} + \boxed{-2} = \boxed{-2}$

$\boxed{-2} + \boxed{-2} + \boxed{-2} + \boxed{+2} + \boxed{+2} + \boxed{+2} + \boxed{-2} = \boxed{-2}$

$\boxed{+2} + \boxed{-2} + \boxed{-2} + \boxed{+2} + \boxed{+2} + \boxed{+2} + \boxed{-2} = \boxed{+2}$

$\boxed{-2} + \boxed{+2} + \boxed{+2} + \boxed{+2} + \boxed{-2} + \boxed{-2} + \boxed{-2} = \boxed{-2}$

Step 2
The sum of the sequences in alternatives A, B, and D is −2 while the sequence in alternative C has the sum of +2.

Therefore, the sequence in alternative C is correct.

76.

Starting at 0, draw an arrow to the value of the first integer, which is +3. Then, starting above the tip of the arrow, draw another arrow that moves the number of places indicated by the value of the second integer, which will be 6 places to the left.

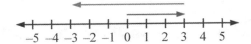

The second arrow stops at −3.
Therefore, (+3) = (−6) = (−3)

77. C

Step 1
Change the integers following the subtraction signs to the additive inverses.
$11 − (−6) − (−12) − 13 − 14 =$
$(+11) + (+6) + (+12) + (−13) + (−14)$

Step 2
Simplify using the order of operations.

Start from the left side of the expression, and follow the same rules that apply for adding integers.
$(+11) + (+6) + (+12) + (−13) + (−14)$
$+17 + (+12) + (−13) + (−14)$
$+29 + (−13) + (−14)$
$+16 + (−14)$
$+2$
The resulting value for $11 − (−6) − (−12) − 13 − 14$ is 2.

78. B

Step 1
Identify integer keywords.

Integer keywords: *rises* indicates positive, and *descends* indicates negative.

The balloon is 89 m above ground → (+89).

Rises 32 m → (+32)
Descends 44 m → (−44)
Descends 27 m → (−27)
Rises 18 m → (+18)

Step 2
Write an expression representing the problem.
$(+89) + (+32) + (-44) + (-27) + (+18)$

Step 3
Solve the equation.
$(+89) + (+32) + (-44) + (-27) + (+18)$
$= (+121) + (-44) + (-27) + (+18)$
$= (+77) + (-27) + (+18)$
$= (+50) + (+18)$
$= (+68)$

The balloon is 68 m above the ground.

79. C

Whenever a negative integer is subtracted from a positive integer, the question can be rewritten to addition, and the negative integer is changed to a positive integer. The sum of two positive integers will always be positive.

80.

Step 1
The signs are different, so subtract the smaller positive value from the larger positive value.

The positive value of –30 is 30. The positive value of +12 is 12.
$30 - 12 = 18$

Step 2
Take the sign of the larger value.

Since 30 is the larger value and has a negative integer sign, apply a negative sign to the answer.
$(+12) + (-30) = -18$

81. B

Step 1
Multiply the positive values.
$3 \times 2 \times 1 \times 1 \times 4 \times 2 = 48$

Step 2
Count the number of negative signs.

Four negative signs in the multiplication equation means the answer will be positive.

Therefore, $-3 \times 2 \times -1 \times -1 \times -4 \times 2 = 48$.

Since Rhonda received her prize, she must have given the value 48 as her answer to the skill-testing question

82.

Step 1
Identify integer and operation keywords.

Integer keywords: *decrease* indicates negative.

Decrease in temperature of 39 degrees → (–39)

Operator keyword: *average* indicates division.

Step 2
Write an expression representing the problem.

Divide the total decrease in temperature by the number of days.
$(-39) \div 13$

Step 3
Simplify.
$(-39) \div 13 = (-3)$

The average daily change in temperature was –3°C.

83.

Step 1
Divide the absolute values.

The absolute values are 28, 7, 2, 2, and 1.
$28 \div 7 \div 2 \div 2 \div 1 = 1$

Step 2
Count the number of negative integer signs.

There is an odd number of negative signs (3) in this expression. The odd number of negatives determines the sign of the solution. Make the solution negative.
$$\frac{-28}{-7} \div (-2) \div (+2) \div (+1) = (-1)$$

84.

To solve this problem, the three distances need to be added. Write the numbers vertically, lining up the decimal points and the place values.

It might be helpful to add three zeros to the end of the whole number 107 and one zero to the end of 223.56 so that the place values line up.
$$107 \to 107.000$$
$$223.56 \to 223.560$$

$$
\begin{array}{r}
{}^{1\,1}\;\;{}^{1}\\
107.00\\
223.560\\
+\ \underline{584.062}\\
914.622
\end{array}
$$

The bus traveled a total distance of 914.622 km.

85.

Write the numbers vertically with the lesser value, 2.73, below the greater value, 6.491. Be sure to line up the decimal points and place values. It might be helpful to add a zero to the end of 2.73 so that the place values line up. Adding a zero to the end will not change the value of the number.

Regroup where necessary.
$$
\begin{array}{r}
{}^{5}\;{}^{1}\\
6.491\\
-\ \underline{2.730}\\
3.761
\end{array}
$$

86. B

Step 1

Multiply numerator by numerator and denominator by denominator.

$$\frac{2}{3} \times \frac{3}{7} = \frac{2 \times 3}{3 \times 7} = \frac{6}{21}$$

Step 2

Reduce the fraction to lowest terms.

Since the greatest common factor that 6 and 21 share is 3, divide both the numerator and the denominator by 3.

$$\frac{6 \div 3}{21 \div 3} = \frac{2}{7}$$

The product of $\frac{2}{3}$ and $\frac{3}{7}$, expressed in lowest terms, is $\frac{2}{7}$.

87.

Step 1

Find the lowest common denominator (LCD).

Write the multiples of each denominator until a common one appears.

- Multiples of 4 are 4, 8, 12, 16, 20.
- Multiples of 5 are 5, 10, 15, 20.

The LCD of 4 and 5 is 20.

Use the LCD to create new equivalent fractions with a denominator of 20.

Multiply the numerator and denominator of each fraction by the same factor.

$$\frac{1 \times 4}{5 \times 4} = \frac{4}{20}, \frac{3 \times 5}{4 \times 5} = \frac{15}{20}$$

Step 2

Add the numerators of the fractions while keeping the denominators the same.

$$\frac{4 + 15}{20} = \frac{19}{20}$$

Step 3

Reduce the resulting fraction to lowest terms.

The fraction is already in lowest terms.

$$\frac{1}{5} + \frac{3}{4} = \frac{19}{20}$$

88. 0.217217

Step 1

Remove the decimal points.

The zeros before the decimal point can be removed as well because having a zero in front does not change the value of the number.

$341 \times 637 =$

Step 2

Line up the numbers based on place value.

$$\begin{array}{r} 341 \\ \times\ 637 \end{array}$$

Step 3

Multiply the two whole numbers.

Start by multiplying 7 by the top number.

$$\begin{array}{r} \overset{2}{341} \\ \times\ \ \ 7 \\ \hline 2{,}387 \end{array}$$

Multiply 30 by the top number.

Remember to add a zero on the right side before multiplying to hold the place value of the tens. Continue to multiply the top number by 3.

$$\begin{array}{r} \overset{1}{341} \\ \times\ \ \ 30 \\ \hline 10{,}230 \end{array}$$

Multiply 600 by the top number.

Remember to add two zeros on the right side before multiplying to hold the place value of the hundreds. Continue multiplying the top number by 6.

$$\begin{array}{r} \overset{2}{341} \\ \times\ \ \ 600 \\ \hline 204{,}600 \end{array}$$

Step 4

Add the products.

$$\begin{array}{r} \overset{11}{2387} \\ 10{,}230 \\ +204{,}600 \\ \hline 217{,}217 \end{array}$$

Step 5

Replace the decimal in the answer.

To determine where to put the decimal point, count how many digits are to the right of both of the original decimals. There are 3 digits to the right of each decimal, so that is 6 digits in total.

Move the decimal 6 digits to the left of the sum.

$217{,}217. \rightarrow 0.217217$

89. B

Step 1

Rewrite the divisor as a whole number.

The divisor is 3.13. To rewrite 3.13 as a whole number, move the decimal point two places to the right.

$3.13 \rightarrow 313$

What you do to the divisor, you must also do to the dividend. Move the decimal point two places to the right in the dividend.

$22.223 \rightarrow 2{,}222.3$

Step 2

Set up the division equation. Line up the decimal points above and below the division sign.

Divide.

```
        7.1
313)2,222.3
    2,191
      313
      313
        0
```

2,222.3 ÷ 313 = 7.1

90. A

This is a three-step solution.

Step 1:

Find the sum of the students that liked blue, red, and green, and subtract from the class total to find the number that liked yellow.

(8 + 11 + 7) = 26

32 − 26 = 6

Step 2:

Express as a fraction, and then change it into a decimal by dividing the numerator by the denominator.

$\frac{6}{32}$ = 6 ÷ 32 = 0.1875

Step 3:

Round 0.1875 to the nearest thousandth.

0.1875 → 0.188

91.

To determine whether or not it is a repeating decimal, the fraction must be converted to a decimal.

Change $\frac{2}{13}$ into decimal form by dividing the numerator by the denominator.

2 ÷ 13 = 0.153846153846

The group of digits 153,846 is repeating.

Therefore, $\frac{2}{13}$ is equivalent to a repeating decimal.

92.

Step 1

Determine what the problem is asking.

The problem is asking how far the balloon is from the ground after rising twice.

Step 2

Identify the information that is given.

The initial distance of the balloon from the ground is 33.5 m. The balloon rises 2.8 m, and then it rises another 1.22 m. The keyword is *rises*.

Step 3

Decide on the strategy or operation to use.

The keyword *rises* implies addition.

Step 4

Apply the strategy or operation.

Write the decimal numbers in a vertical column, lining up the decimal points and place values. Starting at the far right and working left, add the digits in each vertical column.

```
   1
 33.50
  2.80
+1.22
 37.52
```

Step 5

Check by estimating.

```
33.50→  34
 2.80→   3
 1.22→  +1
        38
```

The balloon is 37.52 m from the ground.

93.

Step 1

Identify the given information.

The balloon is 47.2 m above the ground. It falls 3.26 m, and then it falls 8.6 m.

Step 2

Decide on the strategy or operation to use.

The keyword *falls* implies subtraction.

Step 3

Apply the strategy or operation.

Write the minuend above the subtrahend in a vertical column, lining up the decimal points and place values. Starting at the far right and working left, subtract the bottom number from the top number.

```
  6 11 1
 47.20
 −3.26
 43.94
```

Subtract 8.6 from the result.

```
  3 1
 43.94
  8.6
 35.34
```

Step 4

Check by estimating.

```
47.20→  47
 3.26→   3
 8.6→    9
```

Subtract.

47 − 3= 44

44 − 9= 35

The balloon is 35.34 m above the ground.

94. 1.56

Mrs. Singh bought 0.78 kg of rice at a cost of $2 / kg. Multiply the two numbers together to find out the total cost of the rice. $0.78 \times 2 = \$1.56$

Because the decimal is located two places to the left in the number being multiplied, it must be placed two places to the left in the product.

95. B

Step 1
Identify the important information.

Jasdeep read $\frac{3}{8}$ of the book, and Marco read $\frac{1}{4}$ of the book. The question is asking for the total fraction of the book the two students read.

Step 2
Create equivalent fractions.

Fractions must have the same denominator before they can be added together. Determine the lowest common multiple of the two denominators, and use it to create new fractions.

Multiples of 4 include 4, 8, 12, and 16. Multiples of 8 include 8, 16, and 24.

The lowest common multiple is 8. Use 8 as the denominator to create new fractions. Remember that any operation done to the denominator must be done to the numerator.

$$\frac{1}{4} = \frac{1 \times 2}{4 \times 2} = \frac{2}{8}$$

The fraction $\frac{3}{8}$ already has a denominator of 8, so it will remain the same.

Step 3
Add the equivalent fractions.

$$\frac{2}{8} + \frac{3}{8} = \frac{5}{8}$$

96. C

Step 1
The length of the pole is 180 cm.

The blue-colored portion is three-fifths $\left(\frac{3}{5}\right)$ of the total length.

Step 2
Determine the length of the blue-colored portion.

$$\frac{3}{5} \times 180 = \frac{3}{5} \times \frac{180}{1}$$
$$= \frac{3 \times 180}{5 \times 1}$$
$$= \frac{540}{5}$$
$$= 108 \text{cm}$$

97. B

Step 1
Convert the mixed number into an improper fraction.
$$3\frac{3}{5} = \frac{3 \times 5 + 3}{5} = \frac{18}{5}$$

Step 2
Multiply the first fraction by the reciprocal of the second fraction.
Determine the reciprocal of the second fraction.

The reciprocal of $\frac{2}{1}$ is $\frac{1}{2}$.

$$\frac{18}{5} \div \frac{2}{1} = \frac{18}{5} \times \frac{1}{2}$$

Step 3
Multiply numerator by numerator and denominator by denominator.
$$\frac{18}{5} \times \frac{1}{2} = \frac{18 \times 1}{5 \times 2}$$
$$= \frac{18}{10}$$

Step 4
Reduce the fraction to lowest terms.

Since the greatest common factor that 18 and 10 share is 2, divide both the numerator and the denominator by 2.
$$\frac{18 \div 2}{10 \div 2} = \frac{9}{5}$$

Step 5
Convert the improper fraction into a mixed number.
Numerator of improper fraction ÷ denominator
$$= \text{quotient} + \frac{\text{remainder}}{\text{denominator}}$$
$$9 \div 5 = 1 + \frac{4}{5}$$
$$= 1\frac{4}{5}$$

Therefore, the length of each piece will be $1\frac{4}{5}$ m.

98. 47

To calculate how many bags of sugar were received in the shipment, divide the total weight of the shipment by the individual weight of each individual bag of sugar.

To divide by a decimal number, move the decimal (in the divisor) to the right until you get a whole number. Move the decimal in the dividend the same number of places.
$$117.5 \div 2.5 \rightarrow 1{,}175 \div 25$$
$$\frac{1{,}175}{25} = 47$$

The general store received 47 bags of sugar.

NOTES

Expressions and Equations

EXPRESSIONS AND EQUATIONS

Table of Correlations

Standard		Concepts	Exercise #1	Exercise #2
7.EE	Expressions and Equations			
7.EE. 1	*Apply properties of operations as strategies to add, subtract, factor, and expand linear expressions with rational coefficients.*	Identifying Like and Unlike Terms	99	124
		Factoring Simple Polynomials	100	125
		Identifying the Greatest Common Factor of Monomials	101	126
		Adding and Subtracting Monomials	102	127
		Simplifying Expressions	104	129
7.EE. 2	*Understand that rewriting an expression in different forms in a problem context can shed light on the problem and how the quantities in it are related.*	Adding and Subtracting Monomials	102	127
		Rewriting Expressions to Solve Problems	103	128
		Simplifying Expressions	104	129
7.EE. 3	*Solve multi–step real–life and mathematical problems posed with positive and negative rational numbers in any form (whole numbers, fractions, and decimals), using tools strategically. Apply properties of operations to calculate with numbers in any form; convert between forms as appropriate; and assess the reasonableness of answers using mental computation and estimation strategies.*	Dividing Fractions	1	25
		Converting Decimals to Percentages	12	36
		Converting Percentages to Decimals	13	37
		Converting Percentages to Decimals	13	37
		Solving Problems Involving the Addition & Subtraction of Integers	53	78
		Understanding Negative Fractions and Decimals		
		Solving Problems Involving the Multiplication & Division of Integers	57	82
		Multiplying Fractions	61	86
		Adding Fractions with Unlike Denominators	62	87
		Multiplying Decimals by Decimals	63	88
		Dividing Decimals by Decimals	64	89
		Converting Fractions to Terminating Decimals	65	90
		Converting Fractions to Repeating Decimals	66	91
		Solving Addition Problems	67	92
		Solving Problems by Subtracting Decimals	68	93
		Solving Problems by Multiplying Decimals	73	94
		Solving Problems by Adding and Subtracting Fractions	72	95
		Solving Problems Involving the Simple Multiplication of Fractions	70	96
		Solving Problems Involving the Simple Division of Fractions	71	97
		Solving Problems by Dividing Decimals	69	98
		Solving Problems by Adding Decimals	67	92

		Converting Percentages to Fractions	105	130
		Converting Fractions to Percentages	106	131
		Converting Repeating Decimals to Fractions	107	132
		Converting Terminating Decimals to Fractions	108	133
		Estimating Solutions to Multiplication Problems Involving Decimals	109	134
		Estimating Solutions to Division Problems Involving Decimals	110	135
		Estimating Sums of Decimals to the Thousandths	111	136
		Estimate the Difference of Decimal Numbers to Thousandths	112	137
		Subtracting Fractions with Unlike Denominators	113	138
		Estimating Sums of Fractions	114	139
		Estimating Differences of Fractions	115	140
7.EE. 4A	Use variables to represent quantities in a real-world or mathematical problem, and construct simple equations and inequalities to solve problems by reasoning about the quantities. Solve word problems leading to equations of the form px + q = r and p(x + q) = r, where p, q, and r are specific rational numbers. Solve equations of these forms fluently. Compare an algebraic solution to an arithmetic solution, identifying the sequence of the operations used in each approach.	Writing Equations to Represent Real-Life Relationships with One Variable	116	141
7.EE. 4B	Use variables to represent quantities in a real-world or mathematical problem, and construct simple equations and inequalities to solve problems by reasoning about the quantities. Solve word problems leading to inequalities of the form px + q > r or px + q < r, where p, q, and r are specific rational numbers. Graph the solution set of the inequality and interpret it in the context of the problem.	Solving Linear Inequalities by Adding and Subtracting	117	142
		Solving Linear Inequalities Using Positive Multipliers and Divisors	118	143
		Solving Linear Inequalities Using Negative Multipliers and Divisors	119	144
		Solving Problems Using Linear Inequalities	120	145
		Using Inequalities to Represent Situations Described in Words	121	146
		Solving Two-Step Linear Inequalities	122	148
		Graphing Linear Inequalities on a Number Line	123	147

7.EE.1 Apply properties of operations as strategies to add, subtract, factor, and expand linear expressions with rational coefficients.

IDENTIFYING LIKE AND UNLIKE TERMS

In algebra, a **term** is a part of an expression or equation and can be made up of numbers, variables, or a combination of both. Each term is separated by a plus, minus, or equal sign.

Like terms are terms that have the same combination of variables.

If a term has only a single variable, then like terms will have the same single variable:

- The terms $3a$, a, and $5a$ are all like terms.
- The terms $3a$ and $3b$ are unlike terms because they have different variables.

If a term has exponents on the variables, then like terms will have the same exponents on the same variables:

- The terms $3m^3$, $2m^3$, and $-5m^3$ are like terms because they have the same variable with the same exponent.
- The terms $2n^5$ and $3n^3$ are unlike terms because the variables have different exponents.
- The terms $3x^2$ and $3y^2$ are unlike terms because the variables are different.

If a term has more than one variable, the like terms will have the same combination of variables. The order of the variables does not matter, so if they are the same variables, but in a different order, they are like terms. Usually, variables in a term are written in alphabetical order, which helps to identify like terms:

- The terms $4gh$, gh, and $-3gh$ are like terms because they have the same combination of variables.
- The terms $6xyz$, $5xzy$, and $3yxz$ are like terms because they have the same combination of variables.
- The terms $4rs$, $3r$, and $5st$ are unlike terms because they do not have the same variables.
- The terms $3gh^2$ and $3g^2h$ are unlike terms because the exponent is on different variables.

FACTORING SIMPLE POLYNOMIALS

Factoring is a way to work with expressions in algebra. When you use the distributive property to remove brackets from an expression, you take a value on the outside of the brackets and multiply it by both terms on the inside. For example, $3(x + 2)$ becomes $3x + 6$. Factoring is the opposite of this. You put the brackets back into an expression by dividing both terms by a common factor, so $3x + 6$ becomes $3(x + 2)$.

Factoring changes the way an expression is written, but not the value of the expression. A factored form of an expression will always equal the original expression, just like when the distributive property is used. The factor is written on the outside of a set of brackets, and what is left of the expression is written on the inside of the brackets. An expression is fully factored when the greatest common factor (GCF) is removed from the expression.

In order to factor a polynomial by removing the greatest common factor, follow these steps:

1. Find the greatest common factor of the terms.
2. Divide the expression by the GCF.
3. Write the factored expression.

Example

Factor the expression $4m + 6$.

Solution

Step 1
Find the greatest common factor (GCF) of the terms.
The GCF of $4m$ and 6 is 2.

Step 2
Divide the expression by the GCF.
$$\frac{4m + 6}{2} = \frac{4m}{2} + \frac{6}{2}$$
$$= 2m + 3$$

Step 3
Write the factored expression.
Write the GCF (2) outside the brackets, and place the result of the division ($2m + 3$) inside the brackets.
$2(2m + 3)$
The factored form of $4m + 6$ is $2(2m + 3)$.

Example

Factor the expression $2p - 5pq$.

Solution

Step 1

Find the greatest common factor (GCF) of the terms.

The GCF of $2p$ and $5pq$ is p.

Step 2

Divide the expression by the GCF.

$$\frac{2p - 5pq}{p}$$

$$= \frac{2p}{p} - \frac{5pq}{p}$$

$$= 2 - 5q$$

Step 3

Write the factored expression.

Write the GCF outside the brackets, and place the result of the division inside the brackets.

$p(2 - 5q)$

The factored form of $2p - 5pq$ is $p(2 - 5q)$.

Example

Factor the expression $3m^2 + 6mn - 3m$.

Solution

Step 1

Find the greatest common factor (GCF) of the terms.

The GCF of $3m^2$, $6mn$, and $3m$ is $3m$.

Step 2

Divide the expression by the GCF.

$$\frac{3m^2 + 6mn - 3m}{3m}$$

$$= \frac{3m^2}{3m} + \frac{6mn}{3m} - \frac{3m}{3m}$$

$$= m + 2n - 1$$

Step 3

Write the factored expression.

Write the GCF outside the brackets, and place the result of the division inside the brackets.

$3m(m + 2n - 1)$

The factored form of $3m^2 + 6mn - 3m$ is $3m(m + 2n - 1)$.

IDENTIFYING THE GREATEST COMMON FACTOR OF MONOMIALS

A factor is a whole number that divides evenly into another number. For example, factors of 8 include 1, 2, 4, and 8.

In algebra, it is possible to find the factors of monomials, which can include a combination of both numbers and letters. For example, the factors of $3b$ are 1, 3, b, and $3b$. The factors of y^2 are 1, y, and y^2.

The **greatest common factor** (GCF) of two numbers is the largest number that is a factor of both numbers. The definition is the same in algebra, and the greatest common factor can include numbers, variables, or a combination of both.

Example

The GCF of $12mn$ and $8m$ can be found by looking at the coefficients and then looking at the variables.

Begin with the coefficients 12 and 8. The GCF of these two numbers is 4, so that will be included in the GCF of the two terms.

Next, look at the variables in the terms. The term $12mn$ has the variables of m and n, but the term $8m$ only has the variable m. The only common variable is m, so that will also be a part of the GCF.

The GCF of $12mn$ and $8m$ is $4m$.

To find the greatest common factor of two or more monomials, follow these steps:

1. Find the GCF of the coefficients of all the terms.
2. Find the GCF of the variables in the terms.
3. Combine the two to find the GCF of the terms.

Example

What is the greatest common factor of $4s$ and $6t$?

Solution

Step 1

Find the greatest common factor (GCF) of the coefficients of all the terms.

The coefficients are 4 and 6. The GCF of 4 and 6 is 2.

Step 2

Find the GCF of the variables in the terms. The monomials $4s$ and $6t$ do not have any variables in common.

Step 3

Combine the two to find the GCF of the terms. The GCF of $4s$ and $6t$ is 2.

Example

What is the greatest common factor of $2m$, $3mn$, and $5mo$?

Solution

Step 1

Find the greatest common factor (GCF) of the coefficients of all the terms.

The coefficients of the monomials are 2, 3, and 5. The GCF of these is 1.

Step 2

Find the GCF of the variables in the terms. The variables of the monomials are m, mn, and mo. The GCF of these is m.

Step 3

Combine the two to find the GCF of the terms. The GCF of $2m$, $3mn$, and $5mo$ is $1m$, which can be written as m.

Example

What is the greatest common factor of $6a^2$ and $3a^2b$?

Solution

Step 1

Find the greatest common factor (GCF) of the coefficients of all the terms.

The coefficients are 6 and 3. The GCF of these is 3.

Step 2

Find the GCF of the variables in the terms. The variables are a^2 in the first term, and a^2 and b in the second term. The GCF of these is a^2.

Step 3

Combine the two to find the GCF of the terms. The GCF of $6a^2$ and $3a^2b$ is $3a^2$.

7.EE.2 Understand that rewriting an expression in different forms in a problem context can shed light on the problem and how the quantities in it are related.

ADDING AND SUBTRACTING MONOMIALS

A monomial is an algebraic expression that contains only one term. It is the product of a number and a variable. Both $4c$ and d are monomials. The number represents how many times the variable is added when written in expanded form. The monomial $4c$, in expanded form, is written $4c = c + c + c + c$. If the variable in the monomial is multiplied by 1, it is not written. For example, $1d = d$.

When you are adding and subtracting monomials, the expression can be simplified if the monomials have the **same** variable.

Example

Simplify the expression $3x + 5x$.

Solution

The expression contains two monomials with the same variable. Write the monomials in expanded form.
$3x = x + x + x$
$5x = x + x + x + x + x$

Rewrite the expression to simplify.
$3x + 5x$
$= (x + x + x) + (x + x + x + x + x)$
$8x$

The simplified expression can also be found by adding the numbers before the variable and writing the answer with the given variable.

Example

To simplify $3x + 5x$, add the numbers before the variable, and write the answer with the given variable.
$3x + 5x$
$= (3 + 5)x$
$= 8x$

If the monomials have **different** variables, you cannot combine them.

Example

Simplify the expression $5a + 4b$.

Solution

The expression contains two monomials with different variables. Write the monomials in expanded form.
$5a = a + a + a + a + a$
$4b = b + b + b + b$

Rewrite the expression to simplify.
$5a + 4b$
$= (a + a + a + a + a) + (b + b + b + b)$
$5a + 4b$

Since the monomials have different variables, they cannot be combined. The expression must be kept as it is given.

You can use all of the concepts mentioned to subtract monomials or to work with more than two monomials.

Example

Simplify the expression $13z - 8z$.

Solution

Perform operations on the numbers before the variable.

The expression contains two monomials with the same variable. The numbers before the variable are 13 and –8.

To simplify, subtract the numbers before the variable, and write the answer with the given variable.
$13z - 8z = (13 - 8)z$
$\qquad\qquad = 5z$

Example

Simplify the expression $5y + 11y - 3y$.

Solution

Perform operations on the numbers before the variable.

The expression contains three monomials with the same variable. The numbers before the variable are 5, 11, and –3.

Add and subtract the numbers before the variable in the order they appear, and write the answer with the given variable.
$5y + 11y - 3y = (5 + 11 - 3)y$
$\qquad\qquad\qquad = 13y$

REWRITING EXPRESSIONS TO SOLVE PROBLEMS

You can use expressions to help solve problems. Often, there is more than one way to write an expression to help solve the problem.

Example

Brandy works at a clothing store. The store is having a huge sale where everything in the store is 30% off. She knows that 30% is the same as 0.3. She decides to multiply 0.3 by the original price. Then, she can subtract that amount from the original price to find the sale price. To do this, she uses the expression $p - 0.3p$, where p is the price of the item.

Her boss tells her that there is actually an easier way to figure out the sale price. He says that you can just multiply the original price by 0.7 since $1 - 0.3 = 0.7$.

The expression to represent this statement is $0.7p$.
$p - 0.3p$
$= 1p - 0.3p$
$= 0.7p$

This means that a decrease of 30% is the same as multiplying by 0.7.

If you have an expression with more than one term in the same variable, you can add or subtract the numbers before the variable to write it in a different way.

Example

At Greenfield Primary School, each of the teachers needs to choose $\frac{1}{6}$ of their students to participate in a special activity. The principal asks the teachers to tell her how many students they will have left in their classes.

Show how the teachers could calculate the number of remaining students.

Solution

One way to find the answer is to calculate $\frac{1}{6}$ of the students in the class and then subtract that number from the total number of students in the class.

Let *s* represent the total number of students in a class. The number of students remaining will be $s - \frac{1}{6}s$.

It is also possible to do the calculation in one step.

Simplify $s - \frac{1}{6}s$.

$$s - \frac{1}{6}s = 1s - \frac{1}{6}s$$
$$= \frac{5}{6}s$$

The teachers can find the number of students that will be left in their classrooms by calculating $\frac{5}{6}$ of the total number of students in their classes.

SIMPLIFYING EXPRESSIONS

Properties of numbers can be used to help simplify algebraic expressions. There are three properties you can use:

- Commutative property
- Associative property
- Distributive property

COMMUTATIVE PROPERTY

The **commutative property of addition** states that when two or more numbers are added, the order in which they are added does not matter: $a + b = b + a$. For example, $7 + 3$ and $3 + 7$ both equal 10. This means that $7 + 3 = 3 + 7$.

The **commutative property of multiplication** states that when two or more numbers are multiplied, the order in which they are multiplied does not matter: $ab = ba$. For example, 4×5 and 5×4 both equal 20. This means that $4 \times 5 = 5 \times 4$.

Example

Simplify the expression $2x + 4y + z - x + 7z$.

Solution

Apply the commutative property of addition.

Place like terms together, and combine.
$$2x + 4y + z - x + 7z$$
$$= 2x - x + 4y + z + 7z$$
$$= x + 4y + 8z$$

ASSOCIATIVE PROPERTY

The **associative property** states that a change in the grouping of three or more numbers being added or multiplied does not change their sum or product:

- $(a + b) + c = a + (b + c)$
- $(a \times b) \times c = a \times (b \times c)$

Example

Simplify the expression $2 \times 8m$.

Solution

Apply the associative property of multiplication.

Regroup terms to make multiplication easier.
$$2 \times 8m = 2 \times (8 \times m)$$
$$= (2 \times 8) \times m$$
$$= 16 \times m$$
$$= 16m$$

DISTRIBUTIVE PROPERTY

The **distributive property** is an algebraic property used to multiply the term outside a set of brackets by each term inside the set of brackets:
$a(b + c) = (a \times b) + (a \times c)$.

A common mistake is not multiplying the number outside the brackets by both terms inside the brackets. For example, when asked to apply the distributive property to $2(x + 1)$, people often write $2(x + 1) = 2x + 1$, but this statement is incorrect. The correct way to multiply is
$2(x + 1) = 2(x) + 2(1) = 2x + 2$.

Example
Simplify the expression $(y + 2z)7$.

Solution

Expand using the distributive property.
$(y + 3z)7$
$= (7 \times y) + (7 \times 3z)$
$= 7y + 21z$

COMBINING PROPERTIES

Sometimes, you will need to use a combination of these properties to simplify expressions.

Example
Simplify the expression $5(2a + b) - c + 6b$.

Solution

Step 1
Apply the distributive property.

Multiply 5 by both $2a$ and b.
$5(2a + b) - c + 6b$
$= (5 \times 2a) + (5 \times b) - c + 6b$
$= 10a + 5b - c + 6b$

Step 2
Apply the commutative property.

Place like terms together, and combine.
$10a + 5b - c + 6b$
$10a + 5b + 6b - c$
$10a + 11b - c$

7.EE.3 Solve multi–step real–life and mathematical problems posed with positive and negative rational numbers in any form (whole numbers, fractions, and decimals), using tools strategically. Apply properties of operations to calculate with numbers in any form; convert between forms as appropriate; and assess the reasonableness of answers using mental computation and estimation strategies.

CONVERTING PERCENTAGES TO FRACTIONS

A percentage is a number out of 100. It can be expressed as a fraction where the denominator is 100. For example, $85\% = \dfrac{85}{100}$.

To express a percentage as a fraction, follow these steps:

1. Write the value of the percentage over a denominator of 100.
2. Reduce the fraction to lowest terms.

Example
Write 30% as a fraction.

Solution

Step 1
Write the value of the percentage over a denominator of 100.
The value of the percentage is 30, so it is the numerator.
$30\% = \dfrac{30}{100}$

Step 2
Reduce the fraction to lowest terms.
Divide the numerator and denominator by the greatest common factor (GCF). The GCF of 30 and 100 is 10.
$\dfrac{30}{100} = \dfrac{30 \div 10}{100 \div 10} = \dfrac{3}{10}$

Expressed as a fraction, 30% is $\dfrac{3}{10}$.

CONVERTING FRACTIONS TO PERCENTAGES

Fractions and percentages are related to one another. In mathematics, conversions between fractions and percentages are frequently done as a first step in solving problems.

There are two methods for converting a fraction into a percentage.

Method 1
Division followed by multiplication

To change a fraction to a percentage using division then multiplication, follow these steps:

1. Divide the numerator by the denominator
2. Multiply the result by 100
3. Place a % sign behind the answer

Example

Express $\frac{3}{8}$ as a percentage.

Solution

Step 1
Divide the numerator by the denominator.
The numerator is 3. The denominator is 8.
$3 \div 8 = 0.375$

Step 2
Multiply the result by 100.
$0.375 \times 100 = 37.5$

Step 3
Place the % sign behind the answer.
37.5%
If you are using a calculator, combine the first two steps into one:
numerator ÷ denominator × 100 = percent
$3 \div 8 \times 100 = 37.5$

$\frac{3}{8}$ expressed as a percentage is 37.5%.

Method 2
Use cross-products
To change a fraction to a percentage using cross-products, follow these steps:

1. Set up equivalent fractions in which the second fraction has an unknown numerator and a denominator of 100.
2. Multiply the numerator of the **first** fraction by the denominator of the **second** fraction.
3. Multiply the numerator of the **second** fraction by the denominator of the **first** fraction.
4. Solve for the unknown numerator.

Example

Express $\frac{4}{7}$ as a percentage, rounded to the nearest hundredth.

Solution

Step 1
Set up equivalent fractions.
The second fraction is the percentage.
The numerator is unknown and the denominator is 100.
$$\frac{4}{7} = \frac{x}{100}$$

Step 2
Multiply the numerator of the **first** fraction by the denominator of the **second** fraction.
$$\frac{4}{7} = \frac{x}{100}$$
$4 \times 100 = 400$

Step 3
Multiply the numerator of the **second** fraction by the denominator of the **first** fraction.
$$\frac{4}{7} = \frac{x}{100}$$
$x \times 7 = 7x$

Step 4
Solve for the unknown number.
Because cross-products are equal: $400 = 7x$
Divide each side by 7 to isolate the variable.
$$400 = 7x$$
$$\frac{400}{7} = \frac{7x}{7}$$
$57.143 = x$

$\frac{4}{7}$ expressed as a percentage is 57.14%.

Mixed numbers are converted into percentages greater than 100.

Example

Express $1\frac{2}{10}$ as a percentage.

Solution

Method 1
Division, then multiplication

Step 1
Convert the mixed number to an improper fraction.

$a\frac{b}{c}$ becomes $\frac{(a \times c) + b}{c}$

So, $1\frac{2}{10}$ becomes $\frac{(1 \times 10) + 2}{10} = \frac{12}{10}$

Step 2
Divide the numerator by the denominator and multiply the result by 100.
The numerator is 12. The denominator is 10.
$12 \div 10 \times 100 = 1.2 \times 100$
$\qquad\qquad\qquad\quad = 120$

Step 3
Place the % sign behind the answer.
120%

Method 2
Use cross-products

Step 1
Convert the mixed number to an improper fraction.

$1\frac{2}{10}$ becomes $\frac{(1 \times 10) + 2}{10} = \frac{12}{10}$

Step 2
Set up equivalent fractions.

$\frac{12}{10} = \frac{x}{100}$

Step 3
Multiply each numerator by the denominator on the other side of the equal sign.
$12 \times 100 = x \times 10$
$\qquad 1{,}200 = 10x$

Step 4
Solve for the unknown value.
Divide each side by 10 to isolate the variable.
$\frac{1{,}200}{10} = \frac{10x}{10}$
$\qquad 120 = x$

Step 5
Place the % sign behind the answer.
120%

Expressed as a percentage, $1\frac{2}{10}$ is 120%.

CONVERTING REPEATING DECIMALS TO FRACTIONS

Repeating decimals are decimal numbers where the numbers continue on forever, with one or more digits repeating. If one digit after the decimal repeats, it is referred to as a single-digit repeating decimal. Some examples include 0.999… and 6.22222….

If more than one digit repeats, it is referred to as a multi-digit repeating decimal. Some examples include 4.125125… and 17.080808….

Since writing the same number or numbers over and over again is not practical or efficient, a bar is placed above the repeating digits. This is referred to as bar notation. For example, 6.22222 is written as $6.\bar{2}$ and 17.080808… is written as $17.\overline{8}$.

When converting a repeating decimal to a fraction, place the repeating number over a denominator of 9. If there are two numbers that repeat, then place the numbers over 99, and so on.

To represent a repeating decimal as a fraction, follow these steps:

1. Determine the denominator.
2. Determine the numerator.
3. Reduce the fraction to lowest terms.

Example

Express $0.\bar{6}$ as a fraction in lowest terms.

Solution

Step 1
Determine the denominator.
Since the number is a repeating decimal, determine the number of 9s needed in the denominator.
Use the number of repeating digits to determine how many 9s are written in the denominator.
One digit repeats in $0.\bar{6}$. The denominator is 9.
$\frac{?}{9}$

Step 2

Determine the numerator.

Remove the decimal point and bar.

The number becomes 6.

$\dfrac{6}{9}$

Step 3

Reduce the fraction to lowest terms.

Divide the numerator and denominator by the greatest common factor (GCF): 3.

$\dfrac{6 \div 3}{9 \div 3} = \dfrac{2}{3}$

Expressed as a fraction in lowest terms

$0.\bar{6}$ is $\dfrac{2}{3}$

Example

Express $0.\overline{87}$ as a fraction in lowest terms.

Solution

Step 1

Determine the denominator.

Since the number is a repeating decimal, determine the number of 9s needed in the denominator.

Use the number of repeating digits to determine how many 9s are written in the denominator.

Two digits repeat in $0.\overline{87}$. The denominator is 99.

$\dfrac{?}{99}$

Step 2

Determine the numerator.

Remove the decimal point and bar.

The number becomes 87.

$\dfrac{87}{99}$

Step 3

Reduce the fraction to lowest terms.

Divide the numerator and denominator by the greatest common factor (GCF): 3.

$\dfrac{87 \div 3}{99 \div 3} = \dfrac{29}{33}$

Expressed as a fraction in lowest terms

$0.\overline{87}$ is $\dfrac{29}{33}$

Example

Express 0.972972972... as a fraction in lowest terms.

Solution

Step 1

Determine the denominator.

Since the number is a repeating decimal, determine the number of 9s needed in the denominator.

Use the number of repeating digits to determine how many 9s are written in the denominator.

Three digits repeat in $0.\overline{972}$. The denominator is 999.

$\dfrac{?}{999}$

Step 2

Determine the numerator.

Remove the decimal point and bar.

The number becomes 972.

$\dfrac{972 \div 27}{999 \div 27} = \dfrac{36}{37}$

Expressed as a fraction in lowest terms

$0.\overline{972}$ is $\dfrac{36}{37}$

If you cannot see the greatest common factor (GCF) that both numbers share, use the largest factor you see and keep reducing.

For example, the fraction $\dfrac{972}{999}$ could be reduced like this:

$\dfrac{972 \div 9}{999 \div 9} = \dfrac{108 \div 3}{111 \div 3} = \dfrac{36}{37}$

When the single digit that repeats is the number 9 $(0.\bar{9})$, the resulting fraction is $\dfrac{9}{9} = 1$.

The answer is 1 because the number that separates $0.\bar{9}$ from 1 is represented by a decimal point followed by an infinite number of zeros followed by a one. That number is impossibly small. Since there is no practical difference between the numbers, 1 is the accepted way of expressing the value.

CONVERTING TERMINATING DECIMALS TO FRACTIONS

Terminating decimals are decimal numbers that come to an end. All the digits are written down. Some examples include 0.174, 3.24, and 9.81902.

To convert a terminating decimal into a fraction, determine the place value of the last number in the terminating decimal and use that value as the denominator in the fraction. The numbers after the decimal are used in the numerator.

To represent a terminating decimal as a fraction, follow these steps:

1. Determine the denominator.
2. Determine the numerator.
3. Reduce the fraction to lowest terms.

Example

Change 0.375 to a fraction in lowest terms.

Solution

Step 1

Determine the denominator.
Use the place value of the last digit in the decimal number as the denominator of the fraction.
The 5 is in the thousandths position.
The denominator is 1,000:

$$\frac{}{1,000}$$

Step 2

Determine the numerator.
Remove the decimal point. The number becomes 375.
The numerator is 375

$$\frac{375}{1,000}$$

Step 3

Reduce the fraction to lowest terms.
Divide the numerator and denominator by the greatest common factor (GCF). In this case, the GCF is 125.

$$\frac{375}{1,000} = \frac{375 \div 125}{1,000 \div 125}$$
$$= \frac{3}{8}$$

Written as a fraction in lowest terms
0.375 is $\frac{3}{8}$

ESTIMATING SOLUTIONS TO MULTIPLICATION PROBLEMS INVOLVING DECIMALS

Estimating the product of a decimal number and a whole number is similar to estimating the product of two whole numbers. You round the numbers to make the calculation easier and to get an approximate solution.

When multiplying a decimal number by a whole number, the decimal number is usually rounded to the nearest whole number. The whole number is usually rounded to its greatest place value.

The difference between rounding decimals and whole numbers is that when rounding decimals, you drop the numbers to the right of the number you are rounding to. With whole numbers, you replace them with zeros.

Regardless of the place value you are rounding to, the same rules of rounding apply to decimal numbers as to whole numbers.

- If the digit to the right is 5 or greater, round up.
- If the digit to the right is less than 5, round down

Example

Jackie has 68 straws. Each straw is 20.4 cm long.

If Jackie places all the straws in a straight line end to end, about how long will the line be?

Solution

Step 1

To estimate the length of the line of straws, round the numbers so they can be multiplied mentally.

The whole number 68 → 70 because 8 > 5.

The decimal number 20.4 → 20 because 4 < 5.

Step 2

Multiply the two estimates.

70 × 20 = 1,400

The length of the line will be about 1,400 cm.

ESTIMATING SOLUTIONS TO DIVISION PROBLEMS INVOLVING DECIMALS

Estimating the quotient of a decimal number and a whole number is similar to estimating the quotient of two whole numbers. You round the numbers to make the calculation easier and to get an approximate solution.

When dividing a decimal number by a whole number, the decimal number is usually rounded to the nearest whole number. The whole number is usually rounded to its greatest place value.

The difference between rounding decimals and whole numbers is that when rounding decimals, you drop the numbers to the right of the number you are rounding to. With whole numbers, you replace them with zeros.

Regardless of the place value you are rounding to, the same rules of rounding apply to decimal numbers as to whole numbers.

• If the digit to the right is 5 or greater, round up.
• If the digit to the right is less than 5, round down

Example

An art teacher bought 17.7 m of canvas for an art project. He cut the canvas into 6 equal lengths.

After the canvas was cut, about how long was each piece?

Solution

Step 1

Round the decimal number to the nearest whole number.

The decimal number 17.7 becomes 18 because 7 > 5.

Step 2

Estimate the answer.

The whole number 6 does not need to be rounded because 6 is a factor of 18.

18 ÷ 6 = 3

Each piece of canvas was about 3 m long.

ESTIMATING SUMS OF DECIMALS TO THE THOUSANDTHS

There are several strategies for estimating sums when adding decimals. Two examples are: **rounding** the decimal numbers to the nearest whole numbers and using **front-end estimation**.

ROUNDING TO THE NEAREST WHOLE NUMBER

You can round the decimals to the nearest whole number, and then add estimated numbers.

Regardless of the place value you are rounding to, follow these rules:

1. If the digit to the right is 5 or greater, round up.
2. If the digit to the right is less than 5, round down.

Example

• Rounded to the nearest whole number, 3.461 → 3 because 4 < 5.
• Rounded to the nearest tenth, 3.461 → 3.5 because 6 > 5.
• Rounded to the nearest hundredth, 3.461 → 3.46 because 1 < 5.

Example

Hazel delivers 5.356 kg of papers and 1.768 kg of fliers in one day. She wonders what the total weight of the papers and fliers is that she delivers in one day.

Estimate and then compare to the actual answer.

Solution

Step 1

Estimate.

To find the approximate total weight of the papers and fliers, round each number to the nearest whole number.

5.356 → 5 because 3 < 5.

1.786 → 2 because 7 > 5.

Now, add the two estimated weights.

5 + 2 = 7 kg

Step 2

Calculate.

To find the actual total, add the two given weights.

$$\begin{array}{r} {\scriptstyle 1\ 11} \\ 5.356 \\ +\ 1.786 \\ \hline 7.142 \end{array}$$

Step 3

Since the estimate of 7 kg is so close to the actual weight of 7.142 kg, you know that a reasonable estimate was made.

Also, since the actual answer of 7.142 kg is so close to the estimate of 7 kg, you know that the actual answer is reasonable and most likely correct.

USING FRONT END ESTIMATION

You can use the first digit (greatest place value) of the numbers, turn the rest of the digits into zeros. Then add the estimated numbers. Remember that front-end estimation always gives a lower "about" answer when adding.

Example

Using the strategy of front-end estimation, describe the sum of 9.459, 1.123, and 125.735.

Solution

Step 1

Use front-end estimation.

9.459 → 9

1.123 → 1

125.735 → 125

Step 2

Calculate the estimated sum.

9 + 1 + 125 = 135

Step 3

Describe the sum of 9.459, 1.123, and 125.735. Since all three numbers were rounded down, the estimated sum is less than the actual sum. Therefore, you can describe the sum of 9.459, 1.123, and 125.735 as being greater than 135.

ESTIMATE THE DIFFERENCE OF DECIMAL NUMBERS TO THOUSANDTHS

There are several strategies for estimating differences when subtracting decimals. Two examples are: **rounding** the decimal numbers to the nearest whole numbers and using **front-end estimation**.

ROUNDING DECIMALS TO THE NEAREST WHOLE NUMBER

To round the decimals to the nearest whole number, follow these rules:

1. If the digit to the right is 5 or greater, round up.
2. If the digit to the right is less than 5, round down.

After rounding each number to its nearest whole number, subtract the rounded numbers to find the difference.

Example

23.567 – 13.446 = □

What is the estimated difference of the two given decimals?

Solution

Step 1

Round both decimals to the nearest whole number.

You need to use the value of the digit to the right of the ones place to round the decimals to the nearest whole number. This is called the tenths place.

- In the number 23.567, the digit in the tenths place is 5, so the whole number rounds up to 24.
  23.567 → 24
- In the number 13.446, the digit in the tenths place is 4, so the whole number rounds down to 13.
  13.446 → 13

Step 2

Subtract the two estimated numbers.
24 – 13 = 11.
The estimated difference of 23.567 – 13.446 is 11.

FRONT-END ESTIMATION

To round using front-end estimation, use the first digit (greatest place value) of each number, and turn the rest of the digits into zeros. Then subtract the estimated numbers. Remember that front-end estimation always gives a less exact estimate.

Example

Use front-end estimation to solve
23.567 – 13.446 = □.

Solution

When you use front-end estimation, you use the first digit in the number and turn the rest of the digits into zeros.
23.567 → 20.000
13.446 → 10.000
20 – 10 = 10

The estimated difference using front-end estimation is 10.

SUBTRACTING FRACTIONS WITH UNLIKE DENOMINATORS

To subtract fractions with different denominators, follow these steps:

1. Write the fractions with the lowest common denominator (LCD).
2. Subtract the numerators of the fractions while keeping the denominators the same.
3. Reduce the resulting fraction to lowest terms.

Example

Solve $\dfrac{2}{3} - \dfrac{1}{4}$.

Solution

Step 1

Write the fractions with the lowest common denominator (LCD).

Write the multiples of each denominator until a common one appears.

- Multiples of 3: 3, 6, 9, 12, 15
- Multiples of 4: 4, 8, 12, 16, 20

The lowest common denominator for 3 and 4 is 12.

Use the LCD to create new equivalent fractions with a denominator of 12.

$$\frac{2 \times 4}{3 \times 4} = \frac{8}{12}, \frac{1 \times 3}{4 \times 3} = \frac{3}{12}$$

Step 2

Subtract the numerators of the fractions while keeping the denominators the same.

$$\frac{8-3}{12} = \frac{5}{12}$$

Step 3

Reduce the resulting fraction to lowest terms. The fraction is in lowest terms.

$$\frac{2}{3} - \frac{1}{4} = \frac{5}{12}$$

Example

When $\dfrac{2}{8}$ is subtracted from $\dfrac{3}{5}$, what is the difference?

Solution

Step 1

Write the fractions with the lowest common denominator (LCD).

Write the multiples of each denominator until a common one appears.

- Multiples of 8: 8, 16, 24, 32, 40
- Multiples of 5: 5, 10, 15, 20, 25, 30, 35, 40

The lowest common denominator for 8 and 5 is 40.

Use the LCD to create new equivalent fractions with a denominator of 40.

$$\frac{3 \times 8}{5 \times 8} = \frac{24}{40}$$

$$\frac{2 \times 5}{8 \times 5} = \frac{10}{40}$$

Step 2

Subtract the numerators of the fractions while keeping the denominators the same.

$$\frac{24-10}{40} = \frac{14}{40}$$

Step 3

Reduce the resulting fraction to lowest terms.

$$\frac{14}{40} = \frac{7}{20}$$

Therefore, $\dfrac{3}{5} - \dfrac{2}{8} = \dfrac{7}{20}$.

ESTIMATING SUMS OF FRACTIONS

When you do not need an exact answer, you can estimate to find the sum of fractions. To find the sum of fractions, follow these steps:

1. Round each fraction to the nearest half or whole.
2. Add the rounded fractions.

When you want to round fractions, you can use your number sense to know what to round the fraction to. For example, you can round $3\frac{1}{50}$ to 3 because $\frac{1}{50}$ is so small. Or, you can round $6\frac{14}{15}$ to 7 because $\frac{14}{15}$ is almost a whole.

Another way to round fractions is by using representations. For example, if you need to round $\frac{3}{8}$, you can draw a picture.

The picture shows that $\frac{3}{8}$ is pretty close to $\frac{1}{2}$.

Example

Estimate the sum of $3\frac{1}{50} + 2\frac{3}{8}$.

Solution

Step 1
Round each fraction to the nearest half or whole.

$3\frac{1}{50} \rightarrow 3$

$2\frac{3}{8} \rightarrow 2\frac{1}{2}$

Step 2
Add the rounded fractions.

$3 + 2\frac{1}{2} = 5\frac{1}{2}$

The sum of $3\frac{1}{50}$ and $2\frac{3}{8}$ is about $5\frac{1}{2}$.

ESTIMATING DIFFERENCES OF FRACTIONS

When you do not need an exact answer, you can estimate to find the difference of two fractions. To estimate the difference of two fractions, take the following steps:

1. Round each fraction to the nearest half or whole.
2. Subtract the rounded fractions.

When you want to round fractions, you can use your number sense to know what to round the fraction to. For example, you can round $1\frac{1}{10}$ to 1 because $\frac{1}{10}$ is so small. Or, you can round $3\frac{19}{20}$ to 4 because $\frac{19}{20}$ is almost a whole.

Another way to round fractions is by drawing a picture. For example, if you draw $\frac{7}{12}$, you can see that it is pretty close to $\frac{1}{2}$.

Example

Estimate the difference of $3\frac{19}{20} - 1\frac{7}{12}$.

Solution

Step 1
Round each fraction to the nearest half or whole.

$3\frac{19}{20} \rightarrow 4$

$1\frac{7}{12} \rightarrow 1\frac{1}{2}$

Step 2
Subtract the rounded fractions.

$4 - 1\frac{1}{2} = 2\frac{1}{2}$

The difference between $3\frac{19}{20}$ and $1\frac{7}{12}$ is about $2\frac{1}{2}$.

7.EE.4A Use variables to represent quantities in a real-world or mathematical problem, and construct simple equations and inequalities to solve problems by reasoning about the quantities. Solve word problems leading to equations of the form px + q = r and p(x + q) = r, where p, q, and r are specific rational numbers. Solve equations of these forms fluently. Compare an algebraic solution to an arithmetic solution, identifying the sequence of the operations used in each approach.

WRITING EQUATIONS TO REPRESENT REAL-LIFE RELATIONSHIPS WITH ONE VARIABLE

Mathematical expressions can consist of numbers, variables, and operational symbols ($+$, $-$, $\times$, and $\div$). Expressions can be as short as a single term, or they can consist of two or more terms joined by an operation. For example, $3x + 5$ has two terms ($3x$ and 5) and the addition operation.

You write an **equation** by putting an equal sign between two expressions. The equal symbol means that the expressions on both the left side and right side of the equal sign have the same value.

To convert a word problem into an equation, follow these steps:

1. Define the variable that represents the unknown value for which you need to solve.
2. Identify mathematical keywords, and translate them into mathematical symbols.
3. Using the variable, create an equation to represent the problem.

Some examples of mathematical keywords are listed in this table.

Add ($+$)	Increase, more than, sum, all together, greater than
Subtract ($-$)	Minus, remaining, reduce, less than, decrease, difference
Multiply ($\times$)	Times, per, rate, of, product
Divide ($\div$)	Into, quotient, how many times, divided by
Equal to ($=$)	Result, answer, sum, total

Example

The cost to rent a DVD player is $5 per day, plus a $15 deposit. Bill paid $30 for his DVD player rental. Write an equation to find the number of days that he rented the DVD player for.

Solution

Step 1
Define the variable.
Let x = the number of days that Bill rented the DVD player for.

Step 2
Identify the keywords.
"$5 per day" $\rightarrow 5x$
"Plus $15" $\rightarrow +15$
"Paid $30" $\rightarrow = 30$

Step 3
Write the equation.
$5x + 15 = 30$

Example

The area of Lake Superior is 5 times the area of Lake Ontario. The sum of the areas of the two lakes is 105,000 km². Write an equation that represents this word problem.

Solution

Step 1
Define the variable.
Let x = the area of Lake Ontario.

Step 2
Identify the keywords.
"5 times the area of Lake Ontario" $\rightarrow 5x$
"Sum of the areas of the two lakes is 105,000 km²" $\rightarrow\ = 105,000$

Step 3
Write the equation.
$x + 5x = 105,000$

7.EE.4B Use variables to represent quantities in a real-world or mathematical problem, and construct simple equations and inequalities to solve problems by reasoning about the quantities. Solve word problems leading to inequalities of the form px + q > r or px + q < r, where p, q, and r are specific rational numbers. Graph the solution set of the inequality and interpret it in the context of the problem.

SOLVING LINEAR INEQUALITIES BY ADDING AND SUBTRACTING

Inequalities are solved in much the same way that equations are solved: all the variables are moved to one side of the equation, and all the numbers are moved to the other side by applying inverse operations.

To solve linear inequalities using addition and subtraction, follow these steps:

1. Isolate the variable by completing the inverse operation.
2. Verify the solution set using a test point.

Example

Solve for x in the linear inequality $x + 4 < 10$.

Solution

Step 1

Isolate the variable by completing the inverse operation.

$$x + 4 < 10$$
$$x + 4 - 4 < 10 - 4$$
$$x < 6$$

Step 2

Verify the solution set using a test point.

Since $4 < 6$, 4 can be used as the test point.

$$x + 4 < 10$$
$$(4) + 4 < 10$$
$$8 < 10$$

The resulting statement is true, so it can be assumed that all numbers less than 6 are part of the solution set.

Example

Solve for x in the linear inequality $x - 7 \geq 25$.

Solution

Step 1

Isolate the variable by completing the inverse operation.

$$x - 7 \geq 25$$
$$x - 7 + 7 \geq 25 + 7$$
$$x \geq 32$$

Step 2

Verify the solution set using a test point.

Since $35 \geq 32$, 35 can be used as the test point.

$$x - 7 \geq 25$$
$$(35) - 7 \geq 25$$
$$28 \geq 25$$

The resulting statement is true; therefore, it can be assumed that all numbers greater than or equal to 32 are part of the solution set.

SOLVING LINEAR INEQUALITIES USING POSITIVE MULTIPLIERS AND DIVISORS

Inequalities are solved in much the same way that equations are solved: all the variables are moved to one side of the equation, and all the numbers are moved to the other side by applying inverse operations. Once a solution is obtained, a test point within the solution set can be substituted into the inequality to verify that the solution is correct.

To solve linear inequalities using positive multipliers and divisors, follow these steps:

1. Isolate the variable by completing the inverse operation.
2. Verify the solution set using a test point.

Example

Solve for x in the linear inequality $15x \geq 120$.

Solution

Step 1

Isolate the variable by completing the inverse operation.

$$15x \geq 120$$
$$\frac{15x}{15} \geq \frac{120}{15}$$
$$x \geq 8$$

Step 2

Verify the solution set using a test point.

Since 10 ≥ 8, 10 will be the test point.

$$15x \geq 120$$
$$15(10) \geq 120$$
$$150 \geq 120$$

The resulting statement is true, so it can be assumed that all numbers greater than or equal to 8 are part of the solution set.

Example

Solve for x in the linear inequality $\dfrac{x}{9} < 36$.

Solution

Step 1

Isolate the variable by completing the inverse operation.

$$\frac{x}{9} < 36$$
$$9\left(\frac{x}{9}\right) < 9(36)$$
$$x < 324$$

Step 2

Verify the solution set using a test point.

Since 270 < 324, 270 will be the test point.

$$\frac{x}{9} < 36$$
$$\frac{270}{9} < 36$$
$$30 < 36$$

The resulting statement is true, so it can be assumed that all numbers less than 324 are part of the solution set.

SOLVING LINEAR INEQUALITIES USING NEGATIVE MULTIPLIERS AND DIVISORS

Inequalities are solved in the same way that equations are solved: all the variables are moved to one side of the equation, and all the numbers are moved to the other side by applying inverse operations.

However, if an inequality is multiplied or divided by a negative number, the direction of the inequality symbol must be reversed.

To solve linear inequalities using negative multipliers and divisors, follow these steps:

1. Isolate the variable by completing the inverse operation.
2. Reverse the direction of the inequality symbol.
3. Verify the solution set using a test point.

Example

Solve for x in the linear inequality $\dfrac{x}{-3} \leq 27$.

Solution

Step 1

Isolate the variable by completing the inverse operation.

$$\frac{x}{-3} \leq 27$$
$$-3\left(\frac{x}{-3}\right) \leq -3(27)$$
$$x \leq -81$$

Step 2

Reverse the direction of the inequality symbol.

$$x \leq -81 \Rightarrow x \geq -81$$

Step 3

Verify the solution set using a test point.

Since $-30 \geq -81$, -30 can be used as a test point.

$$\frac{x}{-3} \leq 27$$
$$\frac{-30}{-3} \leq 27$$
$$-10 \leq 27$$

The resulting statement is true, so it can be assumed that all numbers greater than or equal to -81 are part of the solution set.

Example

Solve for x in the linear inequality $-9x \geq 12$.

Solution

Step 1

Isolate the variable by completing the inverse operation.

$$-9x \geq 12$$
$$\frac{-9x}{-9} \geq \frac{12}{-9}$$
$$x \geq -\frac{4}{3}$$

Step 2

Reverse the direction of the inequality symbol.

$$x \geq -\frac{4}{3} \Rightarrow x \leq -\frac{4}{3}$$

Step 3

Verify the solution set using a test point.

Since $-4 \leq -\frac{4}{3}$, -4 can be used as a test point.

$$-9x \geq 12$$
$$-9(-4) \geq 12$$
$$36 \geq 12$$

The resulting statement is true; therefore, it can be assumed that all numbers less than or equal to $-\frac{4}{3}$ are part of the solution set.

SOLVING PROBLEMS USING LINEAR INEQUALITIES

A mathematical sentence that does not have an exact value is called an **inequality**. Inequalities are written using the symbols $>$, $<$, $\geq$, $\leq$, and $\neq$.

Inequalities can be used to model and solve problems about real-life situations. To solve problems involving inequalities, follow these steps:

1. Create an inequality to model the problem. Assign meaningful variables to the quantities involved, and use keywords from the problem to determine the type of inequality and the mathematical operations involved.

Symbol	Meaning
$>$	greater than, more than
$\geq$	greater than or equal to, minimum, at least, cannot fall below
$<$	less than, fewer than
$\leq$	less than or equal to, maximum, at most, cannot exceed
$\neq$	not equal, does not equal

Operation	Keywords
Add	add, increased by, sum, total, altogether, more than
Subtract	minus, decreased by, difference, less than, take away, taken from
Multiply	of, times, times greater than, product, by
Divide	quotient, times less than, divided into, groups

2. Apply inverse operations to isolate the variable.
3. Verify the solution set using a test point.

Example

Lindsay has to go to a workshop for a project she is working on in school. While at the workshop, she has to park her car underground. The cost of parking underground is $3.00 for the first hour and $4.25 for each additional hour or portion of an hour. She has $20.00 to spend on parking.

What is the maximum number of additional hours Lindsay can park?

Solution

Step 1

Create an inequality to model the problem.

Let h represent the additional hours Lindsay can park. It costs $4.25 for each additional hour of parking, so this can be represented as $4.25h$ in the inequality.

The total cost of parking includes $3.00 for the first hour, which can be represented as $+3$ in the inequality.

The total amount of money that Lindsay can spend on parking is $20; therefore, the maximum number of additional hours that she can park can be represented by $4.25h + 3 \leq 20$.

Step 2

Apply inverse operations to isolate the variable.

$$4.25h + 3 \leq 20$$
$$4.25h + 3 - 3 \leq 20 - 3$$
$$\frac{4.25h}{4.25} \leq \frac{17}{4.25}$$
$$h \leq 4$$

Step 3

Verify the solution set using a test point.

Since $3 \leq 4$, one test point that can be used is 3.

$$4.25h + 3 \leq 20$$
$$4.25(3) + 3 \leq 20$$
$$12.75 + 3 \leq 20$$
$$15.75 \leq 20$$

Since the resulting statement is true, the solution set is correct.

Lindsay can park for a maximum of 4 additional hours.

USING INEQUALITIES TO REPRESENT SITUATIONS DESCRIBED IN WORDS

A mathematical sentence that does not have an exact value is called an **inequality**. Inequalities are written using the symbols $>$, $<$, $\geq$, $\leq$, and $\neq$.

Inequalities represent relationships between different quantities. When a relationship between different quantities is initially described in words, it is useful to write an inequality that represents the relationship. The inequality can then be used for further problem solving.

When inequalities are initially described in words, they can be translated into mathematical expressions by following these steps:

1. Assign meaningful variables to the quantities involved.
2. Find keywords that describe the type of inequality involved.

Symbol	Keywords
$>$	greater than, more than
$\geq$	greater than or equal to, minimum, at least, cannot fall below
$<$	less than, fewer than
$\leq$	less than or equal to, maximum, at most, cannot exceed
$\neq$	not equal to

3. Find keywords that describe the operations involved.

Operation	Keywords
Add	add, increased by, sum, total, altogether, more than
Subtract	minus, decreased by, difference, less than, take away, taken from
Multiply	of, times, times greater than, product, by
Divide	quotient, times less than, divided into, groups

4. Write the inequality.

Example

For her birthday, Charlene received a $500.00 gift card to a local sporting goods store. She wants to buy a pair of basketball shoes that cost $250.00, and she would like to spend the rest of the money on track suits, which are on sale for $20.00 each.

Write an inequality to describe the maximum number of track suits that Charlene can buy.

Solution

Step 1
Assign meaningful variables to the quantities involved.
Let t represent the number of tracksuits Charlene can buy.

Step 2
Find keywords that describe the type of inequality involved.
The phrase "maximum number of track suits" indicates a value less than or equal to a number, so the symbol to use in the inequality will be ≤ .

Step 3
Find keywords that describe the operations involved.
Track suits are on sale for $20.00 each, which can be expressed as $20t$ in the inequality.
The basketball shoes cost $250.00, which can be expressed as +250 in the inequality.

Step 4
Write the inequality.
$20t + 250 \leq 500$

Example

Maria is going on a ski trip, and she wants to save at least $100.00 for spending money for the trip. She currently has $35.00 set aside for this purpose, and she plans to save $2.50 per day from her wages from her part-time job in order to reach her goal.

Write an inequality to represent the number of days that Maria needs to work in order to save at least $100.00.

Solution

Step 1
Assign meaningful variables to the quantities involved.
Let d represent the number of days Maria will have to work.

Step 2
Find keywords that describe the type of inequality involved.
The phrase "at least $100.00" implies a value greater than or equal to $100, so the symbol to use in the inequality will be ≥ .

Step 3
Find keywords that describe the operations involved.
Maria wants to save $2.50 per day, which can be expressed as $2.50d$ in the inequality.
She currently has $35.00 saved, which can be expressed as +35 in the inequality.

Step 4
Write the inequality.
$2.50d + 35 \geq 100$

SOLVING TWO-STEP LINEAR INEQUALITIES

Inequalities are solved in much the same way that equations are solved. Move all the variables to one side of the equation and all the numbers to the other side by applying inverse operations.

To solve linear inequalities, follow these steps:

1. Move all the constants to one side of the inequality.
2. Isolate the variable.
3. Check the solution using a test point.

Example

Solve the inequality $2x + 4 > 10$.

Solution

Step 1

Move all the constants to one side of the inequality.

The inverse of adding 4 is subtracting 4, so subtract 4 from both sides of the inequality.

$$2x + 4 > 10$$
$$2x + 4 - 4 > 10 - 4$$
$$2x > 6$$

Step 2

Isolate the variable.

The inverse of multiplying by 2 is dividing by 2, so divide both sides of the inequality by 2.

$$2x > 6$$
$$\frac{2x}{2} > \frac{6}{2}$$
$$x > 3$$

Step 3

Check the solution using a test point.

The solution is $x > 3$, so pick any number that is greater than 3, and substitute it into the inequality. If it works, the solution is correct. Try using 5.

$$2x + 4 > 10$$
$$2(5) + 4 > 10$$
$$10 + 4 > 10$$
$$14 > 10$$

Since this is true, the solution is correct.
$$x > 3$$

When you multiply or divide an inequality by a negative number, remember to change the direction of the inequality sign.

Example

Solve $-3a - 1 \geq 11$.

Solution

Step 1

Move all the constants to one side of the inequality.

The inverse of subtracting 1 is adding 1, so add 1 to both sides of the inequality.

$$-3a - 1 \geq 11$$
$$-3a - 1 + 1 \geq 11 + 1$$
$$-3a \geq 12$$

Step 2

Isolate the variable.

The inverse of multiplying by -3 is dividing by -3, so divide both sides of the inequality by -3. When multiplying or dividing an inequality by a negative number, reverse the direction of the inequality sign.

$$-3a \geq 12$$
$$\frac{-3a}{-3} \leq \frac{12}{-3}$$
$$a \leq -4$$

Step 3

Check the solution using a test point.

The solution is $a \leq -4$, so pick any number that is less than -4, and substitute it into the inequality. If it works, the solution is correct. Try using -5.

$$-3a - 1 \geq 11$$
$$-3(-5) - 1 \geq 11$$
$$15 - 1 \geq 11$$
$$14 \geq 11$$

Since this is true, the solution is correct.
$$a \leq -4$$

GRAPHING LINEAR INEQUALITIES ON A NUMBER LINE

A number sentence like $x < 3$ is called an inequality. It is possible to show the solution to an inequality on a number line.

The numbers that make $x < 3$ true are 2, 1, 0, and all of the other numbers less than 3. This also includes all of the possible decimals and fractions that are less than 3, like 1.000002 and $2\frac{4}{5}$.

Example

The graph for $x < 3$ is shown.

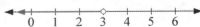

In this graph, 3 is called the boundary point because it is where the arrow starts. The circle around 3 is not shaded, because x cannot equal 3.

To graph the solution to an inequality, follow these steps:

1. Draw a number line and circle the boundary point. Shade in the boundary point if the solution includes that number. Leave it unshaded if it does not.
2. Draw the arrow pointing left for less than (<) and less than or equal to (≤). Draw the arrow pointing right for greater than (>) and greater than or equal to (≥).
3. Check to see if the number line is correct.

Example

Carver found the solution of the linear inequality $3x - 2 \geq 1$ to be $x \geq 1$.

Graph the solution for $x \geq 1$ on a number line.

Solution

Step 1
Draw a number line and circle the boundary point. Shade in the boundary point if the solution includes that number. Leave it unshaded if it does not.

The boundary point in the inequality $x \geq 1$ is 1. Since the inequality includes 1, shade the circle in.

Step 2
Draw the arrow pointing left for less than (<) and less than or equal to (≤). Draw the arrow pointing right for greater than (>) and greater than or equal to (≥).

Since all of the possible values for x are greater than or equal to 1, the arrow will point to the right.

Step 3
Check to see if the number line is correct. Carver's graph shows the solution to $3x - 2 \geq 1$. He should be able to pick any number on the graph and use that to make $3x - 2 \geq 1$ true. Try the number 5.

Substitute 5 back into the original inequality and simplify.

$$3x - 2 \geq 1$$
$$3(5) - 2 \geq 1$$
$$13 \geq 1$$

The graph of $x \geq 1$ is correct.

EXERCISE #1—EXPRESSIONS AND EQUATIONS

Use the following information to answer the next question.

> A list of terms is given.
> p^2, $3pq$, $2q$, $2qp$, $3p$

99. Which of the given terms are like terms?
   - A. p^2 and $3p$
   - B. $3p$ and $2q$
   - C. $2qp$ and $2q$
   - D. $3pq$ and $2qp$

100. What is the factored form of $abc - ad$?
   - A. $ab(c - d)$
   - B. $a(bc - d)$
   - C. $ad(bc - 1)$
   - D. $a(bc - ad)$

101. What is the greatest common factor of $10xz$ and $16x^2y$?
   - A. 2
   - B. 4
   - C. $2x$
   - D. $4x$

102. Which of the following monomials is equal to $7n - 3n - 2m$?
   - A. $2n$
   - B. $12m$
   - C. $4n - 2m$
   - D. $7n - 5m$

Use the following information to answer the next question.

> Leo's telephone plan lets him call anywhere in the country for 4¢ a minute. He also has to pay a 5% tax on his long-distance calls. Leo wants to know how much he will pay for his long-distance calls over 6 months if he uses the same number of minutes every month. He writes the expression $6(4m + 0.05 \times 4m)$, where m is the number of long-distance minutes he uses in a month.

103. Another expression that Leo can use to calculate how much he will pay for long-distance calls in 6 months is
   - A. $\$4.8m$
   - B. $\$24.3m$
   - C. $\$25.2m$
   - D. $\$97.2m$

104. Which of the following binomials represents the expression $(2x - 8) + (4x + 12)$?
   - A. $6x + 4$
   - B. $6x - 4$
   - C. $2x + 4$
   - D. $2x - 4$

Use the following information to answer the next question.

> Potassium makes up 75% of the minerals in an apple. It makes up 60% of the minerals in an orange and 90% of the minerals in a peach.

105. Which of the following tables shows these percents as fractions in lowest terms?

A.
Apple	Orange	Peach
$\frac{2}{3}$	$\frac{2}{5}$	$\frac{45}{50}$

B.
Apple	Orange	Peach
$\frac{1}{4}$	$\frac{2}{5}$	$\frac{1}{10}$

C.
Apple	Orange	Peach
$\frac{15}{20}$	$\frac{6}{10}$	$\frac{18}{20}$

D.
Apple	Orange	Peach
$\frac{3}{4}$	$\frac{3}{5}$	$\frac{9}{10}$

106. The percentage equivalent of the fraction $\frac{1}{4}$ is _____%.

107. The repeating decimal $0.\overline{336}$ converted into a fraction expressed in lowest terms is
   - A. $\frac{112}{333}$
   - B. $\frac{168}{333}$
   - C. $\frac{112}{666}$
   - D. $\frac{168}{666}$

108. The decimal number 0.005 can be written as the fraction
   - A. $\frac{5}{10,000}$
   - B. $\frac{1}{2}$
   - C. $\frac{5}{100}$
   - D. $\frac{1}{200}$

Use the following information to answer the next question.

> Shane bought 9 candy bars to share with his classmates.
>
> He knows that 1 candy bar weighs 46.6 g, but before he brings them to school in his backpack, he wants to estimate how much the candy bars will weigh altogether.

109. Which of the following estimates is **most reasonable** for Shane to make?
   - A. 200 g
   - B. 330 g
   - C. 470 g
   - D. 520 g

110. Use rounding to estimate the solution to $54 \div 5.7$. _____

111. Rounded to the nearest whole number, what is the estimated sum of $549.361 + 85.200$?
   - A. 635
   - B. 622
   - C. 602
   - D. 598

112. Rounded to the nearest whole number, what is the estimated difference of $38.897 - 14.331$?
   - A. 33
   - B. 25
   - C. 14
   - D. 10

113. Solve $\frac{5}{7} - \frac{2}{5}$.

114. The **best** estimate for $\frac{6}{10} + 2\frac{95}{100}$ is
   - A. 2
   - B. 3
   - C. $3\frac{1}{2}$
   - D. $4\frac{1}{2}$

115. The **best** estimate of the solution to the expression $6\frac{5}{9} - 4\frac{1}{12}$ is
   - A. 1
   - B. $1\frac{1}{2}$
   - C. 2
   - D. $2\frac{1}{2}$

Use the following information to answer the next question.

> Vivian has 14 fewer quarters than nickels.

116. If the total value of Vivian's coins is \$8.80, which of the following equations could be used to solve for the number of quarters that Vivian has?
   - A. $0.25x + 0.05(x + 14) = 8.80$
   - B. $0.05x + 0.25(x - 14) = 8.80$
   - C. $0.05x + 0.25(x + 14) = 8.80$
   - D. $0.25x - 0.05(x - 14) = 8.80$

117. The solution set for $7 + x < 67$ is
   - A. $x < 60$
   - B. $x > 60$
   - C. $x < 74$
   - D. $x > 74$

118. What is the solution set for the inequality $80 < \frac{5}{t}$?
   - A. $t < \frac{1}{400}$
   - B. $t < \frac{1}{16}$
   - C. $t < 16$
   - D. $t < 400$

119. What is the solution to the inequality $\frac{-x}{4} < -5$?
   - A. $x > 20$
   - B. $x < 20$
   - C. $x > -20$
   - D. $x < -20$

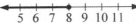

Use the following information to answer the next question.

Sean and Dave ate at a local pizza parlor on all-you-can-eat pizza night. Sean ate at least six more than triple the number of slices of pizza Dave ate.

120. If Sean ate 18 slices of pizza, which inequality represents the number of slices of pizza Dave ate?
- A. $x \geq 8$
- B. $x \leq 8$
- C. $x \geq 4$
- D. $x \leq 4$

Use the following information to answer the next question.

For a class he is taking, Jayson has to complete at least 35 h of volunteer work. He has already completed 7 h at the food bank. He wants to finish his hours at a local animal shelter, where all the shifts are 4 h long.

121. Which of the following inequalities expresses the number of shifts that Jayson needs to volunteer for to complete his class?
- A. $4s + 7 \leq 35$
- B. $4s + 7 \geq 35$
- C. $4s - 7 \leq 35$
- D. $4s - 7 \geq 35$

122. Which of the following inequalities has the solution set $x > 6$?
- A. $3x > 6$
- B. $6x > 12$
- C. $5x - 4 > 26$
- D. $x - 12 > -18$

Use the following information to answer the next question.

The solution to $2x < 8 + x$ is $x < 8$. The given number line shows how Alia graphed this solution.

5 6 7 8 9 10 11

123. Which of the following statements **best** describes Alia's graph of the solution?
- A. The circle is in the wrong place.
- B. The circle should not be filled in.
- C. The arrow is pointing in the wrong direction.
- D. The numbers on the number line are incorrect.

EXERCISE #1—EXPRESSIONS AND EQUATIONS ANSWERS AND SOLUTIONS

99. D	106. 25	113. See solution	120. D
100. B	107. A	114. C	121. B
101. C	108. D	115. D	122. C
102. C	109. C	116. B	123. B
103. C	110. 9	117. A	
104. A	111. A	118. B	
105. D	112. B	119. A	

99. D

Like terms have the same combination of variables:

- The terms $3pq$ and $2qp$ are like terms because both have a p and a q.
- The terms p^2 and $3p$ are unlike because they have different exponents on the variables.
- The terms $3p$ and $2q$ are unlike because they have different variables.
- The terms $2qp$ and $2q$ are unlike because they do not both have a p.

100. B

Step 1
Find the greatest common factor (GCF) of the terms.
The GCF of abc and ad is a.

Step 2
Divide the expression by the GCF.
$$\frac{abc - ad}{a}$$
$$= \frac{abc}{a} - \frac{ad}{a}$$
$$= bc - d$$

Step 3
Write the factored expression.
Write the GCF outside the brackets, and place the result of the division inside the brackets.
$a(bc - d)$
The factored form of $abc - ad$ is $a(bc - d)$.

101. C

Step 1
Find the greatest common factor (GCF) of the coefficients of all the terms.
The coefficients are 10 and 16. The GCF of these is 2.

Step 2
Find the GCF of the variables in the terms.
The variables are xz and x^2y. The GCF of these is x.

Step 3
Combine the two to find the GCF of the terms.
The GCF of $10xy$ and $16x^2y$ is $2x$.

102. C

Perform operations on the numbers before the variable. The expression contains two monomials with the same variable, n. The numbers before that variable are 7 and –3. It also has one monomial with a different variable, m. The number before that variable is –2.

To simplify, subtract the numbers before the variable n, and write the answer with n.
The monomial with a different variable cannot be combined. Keep it as is.
$7n - 3n - 2m = (7 - 3)n - 2m$
$\qquad\qquad\qquad = 4n - 2m$

103. C

Simplify $6(4m + 0.05 \times 4m)$.
$6(4m + 0.05 \times 4m) = 6(4m + 0.2m)$
$\qquad\qquad\qquad\qquad = 6(4.2m)$
$\qquad\qquad\qquad\qquad = 25.2m$

Leo will pay $\$25.2m$ for long-distance calls.

104. A

Apply the associative property of addition.
$(2x - 8) + (4x + 12)$
$= (2x + 4x) + (-8 + 12)$
$= (6x) + (4)$
$= 6x + 4$

105. D

Step 1

Write the percent of potassium in an apple as a fraction in lowest terms.

The value of the percent over a denominator of 100 is $\dfrac{75}{100}$.

To reduce the fraction to lowest terms, divide the numerator and denominator by the greatest common factor (GCF).

The GCF of 75 and 100 is 25.

$$\dfrac{75}{100} = \dfrac{75 \div 25}{100 \div 25} = \dfrac{3}{4}$$

The percent of potassium in an apple as a fraction in lowest terms is $\dfrac{3}{4}$.

Step 2

Write the percent of potassium in an orange as a fraction in lowest terms.

The value of the percent over a denominator of 100 is $\dfrac{60}{100}$.

To reduce the fraction to lowest terms, divide the numerator and denominator by the greatest common factor (GCF).

The GCF of 60 and 100 is 20.

$$\dfrac{60}{100} = \dfrac{60 \div 20}{100 \div 20} = \dfrac{3}{5}$$

The percent of potassium in an orange as a fraction in lowest terms is $\dfrac{3}{5}$.

Step 3

Write the percent of potassium in a peach as a fraction in lowest terms.

The value of the percent over a denominator of 100 is $\dfrac{90}{100}$.

To reduce the fraction to lowest terms, divide the numerator and denominator by the greatest common factor (GCF).

The GCF of 90 and 100 is 10.

$$\dfrac{90}{10} = \dfrac{90 \div 10}{100 \div 10} = \dfrac{9}{10}$$

The percent of potassium in a peach as a fraction in lowest terms is $\dfrac{9}{10}$.

In lowest terms, the fractions are $\dfrac{3}{4}$ (apple), $\dfrac{3}{5}$ (orange), and $\dfrac{9}{10}$ (peach).

106. 25

Step 1

Divide the numerator, 1, by the denominator, 4.

$1 \div 4 = 0.25$

Step 2

Multiply by 100 to convert the decimal to a percentage. Then, add a percentage sign after the solution.

$0.25 \times 100 = 25\%$

The percentage equivalent of the fraction $\dfrac{1}{4}$ is 25%.

107. A

Step 1

Determine the denominator.

Since the number is a repeating decimal, the denominator will consist of a series of 9s. Use the number of repeating digits to determine how many 9s are written in the denominator.

Three digits repeat in $0.\overline{336}$. The denominator is 999.

$$\dfrac{?}{999}$$

Step 2

Determine the numerator.

Remove the decimal point and bar. The numerator is 336.

$$\dfrac{336}{999}$$

Step 3

Reduce the fraction to lowest terms.

Divide the numerator and denominator by the greatest common factor (GCF), 3.

$$\dfrac{336 \div 3}{999 \div 3} = \dfrac{112}{333}$$

Expressed as a fraction in lowest terms, $0.\overline{336}$ is $\dfrac{112}{333}$.

108. D

Step 1

Convert 0.005 to a fraction.

Since there are three digits to the right of the decimal, the denominator of the fraction is 1,000.

$$\dfrac{?}{1,000}$$

The digits to the right of the decimal represent the numerator. Drop the two zeros.

$$\dfrac{5}{1,000} = \dfrac{5}{1,000}$$

Step 2

Since $\dfrac{5}{1,000}$ is not one of the options, reduce the fraction to its lowest form.

Divide both the numerator and the denominator by 5.

$\dfrac{5 \div 5}{1,000 \div 5} = \dfrac{1}{200}$

The decimal number 0.005 can be written as the fraction $\dfrac{1}{200}$.

109. C

Step 1

Round the numbers to make them easier to work with.

Round the decimal number to the nearest whole number.

The decimal number 46.6 can round up to 47 because the digit to the right is 6 and 6 > 5.

Round the whole number to the nearest ten.

The whole number 9 can round up to 10.

Step 2

Multiply the rounded numbers.

47 × 10 = 470 g

From the given choices, the most reasonable estimate for the weight of Shane's candy bars is 470 g.

110. 9

Step 1

Round the decimal number to the nearest whole number.

Because 7 is greater than 5, round up.

5.7 → 6

Step 2

Estimate the answer.

The whole number 6 does not need to be rounded because 6 is a factor of 54.

54 ÷ 6 = 9

The estimated quotient of 54 ÷ 5.7 is 9. Because you rounded up to 6, the actual answer will be slightly lower than 9.

111. A

Step 1

Round both decimals to the nearest whole number. When rounding to the nearest whole number, look at the digit in the tenths place to determine whether the number should be rounded up or down. If the number in the tenths place is equal to or greater than 5, round up. If the number is less than 5, round down.

549.631 → 550

85.200 → 85

Step 2

Add the two estimated numbers.

550 + 85 = 635

The estimated sum is 635.

112. B

Step 1

Round both numbers to the nearest whole number. When rounding to the nearest whole number, look at the digit in the tenths place value to determine whether the number should be rounded up or down. If the number is equal to or greater than 5, round up. If the number is less than 5, round down.

Since 8 is greater than 5, 38.897 rounds up to 39.

Since 3 is less than 5, 14.331 rounds down to 14.

Step 2

Subtract the two estimated numbers.

39 − 14 = 25

The estimated difference is 25.

113.

Step 1

Write the fractions with the lowest common denominator (LCD).

Write the multiples of each denominator until a common one appears.

- Multiples of 7: 7, 14, 21, 28, 35
- Multiples of 5: 5, 10, 15, 20, 25, 30, 35

The LCD for 7 and 5 is 35.

Use the LCD to create new equivalent fractions with a denominator of 35.

$\dfrac{5 \times 5}{7 \times 5} = \dfrac{25}{35}, \dfrac{2 \times 7}{5 \times 7} = \dfrac{14}{35}$

Step 2

Subtract the numerators of the fractions while keeping the denominators the same.

$\dfrac{25 - 14}{35} = \dfrac{11}{35}$

Step 3

Reduce the resulting fraction to lowest terms.

The fraction is already in lowest terms.

Therefore, $\dfrac{5}{7} - \dfrac{2}{5} = \dfrac{11}{35}$.

114. C

Step 1

Round each fraction to the nearest half or whole.

- $\dfrac{6}{10} \to \dfrac{1}{2}$

- $2\dfrac{95}{100} \to 3$

Step 2

Add the rounded fractions.

$$\frac{1}{2} + 3 = 3\frac{1}{2}$$

The sum of $\frac{6}{10}$ and $2\frac{95}{100}$ is about $3\frac{1}{2}$.

115. D

Step 1

Round each fraction to the nearest half or whole.

$$6\frac{5}{9} \rightarrow 6\frac{1}{2}$$

$$4\frac{1}{12} \rightarrow 4$$

Step 2

Subtract the rounded fractions.

$$6\frac{1}{2} - 4 = 2\frac{1}{2}$$

The difference between $6\frac{5}{9}$ and $4\frac{1}{12}$ is about $2\frac{1}{2}$.

116. B

Step 1

Define the variable.

Let x = the number of nickels Vivian has.

Step 2

Create an equation using the variable to represent the situation.

Since x is defined as the number of nickels that Vivian has, $x - 14$ = the number of quarters Vivian has.

value of nickels & quarters = $8.80
(value of nickels) = $0.05x$
(value of quarters) = $0.25(x - 14)$

Given this information it is now possible to put together an equation that satisfies the situation described.

$$0.05x + 0.25(x - 14) = 8.80$$

When dealing with coins, decide whether you will treat everything as dollars or as cents. If you choose to represent the values as cents, then the expression would be as follows:

$$5x + 25(x - 14) = 880$$

117. A

For linear inequalities, the inequality sign can be treated like an equal sign if not multiplying or dividing by a negative value. Whatever operation is done to one side must be done to the other side.

$$7 + x < 67$$
$$7 - 7 + x < 67 - 7$$
$$x < 60$$

118. B

To solve this inequality, isolate the variable (t). When isolating a variable, be sure that the same operations are performed on both sides of the inequality.

$$80 < \frac{5}{t}$$
$$80(t) < \left(\frac{5}{t}\right)t$$
$$80t < 5$$
$$\frac{80t}{80} < \frac{5}{80}$$
$$t < \frac{1}{16}$$

119. A

A linear inequality can be solved like a linear equation by applying inverse operations to isolate the variable. However, when multiplying or dividing a linear inequality by a negative number, the direction of the inequality sign must be changed.

$$\frac{-x}{4} < -5$$
$$\frac{-x}{4} \times 4 < -5 \times 4$$
$$-x < -20$$
$$\frac{-x}{-1} < \frac{-20}{-1}$$
$$x > 20$$

120. D

Let the variable x represent the number of slices of pizza Dave ate.

The phrase "six more than triple the slices of pizza Dave ate" can be represented by the expression $3x + 6$. Therefore, Sean ate at least $3x + 6$ slices of pizza. Since Sean ate 18 slices of pizza, the problem can be represented by the inequality $3x + 6 \leq 18$.

Solve the inequality by applying inverse operations.

$$3x + 6 \leq 18$$
$$3x + 6 - 6 \leq 18 - 6$$
$$3x \leq 12$$
$$\frac{3x}{3} \leq \frac{12}{3}$$
$$x \leq 4$$

The inequality $x \leq 4$ represents the number of slices of pizza Dave ate. In other words, Dave ate a maximum of 4 slices of pizza.

121. B

Step 1
Assign meaningful variables to the quantities involved.

Let s equal the number of shifts that Jayson will need to work at the animal shelter.

Step 2
Find the keywords that describe the type of inequality involved.

Since the question asks for at least 35 h, the type of inequality will be greater than or equal to, $\geq$.

Step 3
Find the keywords that describe the operations involved.

The shifts at the animal shelter are 4 h long. You can write this as $4s$.

Jayson has already completed 7 h at the food bank. You can write this as +7.

Step 4
Write the inequality.

$4s + 7 \geq 35$

122. C

A linear inequality can be solved like a linear equation. Follow the order of operations, and make sure that whatever operation you perform on one side you also perform on the other.

Solve each given inequality until a solution set matches the given solution.

Step 1
$3x > 6$

$\dfrac{3x}{6} > \dfrac{6}{6}$

$x > 2$

This does not satisfy the inequality.

Step 2
$6x > 12$

$\dfrac{6x}{6} > \dfrac{12}{6}$

$x > 2$

This does not satisfy the inequality.

Step 3
$5x - 4 > 26$

$5x - 4 + 4 > 26 + 4$

$5x > 30$

$\dfrac{5x}{5} > \dfrac{30}{5}$

$x > 6$

This matches the given inequality.

123. B

In the solution $x < 8$, x can be any number that is less than 8, but it cannot include the number 8. In Alia's graph, the circle is filled in. This shows that the solution can include the number 8. To correct the graph, she should draw a circle that is not filled in.

EXERCISE #2—EXPRESSIONS AND EQUATIONS

124. Which of the following pairs are **not** like terms?

   A. d^2 and d

   B. $5f^2$ and f^2

   C. def and fed

   D. $3ef$ and $6ef$

125. What is the factored form of $5j + 10k - 15$?

   A. $5(j + 10k - 15)$

   B. $5j(1 + 2k - 3)$

   C. $5k(j + 2 - 3)$

   D. $5(j + 2k - 3)$

126. What is the greatest common factor of $6pq$, $3qs$, and $18ps$?

   A. 3   B. 6

   C. $3p$ D. $6p$

127. Which of the following monomials is equal to the expression $6t + 2t - 7t$?

   A. t B. $3t$

   C. $13t$ D. $15t$

Use the following information to answer the next question.

Elaine and her family are going on a long drive. They decide that they will stop for a half hour rest every 4 h. Elaine wants to know how long this will make their trip. She calculates that the amount of time they spend on breaks will be $\dfrac{h}{4} \times \dfrac{1}{2}$, where h is the number of hours that they drive. The total time of their trip will therefore be equal to $h + \dfrac{h}{4} \times \dfrac{1}{2}$.

128. Which of the following expressions could Elaine also use to calculate the total time of their trip?

   A. $\dfrac{5h}{2}$ B. $\dfrac{9h}{4}$

   C. $\dfrac{5h}{8}$ D. $\dfrac{9h}{8}$

129. In its simplest form, the expression $3 \times x \times 12$ is

   A. $3x \times 12$ B. $12x \times 3$

   C. $36x$ D. $48x$

Use the following information to answer the next question.

Strawberry ice cream is approximately 40% fat.

130. Write this percentage as a fraction in lowest terms.

   A. $\dfrac{40}{100}$ B. $\dfrac{20}{50}$

   C. $\dfrac{10}{25}$ D. $\dfrac{2}{5}$

131. The fraction $\dfrac{1}{5}$ expressed as a percentage is

   A. 2%   B. 5%

   C. 15%   D. 20%

132. To reduce a fraction to lowest terms, it is necessary to divide by the
   A. lowest common factor
   B. greatest common factor
   C. lowest common denominator
   D. greatest common denominator

133. Determine three proper fractions that represent the decimal number 0.75.

Use the following information to answer the next question.

Marcie is making cherry pies for a school bake sale. She wants to make 12 pies. Each pie needs 2.5 cups of cherries. She estimates the total amount of cherries she needs to make all the pies.

134. Which of the following estimates is the **most reasonable**?
   A. 20 cups   B. 30 cups
   C. 40 cups   D. 50 cups

135. Use the strategy of compatible numbers to estimate the quotient of $106.2 \div 9$. _____

136. Rounded to the nearest whole number, the estimated difference of $34.201 + 60.002$ is
   A. 78   B. 90
   C. 94   D. 101

137. Using the strategy of rounding to the nearest hundredth, the difference of $0.369 - 0.048$ is equal to _____.

138. Solve $\dfrac{5}{6} - \dfrac{3}{12}$.

139. The **best** estimate for $2\dfrac{1}{8} + 2\dfrac{18}{20}$ is
   A. 3   B. $3\dfrac{1}{2}$
   C. $4\dfrac{1}{2}$ D. 5

140. What is the **best** estimate of the solution to the expression $9\dfrac{1}{6} - 1\dfrac{7}{8}$?
   A. $6\dfrac{1}{2}$ B. 7
   C. 8   D. $8\dfrac{1}{2}$

141. Jill works in a shoe store where she makes $96 / day plus $3 in commission for each pair of shoes that she sells. If Jill makes $500 in one week and sells n pairs of shoes, which of the following equations represents her earnings for the 5-day work week?
   A. $5(3 + 96n) = 500$
   B. $5(96 + 3n) = 500$
   C. $96(3 + 5n) = 500$
   D. $96(5 + 3n) = 500$

142. What is the solution set for $x + 3 > 4$?
   A. $x > 1$ B. $x > 7$
   C. $x > 12$ D. $x < 12$

143. What is the solution set for $3x < 51$?
   A. $x < 17$ B. $x > 17$
   C. $x < 47$ D. $x > 54$

144. What is the solution set for the inequality
$\frac{w}{-2} \geq 32$?

A. $w \leq -16$ B. $w \geq -16$

C. $w \geq -64$ D. $w \leq -64$

*Use the following information to
answer the next question.*

Rachelle and Lisa are flying to Vancouver.
When they weigh their bags at the airline
counter, they discover that Rachelle's bag
weighs no more than double Lisa's bag
decreased by 5 kg.

145. If Rachelle's bag weighs 45 kg, which of the
following inequalities represents the
possible weight of Lisa's bag?

A. $x \geq 25$ B. $x \leq 25$

C. $x \geq 20$ D. $x \leq 20$

*Use the following information to
answer the next question.*

Maria wants to save $100. She has already
saved $35. She saves $2.50 every day from
her wages.

146. Which of the following inequalities shows the
minimum number of days Maria needs to
work to earn $100?

A. $35 + 2.50x \geq 100$

B. $35 + 2.50x \leq 100$

C. $35x + 2.50 \geq 100$

D. $35x + 2.50 \leq 100$

*Use the following information to
answer the next question.*

Olivia graphs an inequality as shown.

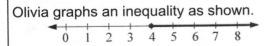

147. What inequality did Olivia graph?

A. $x < 4$ B. $x \leq 4$

C. $x > 4$ D. $x \geq 4$

148. Solve $2x - 3 > 5$, and then identify which of
the numbers –3, –4, –7, or 7 belongs to the
solution set. _____

EXERCISE #2—EXPRESSIONS AND EQUATIONS ANSWERS AND SOLUTIONS

124. A	131. D	138. See solution	145. A
125. D	132. B	139. D	146. A
126. A	133. See solution	140. B	147. D
127. A	134. B	141. B	148. 7
128. D	135. 12	142. A	
129. C	136. C	143. A	
130. D	137. 0.32	144. D	

124. A

Like terms have the same combination of variables.

- *def* and *fed* both have a *d*, an *e*, and an *f*, so they are like terms.
- 3*ef* and 6*ef* both have an *e* and an *f*, so they are like terms.
- 5f^2 and f^2 both have an f^2, so they are like terms.
- d^2 and *d* have different exponents, so they are not like terms.

125. D

Step 1
Find the greatest common factor (GCF) of the terms.
The GCF of 5*j*, 10*k*, and 15 is 5.

Step 2
Divide the expression by the GCF.

$$\frac{5j + 10k - 15}{5}$$
$$= \frac{5j}{5} + \frac{10k}{5} - \frac{15}{5}$$
$$= j + 2k - 3$$

Step 3
Write the factored expression.

Write the GCF outside the brackets, and place the result of the division inside the brackets.
5($j + 2k - 3$)
The factored form of 5j + 10k – 15 is 5($j + 2k - 3$).

126. A

Step 1
Find the greatest common factor (GCF) of the coefficients of all the terms.

The coefficients are 6, 3, and 18. The GCF of these is 3.

Step 2
Find the GCF of the variables in the terms.

The variables are *pq*, *qs*, and *ps*. There is no variable common to all three monomials.

Step 3
Combine the two to find the GCF of the terms.
The GCF of 6*pq*, 3*qs*, and 18*ps* is 3.

127. A

Perform operations on the numbers before the variable.

The expression contains three monomials with the same variable. The numbers before the variable are 6, 2, and –7.

Add and subtract the numbers before the variable in the order that they appear, and write the answer with the given variable.
$6t + 2t - 7t = (6 + 2 - 7)t$
$$= 1t$$
$$= t$$

128. D

Simplify $h + \frac{h}{4} \times \frac{1}{2}$.

$h + \frac{h}{4} \times \frac{1}{2} = h + \frac{h}{8}$
$$= \frac{8h}{8} + \frac{1h}{8}$$
$$= \frac{9h}{8}$$

The total time of the trip is represented by $\frac{9h}{8}$.

Elaine could therefore also use this expression to calculate the total time of their trip.

129. C

Apply the commutative property of multiplication.
$3 \times x \times 12 = 3 \times 12 \times x$
$$= 36 \times x$$
$$= 36x$$

130. D

Step 1

Write the percentage as a fraction with a denominator of 100.

$\dfrac{40}{100}$

Step 2

Reduce the fraction to lowest terms.

Divide both the numerator and denominator by their greatest common factor.

$\dfrac{40 \div 20}{100 \div 20} = \dfrac{2}{5}$

131. D

Step 1

Divide the numerator by the denominator.

The numerator is 1. The denominator is 5.

$1 \div 5 = 0.2$

Step 2

Multiply the result by 100.

$0.2 \times 100 = 20$

Step 3

Place the percent sign behind the answer.

20%

Therefore, $\dfrac{1}{5} = 20\%$.

132. B

Fractions are reduced by dividing by the greatest common factor (GCF).

133.

Step 1

Since there are two digits to the right of the decimal, the denominator of the fraction is 100.

The numerator of the fraction has the same number of digits to the right of the decimal in the decimal number, 75.

One fraction that represents 0.75 is $\dfrac{75}{100}$.

Step 2

It is possible to reduce the fraction $\dfrac{75}{100}$ by dividing both the numerator and the denominator by the same number.

$\dfrac{75}{100} = \dfrac{75 \div 5}{100 \div 5} = \dfrac{15}{20}$

$\dfrac{75}{100} = \dfrac{75 \div 25}{100 \div 25} = \dfrac{3}{4}$

The decimal 0.75 can be represented by the proper fractions $\dfrac{75}{100}$, $\dfrac{15}{20}$, and $\dfrac{3}{4}$.

134. B

Step 1

Round the decimal number to the nearest whole number.

$2.5 \to 3$

Round the number of pies to the nearest ten.

$12 \to 10$

Step 2

Determine the total amount of cherries needed. Multiply the rounded amount of cherries (3 cups) by the rounded number of pies (10).

$3 \times 10 = 30$

Marcie needs about 30 cups of cherries to make 12 pies.

135. 12

Step 1

Recall that compatible numbers are numbers that are close to the actual numbers and divide without a remainder.

A number that is compatible with 9 and is close to 106.2 is 108.

$(9 \times 12 = 108)$

Step 2

Divide the compatible numbers.

$108 \div 9 = 12$

The estimated quotient of $106.2 \div 9$ is 12.

Since the compatible number of 108 is a little greater than the actual number of 106.2, the estimated quotient will be a little less than 12.

136. C

Step 1

Round the two numbers to the nearest whole. When you are rounding to the nearest whole number, you use the digit in the tenths place to determine if you are rounding up or rounding down. If the number is equal to or greater than 5, you round up.

If the number is less than 5, you round down.

$34.201 \to 34$

$60.002 \to 60$

Step 2

Add the two estimated numbers.

$60 + 34 = 94$

The estimated sum is 94.

137. 0.32

Step 1

Round both decimals to the nearest hundredth.

To round to the nearest hundredth, look at the digit in the thousandths place value and determine whether it should be rounded up or down. If the number is equal to or greater than 5, round up. If the number is less than 5, round down.

Since 9 is greater than 5, 0.369 rounds up to 0.37.

Since 8 is greater than 5, 0.048 rounds up to 0.05.

Step 2

Subtract the two numbers.

0.37 − 0.05 = 0.32

Rounded to the nearest hundredth, the estimated difference is 0.32.

138.

Step 1

Write the fractions with the lowest common denominator (LCD).

Write the multiples of each denominator until a common one appears.

- Multiples of 6: 6, 12, 18, 24
- Multiples of 12: 12, 24

The lowest common denominator for 6 and 12 is 12. Use the LCD to create new equivalent fractions with a denominator of 12.

$$\frac{5 \times 2}{6 \times 2} = \frac{10}{12}$$

$$\frac{3 \times 1}{12 \times 1} = \frac{3}{12}$$

Step 2

Subtract the numerators of the fractions while keeping the denominators the same.

$$\frac{10 - 3}{12} = \frac{7}{12}$$

Step 3

Reduce the resulting fraction to lowest terms. The fraction is already in lowest terms.

Therefore, $\frac{5}{6} - \frac{3}{12} = \frac{7}{12}$.

139. D

Step 1

Round each fraction to the nearest half or whole.

- $2\frac{1}{8} \rightarrow 2$

- $2\frac{18}{20} \rightarrow 3$

Step 2

Add the rounded fractions.

2 + 3 = 5

The sum of $2\frac{1}{8}$ and $2\frac{18}{20}$ is about 5.

140. B

Step 1

Round each fraction to the nearest half or whole.

- $9\frac{1}{6} \rightarrow 9$

- $1\frac{7}{8} \rightarrow 2$

Step 2

Subtract the rounded fractions.

9 − 2 = 7

The difference between $9\frac{1}{6}$ and $1\frac{7}{8}$ is about 7.

141. B

Identify keywords that will help to create a mathematical equation to represent the situation.

Jill makes \$96 / day plus another \$3 in commission for each pair of shoes she sells. This is represented by $96 + 3n$.

In one work week, Jill will work 5 days. The expression becomes $5(96 + 3n)$.

If she makes a total of \$500 in one week, the equation now becomes $5(96 + 3n) = 500$.

142. A

When solving linear inequalities, the inequality sign can usually be treated like an equal sign. Whatever operation is done to one side must be done to the other side. The inequality needs to be reversed if multiplying or dividing by a negative value.

$$x + 3 > 4$$
$$x + 3 - 3 > 4 - 3$$
$$x > 1$$

143. A

For linear inequalities, the inequality sign can be treated like an equal sign if the inequality is not being multiplied or divided by a negative value. Whatever operation is done to one side must be done to the other side.

$$3x < 51$$
$$\frac{3x}{3} < \frac{51}{3}$$
$$x < 17$$

144. D

A linear inequality can be solved like a linear equation by applying inverse operations to isolate the variable. However, when multiplying or dividing a linear inequality by a negative number, remember to change the direction of the inequality sign.

$$\frac{w}{-2} \geq 32$$
$$\frac{w}{-2}(-2) \geq 32(-2)$$
$$w \leq -64$$

145. A

Let the weight of Lisa's bag be x. The relationship between the weights of the girls' bags can be represented by the inequality $2x - 5 \geq 45$.

Solve the inequality by applying inverse operations.
$$2x - 5 \geq 45$$
$$2x - 5 + 5 \geq 45 + 5$$
$$\frac{2x}{2} \geq \frac{50}{2}$$
$$x \geq 25$$

The weight of Lisa's bag is greater than or equal to 25 kg.

146. A

Step 1
Look for keywords.
Since the question asks for a minimum, the inequality will be "greater than or equal to."

Step 2
Set up the inequality.
Let x stand for the number of days that Maria needs to work.
The total amount of money Maria will save from her wages will be her daily savings multiplied by the number of days she works: $2.50x$.
The inequality will be the sum of the amount she has already saved plus the amount she saves from her wages each day compared to the total amount of money she wishes to save.
$$35 + 2.50x \geq 100$$

147. D

The boundary point of Olivia's inequality is 4. The circle is filled in, so the solution can be equal to 4. The arrow points to the right, so any possible solution is greater than or equal to 4. Olivia graphed the inequality $x \geq 4$.

148. 7

Step 1
Move the constant to the right side of the equation by adding 3 to both sides of the equation.
$$2x - 3 > 5$$
$$2x - 3 + 3 > 5 + 3$$
$$2x > 8$$

Step 2
Isolate the variable by dividing both sides of the equation by 2.
$$2x > 8$$
$$\frac{2x}{2} > \frac{8}{2}$$
$$x > 4$$

Notice both sides of the equation were divided by a positive value. The inequality sign did not change.

Step 3
Determine the answer.
The solution set is all the values that satisfy the inequality. The only given number that is greater than 4 is 7.

NOTES

Geometry

GEOMETRY

Table of Correlations

Standard		Concepts	Exercise #1	Exercise #2
7.G	Geometry			
7.G.1	Solve problems involving scale drawings of geometric figures, including computing actual lengths and areas from a scale drawing and reproducing a scale drawing at a different scale.	Reductions of Two-Dimensional Shapes	149	194
		Interpreting Scale Drawings	150	195
		Enlargements of Two-Dimensional Shapes	151	196
		Applying Scale Factors of Two-Dimensional Geometric Shapes to Perimeter and Area	152	197
7.G.2	Draw (freehand, with ruler and protractor, and with technology) geometric shapes with given conditions. Focus on constructing triangles from three measures of angles or sides, noticing when the conditions determine a unique triangle, more than one triangle, or no triangle.	Investigating the Angle Sum Theorem		
		Applying the Angle Sum Theorem for Triangles	153	198
		Applying the Triangle Inequality Theorem	154	199
		Determining Unique Triangles	155	200
		Drawing a Triangle Given Two Angles and a Side Length	157	202
		Drawing a Triangle Given the Lengths of Two Sides and the Angle between Them	156	201
7.G.3	Describe the two–dimensional figures that result from slicing three-dimensional figures, as in plane sections of right rectangular prisms and right rectangular pyramids.	Plane Sections of Three-Dimensional Figures	158	203
7.G.4	Know the formulas for the area and circumference of a circle and use them to solve problems; give an informal derivation of the relationship between the circumference and area of a circle.	Pi (π)	159	204
		Developing the Area Formula for Circles		
		Developing the Circumference Formula		
		Calculating the Area of Circles Using 3.14 or $\frac{22}{7}$	160	205, 208
		Calculating the Circumference of Circles Using 3.14 or $\frac{22}{7}$	161	206, 209
		Solving Problems Involving Circumferences	162	209
		Solving Problems Involving the Area of Circles	163	208
		Problem Solving with the Radius or Diameter of a Circle	164	207
7.G.5	Use facts about supplementary, complementary, vertical, and adjacent angles in a multi–step problem to write and solve simple equations for an unknown angle in a figure.	Calculating Complementary Angles	165	210
		Calculating Angle Measures of Opposite and Adjacent Angles of Intersecting Lines	166	211
		Calculating Supplementary Angles	167	212
		Identifying Complementary Angles	168	213
		Identifying Supplementary Angles	169	214

7.G.6	Solve real–world and mathematical problems involving area, volume and surface area of two– and three– dimensional objects composed of triangles, quadrilaterals, polygons, cubes, and right prisms.	Volume Of a Triangular Prism	170, 174	218
		Developing the Area of Trapezoids	179	
		Developing a Volume Formula		
		Calculating the Surface Area of Right Rectangular Prisms	171	215
		Calculating Surface Area of Right Triangular Prisms	172	216
		Calculating Volume of Right Rectangular Prisms	173	217
		Calculating the Volume of a Triangular Prism	174	218, 219
		Solving Problems with Areas of Parallelograms	175	220
		Solving Problems with Areas of Triangles	176	221
		Calculating the Surface Area of a Right Trapezoidal Prism	177	222
		Calculating Surface Area of Pyramids	178	223
		Calculating the Area of Trapezoids	179, 180	224
		Solving Problems Involving the Area of a Rectangle	181	237
		Solving Problems Involving the Volume of a Triangular Prism	182	225
		Solving Problems Involving the Surface Areas of Rectangular Prisms	183	226
		Solving Problems Involving the Surface Area of a Triangular Prism	184	227
		Calculating the Area of a Triangle	185	228
		Calculating the Area of a Parallelogram	186	229
		Calculating the Area of a Rectangle	187	230, 237
		Solving Problems Involving Volume of Rectangular Prisms	188	231
		Calculating the Volume of Two Solid Figures	189	232
		Solving Problems Involving the Surface Area of Pyramids	190	233
		Calculating the Area of Regular Polygons	191	234
		Solving Problems with the Area of a Trapezoid	192	235
		Calculating Missing Side Lengths	193	236

7.G.1 Solve problems involving scale drawings of geometric figures, including computing actual lengths and areas from a scale drawing and reproducing a scale drawing at a different scale.

REDUCTIONS OF TWO-DIMENSIONAL SHAPES

Scale drawings are used when objects are too large or too small to be drawn on a piece of paper.

The **scale factor** between the original shape and the new image is a number that indicates how much larger or smaller than the original shape the image was made. The scale factor can be calculated using the formula

$$\text{scale factor} = \frac{\text{image length}}{\text{original length}}.$$

If the scale factor is less than 1, the image will be a **reduction** of the original shape. In other words, the new image will be smaller than the original figure.

Knowing the scale factor makes it possible to draw the image of a diagram. To draw a scale diagram, follow these steps:

1. Draw and label the original figure.
2. Use the scale factor formula to determine the length of each side of the image diagram.
3. Draw and label the image diagram. Use the prime symbol (′) to indicate that this is the image.
4. Join each original point to its corresponding point on the image, and label the scale factor on the diagram.

Example

The rectangle *ABCD* has a length measuring 12 cm and a width measuring 9 cm.

Using a scale factor of $\frac{1}{3}$, draw the image of the rectangle.

Solution

Step 1
Draw and label the original figure.

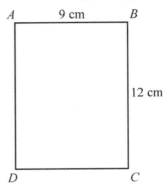

Step 2
Use the scale factor formula to determine the length of each side in the image diagram.
The length of the original rectangle is 12 cm.

$$\text{scale factor} = \frac{\text{image length}}{\text{original length}}$$
$$\frac{1}{3} = \frac{B'C'}{12}$$
$$12\left(\frac{1}{3}\right) = 12\left(\frac{B'C'}{12}\right)$$
$$4 = B'C'$$

The width of the original rectangle is 9 cm.

$$\text{scale factor} = \frac{\text{image width}}{\text{original width}}$$
$$\frac{1}{3} = \frac{A'B'}{9}$$
$$9\left(\frac{1}{3}\right) = 9\left(\frac{A'B'}{9}\right)$$
$$3 = A'B'$$

The image rectangle has a length of 4 cm and a width of 3 cm.

Step 3

Draw and label the image diagram. Use the prime symbol (′) to indicate that this is the image.

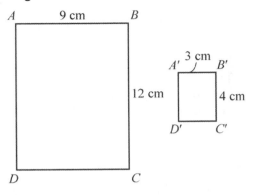

Step 4

Join each original point to its corresponding point on the image, and label the scale factor on the diagram.

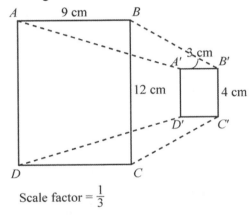

Interpreting Scale Drawings

A **scale drawing**, such as a blueprint or a map, is made when the actual dimensions of an object are either too small or too big to draw clearly.

To interpret a scale drawing, refer to the scale that has been provided with the image. The scale used in a scale drawing is a **ratio** that compares two units of measurement: one unit is used to measure the actual dimensions of an object, and the other unit is used to measure the dimensions of the drawing that represents the object. For example, the scale on a map might be given as 1 inch:10 miles. This means that 1 inch on the map is being used to represent 10 miles in real life.

The information provided in a scale drawing can be used to calculate the measurement of objects that have been represented in the drawing. To use a scale drawing in this way, set up a **proportion** between the ratios that compare the relationship between the units used to measure the actual object and the units used to measure its representation, and then solve for the unknown measurement.

Example

An interior designer wants to show the possible furniture placement in a room to a client. The designer makes a scale drawing.

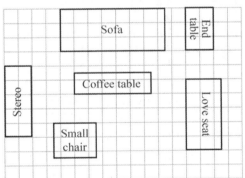

The scale is 1 square:14 inches.

What is the actual length of the sofa in feet and inches?

Solution

Step 1

Set up the proportion.
Write an equation using *x* to represent the actual length of the sofa.

$$\frac{7.5 \text{ squares}}{1 \text{ square}} = \frac{x \text{ inches}}{14 \text{ inches}}$$

Step 2

Solve for the value of x.

Apply the cross-product strategy to solve.

$1x = 14 \text{ in} \times 7.5$

$x = 14 \text{ in} \times 7.5$

$x = 105 \text{ inches}$

The real sofa is 105 inches in length.

Step 3

Determine the number of feet.

Use the scale of 12 inches = 1 foot.

Write an equation using proportions and solve.

$\dfrac{x \text{ ft}}{1 \text{ ft}} = \dfrac{105 \text{ in}}{12 \text{ in}}$

$x = \dfrac{1 \times 105}{12}$

$x = 8.75 \text{ ft}$

The actual measure of the sofa is 8.75 feet. The measure needs to be in feet and inches.

Step 4

Change 0.75 feet into inches.

Write an equation using proportions and solve.

$\dfrac{0.75 \text{ ft}}{1 \text{ ft}} = \dfrac{x \text{ in}}{12 \text{ in}}$

$0.75 \times 12 = 1x$

$9 \text{ in} = x$

The actual measurement of the sofa is 8.75 feet = 8 feet 9 inches.

ENLARGEMENTS OF TWO-DIMENSIONAL SHAPES

Scale drawings are used when objects are too large or too small to be drawn on a piece of paper.

The **scale factor** between the original shape and the new image is a number that indicates how much larger or smaller the shape was made. The scale factor can be calculated using the formula scale factor = $\dfrac{\text{image length}}{\text{original length}}$.

If the scale factor is greater than 1, the image will be an **enlargement** of the original shape. In other words, the new image will be larger than the original figure.

Knowing the scale factor makes it possible to draw the image of a diagram. To draw a scale diagram, use the following steps:

1. Draw and label the original figure.
2. Use the scale factor formula to determine the length of each side in the image diagram.
3. Draw and label the image diagram. Use the prime symbol (′) to indicate that this is the image.
4. Join each original point to its corresponding point on the image, and label the scale factor on the diagram.

Example

Isosceles triangle *ABC* has two legs measuring 2 cm and a base measuring 1.3 cm. Using a scale factor of 2.5, draw the image of the triangle.

Solution

Step 1

Draw and label the original figure.

Step 2

Use the scale factor formula to determine the length of each side in the image diagram.

Two legs of the original triangle measure 2 cm.

scale factor = $\dfrac{\text{image length}}{\text{original length}}$

$2.5 = \dfrac{A'C'}{2}$

$2(2.5) = 2\left(\dfrac{A'C'}{2}\right)$

$5 = A'C'$

The base of the original triangle measures 1.3 cm.

scale factor = $\dfrac{\text{image length}}{\text{original length}}$

$2.5 = \dfrac{B'C'}{1.3}$

$1.3(2.5) = 1.3\left(\dfrac{B'C'}{1.3}\right)$

$3.25 = B'C'$

The image triangle has two legs measuring 5 cm and a base measuring 3.25 cm.

Step 3
Draw and label the image diagram. Use the prime symbol (′) to indicate that this is the image.

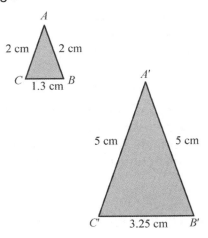

Step 4
Join each original point to its corresponding point on the image, and label the scale factor on the diagram.

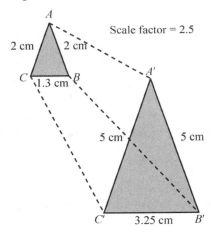

APPLYING SCALE FACTORS OF TWO-DIMENSIONAL GEOMETRIC SHAPES TO PERIMETER AND AREA

If the scale factor is a number greater than 1, the new image is an **enlargement** of the original shape. If the scale factor is a number less than 1, the new image is a **reduction** of the original shape.

To calculate the perimeter of a scaled image, the original perimeter is multiplied by the scale factor.
$P_2 = P_1 \times$ scale factor

Example
Two similar rectangles have lengths of 4 cm and 12 cm.

If the perimeter of the smaller rectangle is 10 cm, it follows that the perimeter of the larger rectangle is _____cm.

Solution
Step 1
Calculate the scale factor.
$$\text{scale factor} = \frac{12 \text{ cm}}{4 \text{ cm}}$$
$$= 3$$
The length of the smaller rectangle is multiplied by 3 to get the length of the larger rectangle.

Step 2
Apply the scale factor to the original perimeter.
$P_2 = P_1 \times$ scale factor
$P_2 = 10 \times 3$
$P_2 = 30$ cm
The perimeter of the larger rectangle is 30 cm.

To calculate the area of a scaled image, the original area is multiplied by the squared scale factor.
$A_2 = A_1 \times$ scale factor^2

Example
Two similar rectangles have lengths of 9 cm and 3 cm.

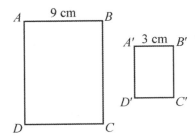

If the area of the larger rectangle is 108 cm², what is the area of the smaller rectangle?

Solution

Step 1
Calculate the scale factor.

scale factor = $\dfrac{\text{image length}}{\text{original length}}$

$= \dfrac{3}{9}$

$= \dfrac{1}{3}$

The smaller rectangle is $\dfrac{1}{3}$ the size of the larger rectangle.

Step 2
Apply the scale factor to the area of the larger rectangle.
The scale factor is squared to calculate the area of the new image.

$A_2 = A_1 \times \text{scale factor}^2$

$= 108 \times \left(\dfrac{1}{3}\right)^2$

$= 12$

The area of the smaller rectangle is 12 cm².

7.G.2 Draw (freehand, with ruler and protractor, and with technology) geometric shapes with given conditions. Focus on constructing triangles from three measures of angles or sides, noticing when the conditions determine a unique triangle, more than one triangle, or no triangle.

INVESTIGATING THE ANGLE SUM THEOREM

When you are working with triangles, it is useful to understand the relationships between the interior angles. The angle sum theorem states that the sum of the measures of the interior angles in any triangle is 180°.

Try This!
Cut a triangle from a piece of paper.

Tear the corners off the triangle, and place them together.

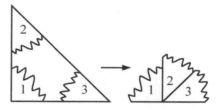

When they are placed together, the angles form a straight line. The measure of a straight line is 180°. Therefore, the combined measures of the interior angles of a triangle must be 180°.

Example
Prove the angle sum theorem for a triangle.

Solution

Step 1
Draw any triangle *ABC*.

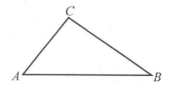

Step 2

Extend line segment *AB*. Draw a line parallel to line segment *AB* through *C*, and label two arbitrary points on either side of *C*.

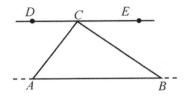

Step 3

Observe that since line segment *AB* and line segment *DE* are parallel, there are two sets of alternate interior angles: ∠*CAB* and ∠*DCA*, and ∠*CBA* and ∠*BCE*. Since alternate interior angles are equal, ∠*CAB* = ∠*DCA* and ∠*CBA* = ∠*BCE*.

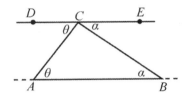

On line segment *DE*, it is clear that ∠*DCA* + ∠*ACB* + ∠*BCE* = 180° because the angles form a straight line when combined. Therefore, since ∠*CAB* + ∠*ACB* + ∠*CBA* = 180°, the angle sum theorem for a triangle is proven.

APPLYING THE ANGLE SUM THEOREM FOR TRIANGLES

The sum of the interior angles of any triangle is 180°. This means that the sum of the interior angles of a triangle can be represented as ∠*a* + ∠*b* + ∠*c* = 180°.

You can use the angle sum theorem to find missing angles in a triangle by following these steps:

1. Determine which angles are given.
2. Substitute the given values into the angle property for a triangle, and simplify.

Example

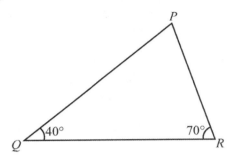

Find the measure of ∠*P*.

Solution

Step 1

Determine which angle measures are given.
∠*Q* = 40°
∠*R* = 70°

Step 2

Substitute the given values into the formula for the angle property for a triangle, and simplify.
∠*P* + ∠*Q* + ∠*R* = 180°
∠*P* + 70° + 40° = 180°
∠*P* + 110° = 180°
∠*P* = 70°

The measure of ∠*P* is 70 °.

Example

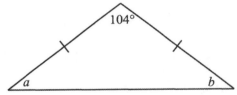

Find the measures of ∠*a* and ∠*b*.

Solution

Step 1

Determine what angle measures are given. Since this is an isosceles triangle, ∠*a* and ∠*b* have the same measure: ∠*a* = ∠*b*.
So, the property is modified and becomes
∠*a* + ∠*b* + ∠*c* = 180°
∠*a* + ∠*a* + ∠*c* = 180°.
2∠*a* + ∠*c* = 180°

Step 2

Substitute the given values into the angle property for a triangle and simplify.

$$2\angle a + (104°) = 180°$$
$$2\angle a + 104° - 104° = 180° - 104°$$
$$\frac{2\angle a}{2} = \frac{76°}{2}$$
$$\angle a = 38°$$

Therefore, $\angle a$ and $\angle b$ each have a measure of 38°.

APPLYING THE TRIANGLE INEQUALITY THEOREM

If you know the lengths of two sides of a triangle, the third side can usually be many different lengths. For example, if you know that the lengths of two sides of a triangle are 4 and 7, the third side could be longer or shorter. If the angle between the known sides is small, then the length of the third side will be short. If the angle between the two known sides is big, then the length of the third side will be long.

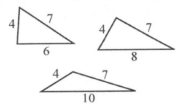

The third side needs to be a certain size to make a triangle. For example, consider again a triangle with side lengths of 4 and 7. If the length of the third side were 2, that would be too short and you would not be able to join up the edges. A length of 15 would be too long to join the edges.

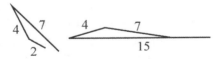

The **triangle inequality theorem** is used to find the side lengths that are possible for the third side. It states that the length of one side of any triangle is less than the sum of the other two sides.

side a < side b + side c

Example

You can use the theorem to show why the triangle described above cannot have a third side length of 2 or 15. Label the side with a length of 7 as a, label the side with a length of 4 as b, and label the third side as c. If side c is 2, the following inequality results:

side a < side b + side c
$$7 < 4 + 2$$
$$7 < 6$$

It is impossible to make this triangle because 7 is not less than 6.

Now label the side with a length of 4 as b, label the side with a length of 7 as c, and label the third side as a. If side a is 15, the following inequality results:

side a < side b + side c
$$15 < 4 + 7$$
$$15 < 11$$

It is impossible to make this triangle because 15 is not less than 11.

To find the possible lengths of the third side of a triangle when the lengths of the first two sides are known, follow these steps:

1. Calculate the minimum length by finding the difference between the lengths of the two known sides.
2. Calculate the maximum length by finding the sum of the lengths of the two known sides.

Example

If a triangle has side lengths of 7, 4, and x, what are the possible values of x?

Solution

Step 1

Calculate the minimum length by finding the difference between the lengths of the two known sides.

Subtract 4 from 7.

$$7 - 4 = 3$$

This means that x has to be greater than 3.

Step 2

Calculate the maximum length by finding the sum of the lengths of the two known sides.

Add 4 and 7.

4 + 7 = 11

This means that x has to be less than 11.

The length of x has to be between 3 and 11.

DETERMINING UNIQUE TRIANGLES

In order for a shape to be a triangle, it must have certain qualities. If you are making a triangle, make sure your shape conforms to the following rules:

- The angles in a triangle must add up to 180°.
- Each angle in a triangle must be between 0° and 180°.
- Each side of a triangle must be shorter than the sum of the other two.

If your shape does not conform to these rules, it is not a triangle.

There are a number of different ways a triangle can be constructed depending on which properties of the triangle are known. It is possible that given properties will not construct a real triangle.

Example

If two people are asked to draw a triangle where all angles are 60°, they could make the two different triangles shown and they would both be correct.

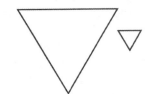

The angles in both of these triangles are 60°.

A unique triangle is one that can be drawn in only one way. If two people are given the properties of a unique triangle, they would construct the exact same triangle. It is possible to determine that a triangle is unique with only limited information about the triangle's properties. Any of the following five conditions provide enough information to determine if a triangle is unique:

1. If three sides of a triangle are given, it is known as the side-side-side (SSS) condition.

2. If two sides of a triangle and the angle included by them are given, it is known as the side-angle-side (SAS) condition.

3. If two angles and the side included by them are given, it is known as the angle-side-angle (ASA) condition.

4. If two angles of a triangle and a non-included side are given, it is known as the angle-angle-side (AAS) condition.

5. If the hypotenuse and leg of a right triangle are given, it is known as the right angle-hypotenuse-leg (RHL) condition.

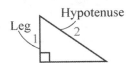

If the measures of a triangle fit the criteria for a unique triangle, only one triangle is possible. If three angles are given, there are multiple possible triangles. If the measures of a triangle break the rules of a triangle, the shape is not a triangle.

Example

A student wants to make a triangle with side lengths of 5 cm and 7 cm. The angle between these sides is 35°.

Determine if these conditions can form more than one, only one, or no possible triangles.

Solution

Since this triangle satisfies the side-angle-side (SAS) condition and does not break any of the rules of a triangle, these conditions form only one possible triangle.

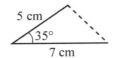

Example

A student wants to make a triangle with side lengths of 10 cm, 8 cm, and 9 cm.

Determine if these conditions can form more than one, only one, or no possible triangles.

Solution

Since these conditions fit the criteria for a side-side-side (SSS) triangle and do not break the rules for a triangle, these conditions form only one possible triangle.

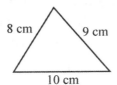

Example

A student wants to make a triangle with side lengths of 3 cm, 5 cm, and 12 cm.

Determine if these conditions can form more than one, only one, or no possible triangles.

Solution

For a triangle to be possible, the length of any one side must be shorter than the sum of the other two.

$3 + 5 \not> 12$
$\quad 8 \not> 12$

Since the sum of 3 and 5 is less than 12, no possible triangle can be formed with these conditions.

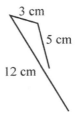

DRAWING A TRIANGLE GIVEN TWO ANGLES AND A SIDE LENGTH

A triangle can be accurately drawn using a ruler and a protractor when you are given the measures of two angles and a side length.

To draw the triangle correctly, you need to know the angles on either side of the given length. If the length you are given is not between the two given angles, then you need to calculate the third angle. Use the fact that the angles in a triangle add up to 180° to find the measure of the third angle.

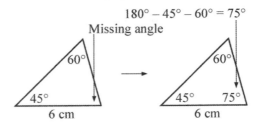

Use the following steps to draw an accurate triangle when you are given two angles and a side length:

1. Draw and label the given side length.
2. Draw and label the first angle at one end of the length.
3. Draw and label the second angle at the other end of the length.
4. Extend the lengths of the second and third lines of the triangle so they meet at a point.

Example

Using a protractor and a ruler, draw a triangle that has angles that measure 35° and 70° with a side length of 4.5 cm between them.

Solution

Step 1

Use a ruler to draw a line that is 4.5 cm long.

Step 2

Use a protractor to draw a 35° angle at one end of the 4.5 cm line.

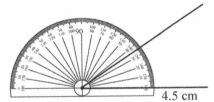

Step 3

Use a protractor to draw a 70° angle at the other end of the 4.5 cm line.

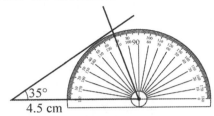

The lines already meet, so they do not need to be extended.

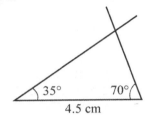

DRAWING A TRIANGLE GIVEN THE LENGTHS OF TWO SIDES AND THE ANGLE BETWEEN THEM

An accurate triangle can be drawn using a ruler and a protractor when you are given the lengths of two sides and the measure of the angle that is between them.

To draw an accurate triangle when you are given two side lengths and the angle between them, use the following steps:

1. Draw and label the first length that is given.
2. Draw and label the given angle at the end of the first line.
3. Measure the second line to the given length, and mark the end of it.
4. Draw a line to connect the end of the first length to the end of the second length.

Example

A triangle has side lengths of 5 cm and 6 cm. The angle between the lengths measures 120°.

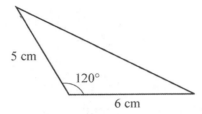

Construct the given triangle.

Solution

Step 1

Draw and label a line that is 6 cm long.

Step 2

Draw and label an angle of 120° at the end of the 6 cm line.

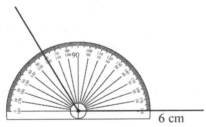

Step 3

Place a mark on the new line 5 cm away from the vertex of the angle.

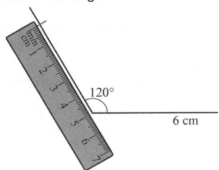

Step 4

Draw a line from the right end of the 6 cm line to where the mark is on the 5 cm line.

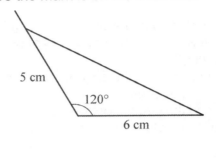

7.G.3 Describe the two–dimensional figures that result from slicing three-dimensional figures, as in plane sections of right rectangular prisms and right rectangular pyramids.

PLANE SECTIONS OF THREE-DIMENSIONAL FIGURES

A plane section is also known as a cross section. A plane section is the image of the intersection of a plane and a three-dimensional figure. This results in a two-dimensional image of a three-dimensional figure. This image can either be on the inside of a figure or the surface.

A real-life example of a plane section is the floor plan of a house.

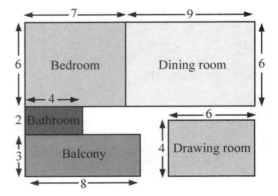

One way to visualize a plane section is to imagine cutting an object into two pieces with a knife. In this case, the knife is comparable to the plane and the newly exposed inside is comparable to the plane section.

Object

Plane

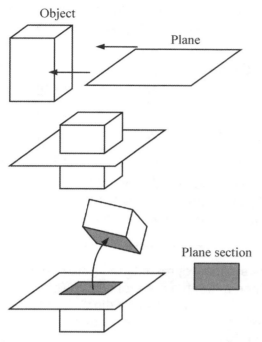

Plane section

Plane sections can be taken from different orientations to produce different images.

Example

Consider plane sections taken from this square pyramid at different orientations.

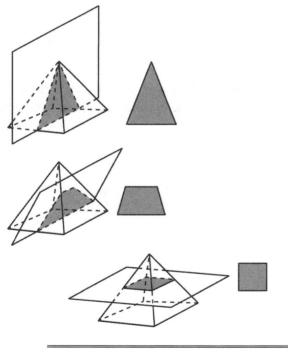

It is important to visualize the entire object when working with three-dimensional figures. Since parts of a three-dimensional object may not be visible, any relevant information must be used to determine the appearance of the figure. Sometimes, it is useful to imagine how many edges or vertices of the three-dimensional figure are intersected by the plane. This will determine how many corners there are on the plane section.

Example

A plane section is taken from the given rectangular pyramid. The plane is parallel to the base of the pyramid.

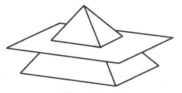

What is the shape of the plane section?

Solution

Although only three edges of the pyramid visibly intersect the plane from this position, it is known that there are actually four edges, since the pyramid is rectangular. Considering that the plane is parallel to the base of the pyramid, the plane section is a rectangle.

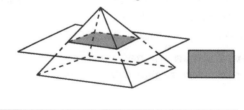

7.G.4 Know the formulas for the area and circumference of a circle and use them to solve problems; give an informal derivation of the relationship between the circumference and area of a circle.

Pi (π)

As mathematicians studied the relationships between the various measurements of the circle, they discovered an important relationship between the **diameter** and the **circumference** of every circle. This relationship was given the Greek symbol π, called pi.

The distance around a circle is called its circumference (*C*). The diameter (*d*) of a circle is the length of the line segment connecting two points on the circumference of the circle and passing through the center of the circle.

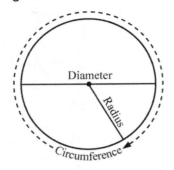

Try This!
You can discover the relationship between circumference and diameter for yourself by conducting the following activity.

1. Collect a number of circular objects from around your house, such as a can, a toilet paper tube, a clock or a bowl.
2. Using a piece of string, measure the distance around the outside of each circular object. This value represents the circumference. Record the value in a table.
3. Then, measure the distance across the center of the object, and record this value in the table as well. This value represents the diameter.

When you have finished your measuring, your table may look similar to the one shown.

Object	*C* (cm)	*d* (cm)	$\frac{C}{d}$
Can	31.5	10	
Tube	18.8	6	
Clock	75.4	24	
Barrel	163.4	52	

To fill in the last column, divide the circumference (*C*) by the diameter (*d*) for each object.

Object	*C* (cm)	*d* (cm)	$\frac{C}{d}$
Can	31.5	10	3.150
Tube	18.8	6	3.133
Clock	75.4	24	3.141
Barrel	163.4	52	3.142

Notice that the value of the quotient for each different object is approximately 3.14. This approximate value is known as π.

Pi is a constant that represents the ratio of the circumference to the diameter of all circles. The value of pi (π) is a non-repeating, non-terminating decimal number known as an irrational number.

$$\pi = \frac{C}{d} = 3.141592653589\ldots$$

The value of pi is often shortened to $\pi = 3.14$ or $\frac{22}{7}$. These values are used when calculating an estimate of circumference or area.

DEVELOPING THE AREA FORMULA FOR CIRCLES

Finding the area of a circle is similar to finding the area of a rectangle. To understand this, cut a circle into equal sections.

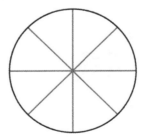

When the sections are arranged to form a parallelogram, they have the following characteristics:

1. The radius is equal to the height.
2. Half the circumference is equal to the base.

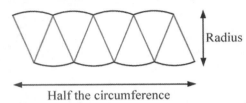

Because the area of a circle is equal to the area of a parallelogram, the formula used to calculate the area of a circle starts from the formula for the area of a parallelogram.

$$A_{circle} = A_{parallelogram}$$
$$= b \times h$$

The base of the parallelogram is half the circumference. Divide the circumference by 2 for the base. Use the radius for the height. Then, simplify the equation.

$$A_{circle} = \frac{circumference}{2} \times r$$
$$= \frac{(2\pi r)}{2} \times r$$
$$= \pi \times r \times r$$
$$= \pi r^2$$

DEVELOPING THE CIRCUMFERENCE FORMULA

The distance around a circle is called its **circumference** (*C*). The **diameter** (*d*) of a circle is the length of a line segment that connects two points on the circumference of a circle and that passes through the center of the circle.

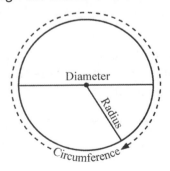

Algebraically, pi is written as $\frac{C}{d} = \pi$. To calculate the circumference, manipulate the variables to isolate *C*. Multiply both sides of the equation by *d*.

$$(d)\frac{C}{d} = \pi(d)$$
$$C = \pi d$$

Use the formula $C = \pi d$ to calculate the value of circumference.

Sometimes, you will be given the radius of a circle. The **radius** (*r*) of a circle is the distance from the center of the circle to a point on the circumference of the circle; it is one-half the length of the diameter.

Since $d = 2r$, substitute this value into the circumference formula to solve for circumference.
$$C = \pi d$$
$$= \pi(2r)$$
$$= 2\pi r$$

Use this formula to solve for circumference when you are given the radius of a circle.

CALCULATING THE AREA OF CIRCLES USING 3.14 OR $\frac{22}{7}$

The values 3.14 or $\frac{22}{7}$ are sometimes used for calculating the area of a circle. This results in a value that is close to the exact answer.

The area of a circle is calculated using the formula $A = \pi r^2$ regardless of whether the radius or diameter is given.

To calculate the area of a circle when given the radius, follow these steps:

1. Determine the given values.
2. Substitute the known values into the area formula, and solve.

Example

Find the area of the circle rounded to the nearest tenths place.

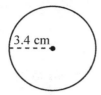

3.4 cm

Solution

Step 1

Determine the given values.

Pi (π) is rounded to 3.14.

The radius is the distance from the center of the circle to the edge: $r = 3.4$ cm.

Step 2

Substitute the known values into the area formula, and solve.

$$A_{circle} = \pi \times r^2$$
$$= 3.14 \times 3.4^2$$
$$= 3.14 \times 11.56$$
$$= 36.2984$$

Rounded to the nearest tenths place, the area of the circle is 36.3 cm^2.

To calculate the area when given the diameter, follow these steps:

1. Determine the given values.
2. Calculate the radius.
3. Substitute the known values into the area formula, and solve.

Example

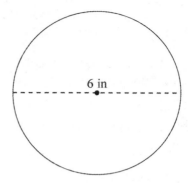

6 in

Calculate the area of the circle rounded to the nearest whole number.

Solution

Step 1

Determine the given values.

Pi (π) is rounded to $\frac{22}{7}$.

The diameter is the distance across the center of the circle from edge to edge: $d = 6$ in.

Step 2

Calculate the radius.

Divide the value of the diameter (6) by 2.

$$r = \frac{d}{2}$$
$$= \frac{6}{2}$$
$$= 3 \text{ in}$$

Step 3

Substitute the known values into the formula, and solve.

$$A = \pi \times r^2$$
$$= \frac{22}{7} \times 3^2$$
$$= \frac{22}{7} \times 9$$
$$= \frac{198}{7}$$
$$= 28.28571429 \text{ in}^2$$

Rounded to the nearest whole number, the area of the circle is 28 in^2.

Calculating the Circumference of Circles Using 3.14 or $\frac{22}{7}$

The approximate values 3.14 or $\frac{22}{7}$ are sometimes used in place of pi for calculating circumference. This results in a value that is close to the exact answer.

The two formulas used for calculating the circumference of a circle are $C = \pi d$ (if the diameter is known) and $C = 2\pi r$ (if the radius is known).

To calculate the circumference of a circle, follow these steps:

1. Choose the appropriate formula using the given values.
2. Substitute the known values into the formula.
3. Solve for the unknown value.

Example

Calculate the circumference of a circle using 3.14 if the diameter of the circle is 5 cm.

Solution

Step 1
Choose the appropriate formula using the given values.
The question is asking for circumference (C) and gives the diameter (d).
$C = \pi d$

Step 2
Substitute in the known values.
$\pi \approx 3.14$
$d = 5$ cm
$C = \pi d$
$ = (3.14) \times (5)$

Step 3
Solve for the unknown.
$C = (3.14) \times (5)$
$ = 15.7$ cm

Example

If the radius of a particular circle is 3 in, calculate the circumference of the circle to the nearest tenths place using $\frac{22}{7}$.

Solution

Step 1
Choose the appropriate formula using the given values.
The question is asking for circumference (C) and gives the radius (r).
Therefore, use the formula $C = 2\pi r$.

Step 2
Substitute the known values into the formula.
$\pi \approx \frac{22}{7}$
$r = 3$ in
$C = 2\pi r$
$ = 2 \times \frac{22}{7} \times 3$

Step 3
Solve for the unknown value.
$C = 2 \times \frac{22}{7} \times 3$
$ = 6 \times \frac{22}{7}$
$ = \frac{132}{7}$
$ = 18.85714286$ in
Rounded to the tenths place, the circumference of the given circle is 18.9 in.

Solving Problems Involving Circumferences

You can use your knowledge about how to calculate circumference to solve a wide variety of real-world problems.

Whenever you have a problem you need to solve, you should follow a four-step problem-solving process:

1. Read the question carefully, and determine what is being asked.
2. Make a plan. Decide which operations you need to use and in which order.
3. Solve the problem. Carry out the plan you made.
4. Decide if your answer is reasonable.

The following ideas can help you better understand a problem and assist you in solving it:

- Look for keywords.
- Decide what information is important.
- Pay close attention to the numbers given in the problem.
- Draw a picture or diagram of the problem.
- Make predictions about what your answer will look like. Will the number be big or small? Will it be a money amount? A length? A unit of time?
- Think about the operation you are using. For example, if you are multiplying, you know that your answer will be larger than the numbers you are multiplying.
- Check your answer with your predictions to see if your answer is reasonable.
- Estimate or round values to see if your answer is reasonable.

Example

Mrs. Solakis is building a circular porch in her backyard. The porch will have a diameter of 4 yd. She wants to make a border around the outside of the porch with red brick, which costs $4.75/yd.

How much will the red brick cost?

Solution

Step 1

Determine what is being asked.

The porch has a diameter of 4 yd, and the brick costs $4.75/yd. The brick will go around the circumference of the patio.

Use this information to determine the cost of the brick.

The answer will be a cost, and it will be more expensive than $4.75 because that is the cost of only 1 yd.

Step 2

Make a plan.

First, find the circumference of the porch. Use the formula for circumference, $C = \pi d$. Next, multiply the cost of 1 yd of brick by the number of yards around the outside of the porch.

Step 3

Solve the problem.

1. Calculate the circumference of the porch.
   $C = \pi d$
   $C \approx 3.14 \times 4$
   $C \approx 12.56$ yd

2. Find the total cost.
   total = cost of 1 yd × 12.56
   total = 4.75 × 12.56
   total = $59.66

Step 4

Decide if the answer is reasonable.

The answer is a cost, and it is more expensive than $4.75, which is what you predicted in Step 1.

You can also use estimation to check the answer.

Round 4.75 to 5, and round 12.56 to 13.
5 × 13 = 65

This is close to your calculation, so the answer is reasonable.

The red brick will cost $59.66.

Solving Problems Involving the Area of Circles

You can use your knowledge about how to calculate the area of a circle to solve a wide variety of real-world problems. Whenever you have a problem you need to solve, you should follow a four-step problem-solving process.

1. Read the question carefully, and determine what is being asked.
2. Make a plan. Decide which operations you need to use and in which order.
3. Solve the problem. Carry out the plan that you made.
4. Decide if your answer is reasonable.

Keep the following ideas in mind when you read a problem. They can help you better understand the problem and assist you in solving it:

- Look for keywords.
- Decide what information is important.
- Pay close attention to the numbers given in the problem.
- Draw a picture or diagram of the problem.
- Make predictions about what your answer will look like. Will the number be big or small? Will it be a money amount? A length? A unit of time?
- Think about the operation you are using. For example, if you are multiplying, you know that your answer will be larger than the numbers you are multiplying.
- Check your answer with your predictions to see if your answer is reasonable.
- Estimate or round values to see if your answer is reasonable.

Example

Mrs. Solakis is building a circular porch in her backyard. The porch will have a diameter of 4 yd. The brick that she chose for the surface of the porch costs $18.75/yd^2.

How much will the brick cost?

Solution

Step 1

Determine what is being asked.

The porch has a diameter of 4 yd, and the brick costs $18.75/yd^2. The brick will cover the surface of the porch.

Use this information to decide the cost of the brick.

The answer will be a cost, and it will be more expensive than $18.75 because that is the cost of only 1 yd^2.

Step 2

Make a plan.

First, find the area of the porch. Use the formula for area of a circle, $A = \pi r^2$. Next, multiply the cost of 1 yd^2 of brick by the area of the porch.

Step 3

Solve the problem.

1. Calculate the area of the porch.
    The diameter of the porch is 4 yd, so the radius is 2 yd.
    $A = \pi r^2$
    $A \approx 3.14 \times 2^2$
    $A \approx 3.14 \times 4$
    $A \approx 12.56 \text{ yd}^2$

2. Find the total cost.
    total = cost of 1 yd × 12.56
    total = 18.75 × 12.56
    total = $235.50

Step 4

Decide if the answer is reasonable.

The answer is a cost, and it is more expensive than $18.75, which is what was predicted in step 1.

Another way to check the answer is by estimation.

Round 18.75 to 20, and round 12.56 to 10.

20 × 10 = 200

This is close to your calculation, so the answer is reasonable.

The brick will cost $235.50.

PROBLEM SOLVING WITH THE RADIUS OR DIAMETER OF A CIRCLE

The distance around the outside of a circle is called the **circumference** (C). The **diameter** (d) of a circle is a line that goes from one point on the circle to another point while passing through the center of the circle. The **radius** (r) of a circle is a line that goes from one point on the circle to the center of the circle. It is equal to half the value of the diameter.

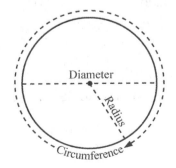

No matter the size of the circle, the circumference of the circle divided by its diameter will always equal the same value. This value is the mathematical constant pi (π). Pi is a non-repeating, non-terminating decimal number.

$$\pi = \frac{C}{d} = 3.141592653589\ldots$$

In mathematics, the value of pi is often shortened to 3.14 to make calculations easier.

The given table shows formulas indicating the relationships among the circumference, diameter, and radius of a circle.

Dimension of a Circle	Formula
Circumference	$C = \pi d$ (if diameter is known)
	$C = 2\pi r$ (if radius is known)
Diameter	$d = \dfrac{C}{\pi}$
Radius	$r = \dfrac{C}{2\pi}$

When you are given the circumference of a circle, the radius or diameter can be calculated by following these steps:

- Determine the appropriate form of the circumference formula to use.
- Substitute the given values into the formula.
- Solve for the unknown value.

Example

The circumference of a circle is 28.26 cm.

Find the radius.

Solution

Step 1

Choose the appropriate formula using the given values.

The question is asking for the radius and gives the circumference.

$$r = \frac{C}{2\pi}$$

Step 2

Substitute in the known values.

In this case, the circumference C is 28.26 cm and the value of π is 3.14.

$$r = \frac{C}{2\pi}$$
$$= \frac{28.26}{2(3.14)}$$

Step 3

Solve for the unknown.

$$r = \frac{C}{2\pi}$$
$$= \frac{28.26}{6.28}$$
$$= 4.5$$

The radius of the circle is about 4.5 cm.

Example

The circumference of a car tire is 120 cm.

Find the diameter of the tire to the nearest tenth of a centimeter.

Solution

Step 1

Choose the appropriate formula using the given values.

The question is asking for diameter (d) and gives the circumference (C).

$$d = \frac{C}{\pi}$$

Step 2

Substitute in the known values.

$C = 120$ cm

$\pi = 3.14$

$$d = \frac{C}{\pi}$$
$$= \frac{120}{3.14}$$

Step 3

Solve for the unknown.

$$d = \frac{C}{\pi}$$
$$= \frac{120}{3.14}$$
$$= 38.21656051\ldots$$

The diameter of the circle, rounded to the tenth position, is 38.2 cm.

7.G.5 Use facts about supplementary, complementary, vertical, and adjacent angles in a multi–step problem to write and solve simple equations for an unknown angle in a figure.

CALCULATING COMPLEMENTARY ANGLES

Complementary angles are two angles whose measures add up to 90°.

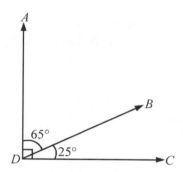

Two angles are given in the diagram. To determine if they are complementary, add them together to see if their sum equals 90.
$\angle ADB + \angle BDC = 65 + 25$
$\qquad\qquad\qquad = 90$

These two angles are complementary angles.

If you know the measure of one of the complements of a complementary angle, you can calculate the measure of the other by subtracting the value of the given complement from 90°.

Example
    A pair of complementary angles are given.

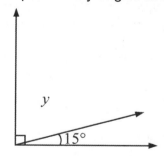

Calculate the value of angle y.

Solution

The question states that the two given angles are complementary. This means that the sum of their measures must equal 90.

The measure of one angle is given. Subtract this given value from 90 to determine the measure of the unknown angle y.

$\angle y = 90 - 15 = 75$

Therefore, angle y equals 75°.

___

CALCULATING ANGLE MEASURES OF OPPOSITE AND ADJACENT ANGLES OF INTERSECTING LINES

Intersecting lines are two lines that cross each other, creating four angles. The given diagram shows two intersecting lines.

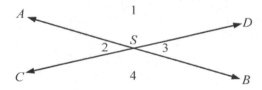

Line $\overleftrightarrow{AB}$ intersects Line $\overleftrightarrow{CD}$ at point S, creating the four angles labeled 1, 2, 3, and 4.

When two lines intersect each other, opposite angles (angles across from each other) have the same measure ($\angle 1 = \angle 4$ and $\angle 2 = \angle 3$).
Adjacent angles (angles beside each other) form a supplementary angle of 180° ($\angle 1 + \angle 3 = 180°$ and $\angle 2 + \angle 4 = 180°$).

If the measure of one angle is known, the relationships of intersecting angles can be used to calculate the measures of the other angles.

Example
    Lines AB and CD intersect to make four angles.

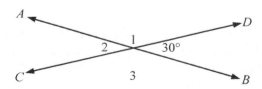

Find the measure of the missing angles.

Solution

Step 1

Determine the measure of ∠2.

The given angle of 30° and ∠2 are opposite angles. Opposite angles have equal measures.

∠2 = 30°

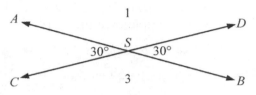

Step 2

Calculate the measure of ∠1 and ∠3.

∠1 and ∠3 are opposite angles.

Their measures will be the same.

The given angle of 30° and ∠1 are adjacent angles that form a supplementary angle of 180°.

Subtract the given angle of 30° from 180°.

The result is the value of ∠1 and ∠3.

∠1 = 180° − 30°
   = 150°

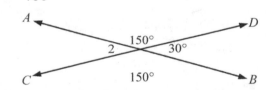

Therefore, ∠1 and ∠3 = 150° and ∠2 = 30°.

CALCULATING SUPPLEMENTARY ANGLES

Supplementary angles are two angles that add to 180°.

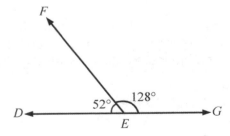

If you know the measure of one of the supplements of a supplementary angle, you can find the measure of the other by subtracting the value of the given supplement from 180°.

Example

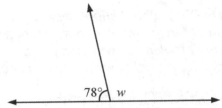

Calculate the value of angle *w*.

Solution

The 78° angle plus angle *w* equal 180°.

Subtract 78° from 180° to calculate the value of *w*.

∠*w* = 180° − 78°

∠*w* = 102°

IDENTIFYING COMPLEMENTARY ANGLES

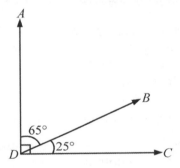

Complementary angles are two angles that add to 90°.

∠*ADB* + ∠*BDC* = 90°

   65° + 25° = 90°

The two angles that make up the complementary angle are called complements. ∠*ADB* is a complement to ∠*BDC*.

Example

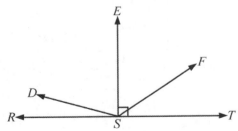

Use the given diagram to find two pairs of complementary angles.

Solution

Step 1
Identify the right angles.
∠*EST* is a right angle.
∠*RSE* is a right angle.

Step 2
Identify the complementary angles within the right angles.
∠*ESF* and ∠*FST* are complementary angles since together they form ∠*EST*.
∠*RSD* and ∠*DSE* are complementary angles since together they form ∠*RSE*.

IDENTIFYING SUPPLEMENTARY ANGLES
Supplementary angles are two angles that add to 180°.

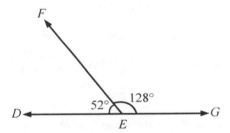

∠*DEF* + ∠*FEG* = 180°
    52° + 128° = 180°
The two angles that make up the supplementary angle are called supplements. ∠*DEF* is a supplement to ∠*FEG*.

Example

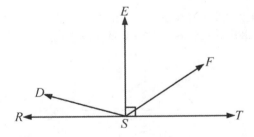

Use the given diagram to find three pairs of supplementary angles.

Solution

Step 1
Identify the straight angle.
∠*RST* is the straight angle (180°).

Step 2
Identify the supplementary angles within the straight angle.
∠*DSR* and ∠*DST* are supplementary since together they form ∠*RST*.
∠*ESR* and ∠*EST* are supplementary since together they form ∠*RST*.
∠*FSR* and ∠*FST* are supplementary since together they form ∠*RST*.

7.G.6 Solve real–world and mathematical problems involving area, volume and surface area of two– and three–dimensional objects composed of triangles, quadrilaterals, polygons, cubes, and right prisms.

VOLUME OF A TRIANGULAR PRISM

A **rectangular prism** has a rectangular base, and a **triangular prism** has a triangular base.

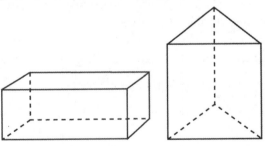

To find the volume of a rectangular prism, take a box in the shape of a rectangular prism and fill the bottom of the box with unit cubes from the base ten materials. A unit cube is 1 cm long, 1 cm wide, and 1 cm high.

To find the volume of the prism, multiply the number of unit cubes in one layer by the number of layers in the box. The number of layers needed is the height of the box in centimeters because each unit cube is 1 cm high.

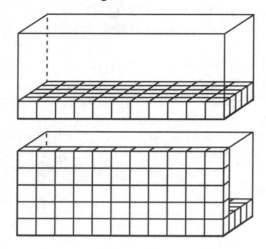

The general formula for the volume of any prism is
Volume = area of the base × height of the prism
Since the area of a rectangle is the length multiplied by the width, the volume of a rectangular prism can also be expressed as
Volume = Length × Width × Height.

A similar procedure can be used to find the volume of a triangular prism. Just as a triangle is one half of a rectangle cut diagonally, if you split the rectangular prism in half diagonally, you would have two triangular prisms.

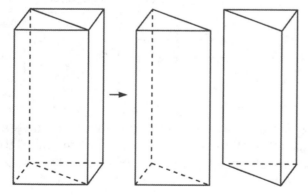

Each triangular prism would be half the volume of the rectangular prism.

You know that the area of a triangle is
$\frac{1}{2}$(base × height). The volume of a triangular prism is the area of the base (triangle) x height of the prism.

Example
The table below shows the dimensions of the two triangular prisms.

Triangular Prisms	Base of the triangle (b)	Height of the triangle (h)	Height of the triangular prism	Volume of the triangular prism
Triangular Prism *A*	5 cm	4 cm	3 cm	30 cm³
Triangular Prism *B*	3 cm	2 cm	4 cm	12 cm³

The process for finding the volume of triangular prisms is summarized in the table below.

Triangular Prism	Area of Triangular Base	Volume of Triangular Prism
Triangular prism *A*	$A_{triangle} = \frac{1}{2}bh$ $= \frac{1}{2}(5)(4)$ $= 10$ cm²	$V = A_{triangle} \times h_{prism}$ $= A_{triangle} \times 3$ $= 10 \times 3$ $= 30$ cm³
Triangular prism *B*	$A_{triangle} = \frac{1}{2}bh$ $= \frac{1}{2}(3)(2)$ $= 3$ cm²	$V = A_{triangle} \times h_{prism}$ $= A_{triangle} \times 4$ $= 3 \times 4$ $= 12$ cm³

By looking at the patterns in the tables, you can see that the volume of a triangular prism can be found by multiplying the area of the triangular base by the height of the prism.

DEVELOPING THE AREA OF TRAPEZOIDS

A **trapezoid** is a quadrilateral that has exactly two parallel sides, such as the given figure.

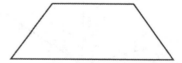

To calculate the area of a trapezoid, decompose the trapezoid into familiar shapes, such as a rectangle and two right triangles.

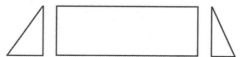

The two right triangles can be joined together to form one triangle.

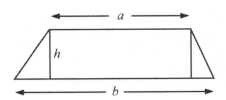

The rectangle and triangle have the same total area as the trapezoid. The area formulas for a triangle and a rectangle are

$$A_{triangle} = \frac{base \times height}{2}$$

$$A_{rectangle} = base \times height$$

The base of the triangle is equal to $b - a$, and the height of the triangle is equal to h. The base of the rectangle is equal to a, and the height of the rectangle is equal to h. The area formulas for a triangle and a rectangle can be combined into a single formula for the area of a trapezoid.

$$A_{trapezoid} = A_{triangle} + A_{rectangle}$$

$$= \frac{(b-a)h}{2} + ah$$

To add the two terms together, a common denominator is needed. Multiply the expression ah by 2 in the numerator and in the denominator:

$$A_{trapezoid} = \frac{(b-a)h}{2} + ah$$

$$= \frac{(b-a)h}{2} + \frac{2ah}{2}$$

$$= \frac{(b-a)h + 2ah}{2}$$

$$= \frac{1}{2}[(b-a)h + 2ah]$$

$$= \frac{1}{2}h(b - a + 2a)$$

$$= \frac{h}{2}(b + a)$$

The area of a trapezoid is therefore

$$A_{trapezoid} = \frac{h}{2}(b + a)$$

DEVELOPING A VOLUME FORMULA

Volume is the amount of space that a 3-D figure holds. Volume is measured in cubic units (units³). A cubic unit is a cube with equal side lengths of 1 unit on all six sides.

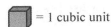 = 1 cubic unit

To find the **volume** of a **rectangular prism**, start by counting the number of cubic units needed to fill the base of the prism.

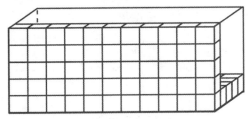

Another way to do this is to find the area of the base of the prism. Use the formula for determining area

Length × Width = Area

The next step is to determine the number of cubic units needed to fill the prism. To do this, it is necessary to know how many layers of cubes are needed to reach the top of the prism.

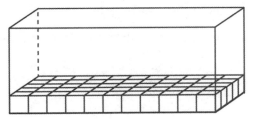

When the height of the prism is known (the number of layers of cubes needed), multiply the area by the height.

Area × Height = Volume

Another way to express this
formula is Length × Width × Height = Volume

The volume of the rectangular prism shown is
275 units^3.

11 × 5 × 5 = 275 units^3

CALCULATING THE SURFACE AREA OF RIGHT RECTANGULAR PRISMS

A right rectangular prism is a three-dimensional
object with six rectangular faces. A prism is called
a right prism if, when placed on one of the bases,
the top base of the prism is directly above the
bottom base of the prism.

An example of a right rectangular prism is given.

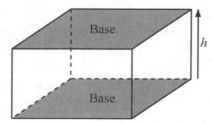

If the rectangular prism is flattened out, the
two-dimensional drawing that results is called a
net.

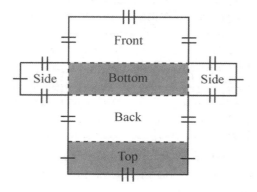

The net is used to calculate the surface area of right
rectangular prisms. The **surface area** of a
rectangular prism is the sum of the areas of all
the faces.

To calculate the surface area of a rectangular right
prism, follow these steps:

1. Draw the net of the rectangular prism.
2. Calculate the area of each face.
3. Add the areas of the faces.

Example

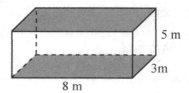

Calculate the surface area of the given right
rectangular prism.

Solution

Step 1
Draw the net of the shape.

A right rectangular prism is made up of four
rectangular faces (front, bottom, back, and top
in the diagram) that join the two rectangular
bases (sides).

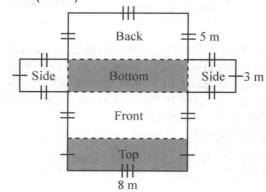

Step 2
Calculate the area of the faces.

Looking at the net, there are some faces that are the same size:

- Top and bottom
- Front and back
- Sides

Find the area for one face, and multiply it by 2 because the measures of the two faces are the same.

$$A_{top\ and\ bottom} = 2(l \times w)$$
$$= 2(8\ m \times 3\ m)$$
$$= 2(24\ m^2)$$
$$= 48\ m^2$$

$$A_{sides} = 2(l \times w)$$
$$= 2(5\ m \times 3\ m)$$
$$= 2(15\ m^2)$$
$$= 30\ m^2$$

$$A_{front\ and\ back} = 2(l \times w)$$
$$= 2(8\ m \times 5\ m)$$
$$= 2(40\ m^2)$$
$$= 80\ m^2$$

$$SA_{right\ rectangular\ prism}$$
$$= A_{top\ and\ bottom} + A_{sides} + A_{front\ and\ back}$$
$$= 48\ m^2 + 30\ m^2 + 80\ m^2$$
$$= 158\ m^2$$

Often, practical problems require similar approach.

Example

Ann wants to paint the walls and door of her basement all one color. The room is 3 m long, 3.5 m wide, and 2.5 m high. There are no windows.

On average, the cost of painting is $1.49 for each square meter painted. How much will it cost to paint the walls?

Solution

First, calculate the total area requiring paint, and then calculate the cost of the paint.

Step 1
Draw the net of the shape.

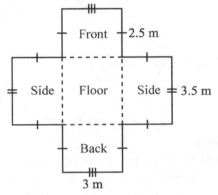

Because Ann is only painting the walls, you only need to calculate the front, back, and sides of the right rectangular prism.

Step 2
Calculate the area of the faces.
Looking at the net, there are some faces that are the same size:

- Front and back
- Sides

Find the area of one face, and multiply it by 2 because the measures of the two faces are the same.

$$A_{\text{front and back}} = 2(l \times w)$$
$$= 2(3 \text{ m} \times 2.5 \text{ m})$$
$$= 2(7.5 \text{ m}^2)$$
$$= 15 \text{ m}^2$$

$$A_{\text{sides}} = 2(l \times w)$$
$$= 2(3.5 \text{ m} \times 2.5 \text{ m})$$
$$= 2(8.75 \text{ m}^2)$$
$$= 17.5 \text{ m}^2$$

$$SA_{\text{walls}} = A_{\text{front and back}} + A_{\text{sides}}$$
$$= 15 \text{ m}^2 + 17.5 \text{ m}^2$$
$$= 32.5 \text{ m}^2$$

Ann will need to paint 32.5 m².

Step 3
Calculate the cost of the paint.
Multiply the total surface area by \$1.49 /m².
32.5 m² × \$1.49/m² = \$48.43
It will cost Ann \$48.43 to paint her room.

CALCULATING SURFACE AREA OF RIGHT TRIANGULAR PRISMS

Prisms are 3-dimensional geometric shapes with flat sides *(polyhedrons)* with two congruent (identical) and parallel faces called bases connected by rectangular faces. A prism is called a **right prism** if, when placed on one of the bases, the top base of the prism is directly above the bottom base of the prism. The number of sides on the base determines the number of rectangular faces in the prism. The shape of the base determines the name of the prism.

These are right triangular prisms with three rectangles. The bases are triangles. This (or any similar) right prism can be sliced parallel to the base. Each cross-section will be in the shape congruent to the bases. Imagine slicing the right prism repeatedly starting at one base and continuing until the other base is reached. It will appear that the cross-section base is "moving" perpendicular to the rectangular faces. The base moves perpendicular to rectangular faces a distance *h*.

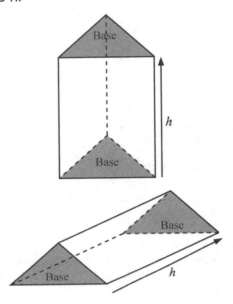

Three-dimensional shapes are shown in different forms. The solid shape is what you see when you have something like a child's building block. Each of the outside surfaces is called a **face**.

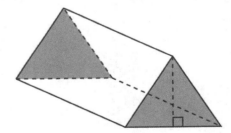

If the three-dimensional shape is flattened out, the two-dimensional drawing that results is called a **net**.

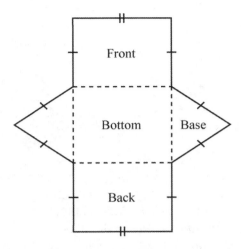

Nets are used to calculate the surface area of different objects. The **surface area** of a three-dimensional solid is the combined area of all the faces.

To calculate the surface area of a right triangular prism, follow these steps:

1. Draw the net.
2. Calculate the area of the faces.
3. Add all areas of the faces.

Example

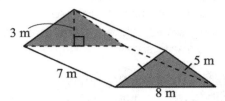

Calculate the surface area of the given right triangular prism.

Solution

Step 1
Draw the net of the shape.
A right triangular prism is made up of three rectangles, which may or may not be the same size, joined to two triangular faces.

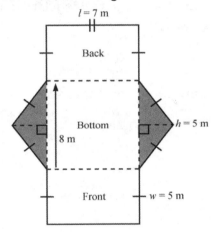

Step 2
Calculate the area of the faces.

Looking at the net, there are some faces that are the same size:

- Front and back (triangular bases)
- Sides (rectangular faces)

For faces that are equal, find the area for one face, and multiply it by the number of times that face repeats.

There is only one bottom. The area of the bottom is:

$A_{bottom} = l \times w$
$= 7 \times 8$
$= 56 \text{ m}^2$

There are two equal rectangular faces:

$A_{rectangular\ sides} = 2(l \times w)$
$= 2(7 \times 5)$
$= 2(35)$
$= 70 \text{ m}^2$

There are two triangular bases:

$A_{triangular\ sides} = 2\left(\dfrac{bh}{2}\right)$
$= 2\left(\dfrac{8 \times 3}{2}\right)$
$= 2(12)$
$= 24 \text{ m}^2$

Step 3

$SA_{right\ triangular\ prism}$
$= A_{triangular\ sides} + A_{rectangular\ sides} + A_{bottom}$
$= 24 + 70 + 56$
$= 150 \text{ m}^2$

Surface area problems such as the one above have many applications. Consider the following example.

Example

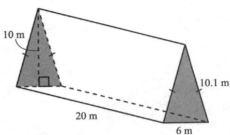

A greenhouse is often built with transparent walls (sides) to let sunlight in on top of soil where plants grow. A particular greenhouse manufacturer uses acrylic glass to construct greenhouses in the shape of a right triangular prisms with dimensions as shown in the diagram.

How much acrylic glass is needed to construct each structure shown above?

Solution

Step 1
Draw the net of the shape.

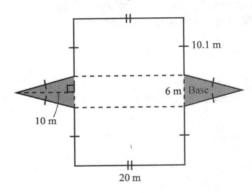

Step 2

Calculate the area of the faces.

Since no acrylic glass is required to make the floor of the greenhouse, you only need to calculate the front, back, and side faces of the right triangular prism.

Looking at the net, there are some faces that are the same size:

- Front and back (triangle bases) Note: Even though the prism does not stand on one of the triangles, traditionally the non-rectangular sides of prisms are called "bases" as described in the introduction to this lesson.
- Sides (rectangle faces)

Find the area for one face, and multiply it by 2 because the measures of the two faces are the same.

$$A_{\text{triangular bases}} = 2\left(\frac{bh}{2}\right)$$
$$= 2\left(\frac{6 \text{ m} \times 10 \text{ m}}{2}\right)$$
$$= 2(30 \text{ m}^2)$$
$$= 60 \text{ m}^2$$
$$A_{\text{rectangular faces}} = 2(l \times w)$$
$$= 2(20 \text{ m} \times 10.1 \text{ m})$$
$$= 2(202 \text{ m}^2)$$
$$= 404 \text{ m}^2$$

Step 3

$$SA_{\text{greenhouse}} = A_{\text{triangular bases}} + A_{\text{rectangular faces}}$$
$$= 60 \text{ m}^2 + 404 \text{ m}^2$$
$$= 464 \text{ m}^2$$

Each greenhouse will require 464 m^2 of acrylic glass.

CALCULATING VOLUME OF RIGHT RECTANGULAR PRISMS

Prisms are polyhedrons with two congruent and parallel faces called bases connected by rectangular faces. *Poly* means many, and *hedra* means faces. The number of sides on the base determines the number of rectangular faces in the prism. The shape of the base determines the name of the prism and moves perpendicular ($\perp$) to the rectangular faces (sides) through space.

A cube is a special type of rectangular prism in that all the sides are the same length.

These are rectangular prisms with four rectangular faces. The bases are rectangles moving perpendicular to the rectangular faces.

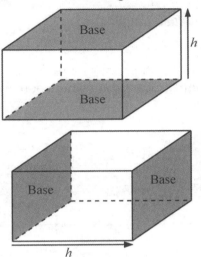

Volume is the space found inside a three-dimensional object. To calculate how much space is inside the rectangular prism, take the area of the rectangle and multiply it by how far it stretched up or across. The stretch is equal to the height of the prism. The general formula for volume is $V = A_{\text{base}} \times h$. The A_{base} is replaced with $l \times w$. Therefore, the formula for the volume of a rectangular prism is $V = (l \times w) \times h$.

To calculate the volume of a rectangular prism, substitute the known values into the volume formula and simplify. When the base is in the shape of a square, it is a special rectangular prism called a square-based prism.

Example

Calculate the volume of the rectangular

prism:

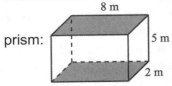

Solution

The shape of the base is a rectangle.
The height is the distance between two parallel base faces.

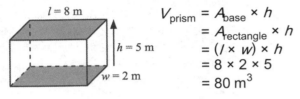

$$V_{prism} = A_{base} \times h$$
$$= A_{rectangle} \times h$$
$$= (l \times w) \times h$$
$$= 8 \times 2 \times 5$$
$$= 80 \text{ m}^3$$

Example

Calculate the volume of the square-based prism:

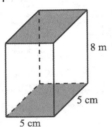

Solution

The shape of the base is a rectangle.
The height is the distance between two parallel base faces.

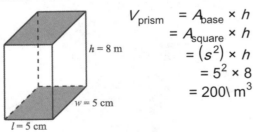

$$V_{prism} = A_{base} \times h$$
$$= A_{square} \times h$$
$$= (s^2) \times h$$
$$= 5^2 \times 8$$
$$= 200\backslash \text{ m}^3$$

Use the same process to solve volume problems in everyday situations.

Example

A juice box has dimensions of
3 cm × 2 cm × 7 cm.

How much juice can it hold in milliliters?

Solution

Step 1

Calculate the volume of the rectangular prism.

The juice box is in the shape of a rectangular prism.

The dimensions are usually given as length, then width, and finally height.

Substitute these values into the volume formula.

$$V_{rectangular\ prism} = A_{base} \times h$$
$$V_{rectangular\ prism} = A_{rectangle} \times h$$
$$= (l \times w) \times h$$
$$= 3 \times 2 \times 7$$
$$= 42 \text{ cm}^3$$

Step 2

Convert the cubic centimeters into milliliters.

Recall that 1 cm^3 = 1 mL.

42 cm^3 = 42 mL

The juice box can hold 42 mL of juice.

CALCULATING THE VOLUME OF A TRIANGULAR PRISM

Prisms are polyhedrons with two congruent and parallel faces called bases connected by rectangular faces. *Poly* means many, and *hedra* means faces. The number of sides on the base determines the number of rectangular faces in the prism. The shape of the base determines the name of a prism and moves perpendicular ($\perp$) to the rectangular faces (sides) through space.

These are triangular prisms with three rectangles. The bases are triangles moving perpendicular to the rectangular faces.

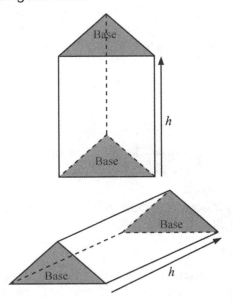

Volume is the space found inside a three-dimensional object. To calculate how much space is inside the rectangular prism, take the area of the triangle and multiply it by the distance between the two parallel congruent faces (bases). The distance is equal to the height of the prism. The general formula for volume is $V = A_{base} \times h$.

The A_{base} is replaced with $\frac{b \times h}{2}$. Because there are two heights in the formula, the height of the triangle is indicated as h_1 and the height of the prism is h_2.

To calculate the volume of a triangular prism, substitute the known values into the volume formula and simplify.

Example

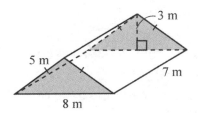

Calculate the volume of the given triangular prism.

Solution

The shape of the base is a triangle. The triangle has a base of 8 m and a height of 3 m.
The height of the prism is the distance between the two triangles: 7 m.

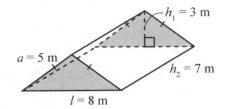

$$V_{\text{triangular prism}} = A_{base} \times h$$
$$V_{\text{triangular prism}} = A_{\text{triangle}} \times h$$
$$= \frac{l \times h_1}{2} \times h_2$$
$$= \frac{8 \times 3}{2} \times 7$$
$$= \frac{24}{2} \times 7$$
$$= 12 \times 7$$
$$= 84 \text{ m}^3$$

Use the same process to solve volume problems in everyday situations.

Example

A wedge of cheese has a volume of 35 cm³, and its height is 5 cm.

What is the area of the base of the wedge of cheese?

Solution

The wedge of cheese is in the shape of a triangular prism.

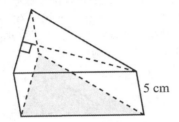

The area of the base is equal to the area of the triangle in the triangular prism.

Substitute the known values into the volume formula.

$$V_{\text{triangular prism}} = A_{\text{triangle}} \times h$$
$$35 = A_{\text{triangle}} \times 5$$
$$\frac{35}{5} = \frac{A_{\text{triangle}} \times 5}{5}$$
$$7 \text{ cm}^2 = A_{\text{triangle}}$$

The area of the triangle is 7 cm².

SOLVING PROBLEMS WITH AREAS OF PARALLELOGRAMS

When solving problems involving finding the area of a parallelogram, draw a diagram of the parallelogram if one is not already provided for you. Include the dimensions on the diagram.

To solve problems with areas of parallelograms, follow these steps:

1. Start with the area formula $A = b \times h$.
2. Substitute the known values for the base and height into the formula.
3. Calculate the answer.

Example

Nikita makes her own notepad so she can write notes to her friends. She makes the paper in her notepad in the shape of a parallelogram. The given diagram illustrates the dimensions of her notepad paper.

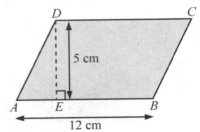

How much room does each piece of paper have for Nikita to write notes on?

Solution

In order to determine how much room Nikita has to write notes, you must calculate the area of the piece of paper.

Step 1
Start with the area formula.
The area formula for a parallelogram is $A = b \times h$.

Step 2
Substitute the known values into the formula. The base is 12 cm. The height is 5 cm.
$$A = b \times h$$
$$A = 12 \times 5 = 60 \text{ cm}^2$$
Nikita will have 60 cm² of space on which to write notes to her friends.

SOLVING PROBLEMS WITH AREAS OF TRIANGLES

When solving problems involving finding the area of a triangle, draw a diagram of the triangle if one is not already provided for you. Include the dimensions on the diagram.

To solve problems with areas of triangles, follow these steps:

1. Start with the area formula $A = \dfrac{b \times h}{2}$.
2. Substitute in the known values.
3. Simplify to get the answer.

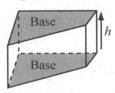

Example

Taran needs to resod part of his backyard. This diagram illustrates the dimensions of the part he needs to resod.

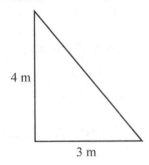

How much sod will Taran need to purchase to completely cover the part of the yard he is resodding?

Solution

In order to determine how much sod Taran will need, you must calculate the area of the part of the backyard that he is resodding.

Step 1

Determine the shape of the part of the backyard that needs to be resodded.

The part that will be resodded is in the shape of a triangle.

The area formula for a triangle is

$A = \dfrac{b \times h}{2}$.

Step 2

Substitute the length of the base (3 m) and the height of the triangle (4 m) into the formula.

$A = \dfrac{b \times h}{2}$

$A = \dfrac{3 \times 4}{2} = \dfrac{12}{2} = 6 \text{ m}^2$

Taran will need 6 m² of sod to cover the triangular shape of the part of the backyard that needs resodding.

CALCULATING THE SURFACE AREA OF A RIGHT TRAPEZOIDAL PRISM

A right trapezoidal prism is a three-dimensional object with six rectangular faces. A prism is called a right prism if the top base of the prism is directly above the bottom base of the prism when it is placed on one of the bases.

An example of a right trapezoidal prism is shown.

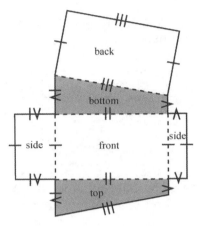

If the right trapezoidal prism is flattened out, the two-dimensional drawing that results is called a **net**.

The net is used to calculate the surface area of right trapezoidal prisms. The **surface area** of a right trapezoidal prism is the sum of the areas of all the faces.

To calculate the surface area of a right trapezoidal prism, follow these steps:

1. Draw the net of the shape.
2. Calculate the area of each face.
3. Add the areas of the faces.

Example

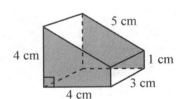

Calculate the surface area of the given right trapezoidal prism.

Solution

Step 1
Draw the net of the shape.
A right trapezoidal prism is made up of four rectangular faces (front, bottom, back, and top in the diagram) that join the two trapezoidal bases (sides).

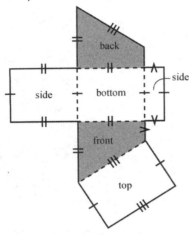

Step 2
Calculate the area of each face.
Solve for the area of each face by applying the appropriate formula.

$$A_{\text{front and back}} = h(b_1 + b_2)$$
$$= (4)(4 + 1)$$
$$= 4 \times 5$$
$$= 20 \text{ cm}^2$$

$$A_{\text{top}} = lw$$
$$= 5 \times 3$$
$$= 15 \text{ cm}^2$$

$$A_{\text{bottom}} = lw$$
$$= 4 \times 3$$
$$= 12 \text{ cm}^2$$

$$A_{\text{small side}} = lw$$
$$= 3 \times 1$$
$$= 3 \text{ cm}^2$$

$$A_{\text{large side}} = lw$$
$$= 4 \times 3$$
$$= 12 \text{ cm}^2$$

Step 3
Add the areas of the faces.

$$SA_{\text{right trapezoidal prism}}$$
$$= A_{\text{front and back}} + A_{\text{top}} + A_{\text{bottom}} + A_{\text{small side}} + A_{\text{large side}}$$
$$= 20 + 15 + 12 + 3 + 12$$
$$= 62 \text{ cm}^2$$

The surface area of the right trapezoidal prism is 62 cm^2.

CALCULATING SURFACE AREA OF PYRAMIDS

Pyramids are made up of a base and triangles that meet at a single point called a vertex. The name of a pyramid is based on the shape of its base; for example, a pyramid with a square base is called a square-based pyramid and a pyramid with a six-sided base is called a hexagonal pyramid.

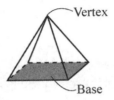

Example

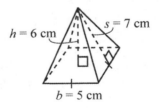

Calculate the surface area of the given square-based pyramid. _____ cm^2

Solution

A square-based pyramid is made up of four equal triangles that join to one square base.

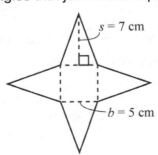

The area of the base is a square. The formula for the area of a square is l^2, and since the length of each side of the base is b, the area of the square base is b^2.

The formula for the area of a triangle is $\dfrac{bh}{2}$.

In a square-based pyramid, the base of each triangle is referred to as b. The height is referred to as the slant height (s).

Therefore, the area of the four equal triangles can be written as follows:

$$A_{\text{four triangles}} = 4\left(\dfrac{bh}{2}\right)$$
$$= 4\left(\dfrac{bs}{2}\right)$$
$$= \overset{2}{4}\left(\dfrac{bs}{2}\right)$$
$$= 2(bs)$$

The surface area of the whole pyramid is defined by the surface area of the square base and the surface area of the four triangular lateral faces.

Square base	Lateral faces
b^2	$2(bs)$

Therefore, the surface area of the given square-based pyramid can be found as follows:

$$SA_{\text{square-based pyramid}} = A_{\text{base}} + A_{\text{lateral faces}}$$
$$= (b^2) + 2(bs)$$
$$= (5^2) + 2(5 \times 7)$$
$$= (25) + 2(35)$$
$$= 25 + 70$$
$$= 95 \text{ cm}^2$$

Example

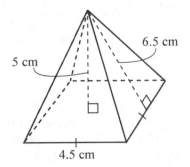

5 cm
6.5 cm
4.5 cm

Draw the net for the given square-based pyramid, and calculate its surface area.

Solution

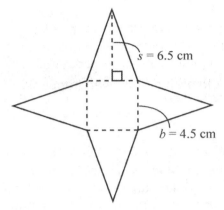

$s = 6.5$ cm
$b = 4.5$ cm

$$SA_{\text{square-based pyramid}}$$
$$= (b^2) + 2(bs)$$
$$= (4.5^2) + 2(4.5 \times 6.5)$$
$$= (4.5 \times 4.5) + 2(4.5 \times 6.5)$$
$$= (20.25) + 2(29.25)$$
$$= 20.25 + 58.5$$
$$= 78.75 \text{ cm}^2$$

CALCULATING THE AREA OF TRAPEZOIDS

A trapezoid has two bases (a and b) and a height (h). The bases are parallel to each other. The height is the shortest distance between the bases. Use these measurements when calculating the area of a trapezoid.

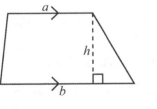

To calculate the area of a trapezoid, follow these steps:

1. Determine the values of h, a, and b.

2. Substitute the known values into the area formula for a trapezoid: $A = \dfrac{1}{2}(a + b)h$.

3. Evaluate the equation to find the area.

Example

A trapezoid is shown.

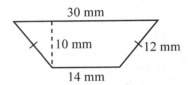

Find the area of the given trapezoid.

Solution

Step 1

Determine the values of *h*, *a*, and *b*.

The height of the trapezoid is 10 mm, so $h = 10$. Make sure you are using the height measurement, and not the side length of 12 mm.

One of the bases measures 30 mm, and the other base measures 14 mm. Therefore, $a = 30$, and $b = 14$.

Step 2

Substitute the known values into the area formula for a trapezoid.

$A = \frac{1}{2}(a + b)h$

$A = \frac{1}{2}(30 + 14)(10)$

Step 3

Evaluate the equation.

$A = \frac{1}{2}(30 + 14)(10)$

$A = \frac{1}{2}(44)(10)$

$A = \frac{1}{2} \times 440$

$A = 220$

The area of the trapezoid is 220 mm².

SOLVING PROBLEMS INVOLVING THE AREA OF A RECTANGLE

To solve problems involving the area of a rectangle, follow these steps:

1. Start with the area formula for a rectangle, $A = l \times w$.
2. Substitute in the known values.
3. Simplify to get the answer.

Example

Callie's teacher asked her to draw a rectangle on the board by using decimal measurements for the length and width. This is the rectangle Callie drew.

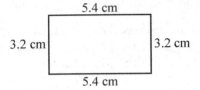

What is the area of the rectangle Callie drew?

Solution

The area of the rectangle is equal to the number of square centimeters that are needed to cover the surface of the rectangle. To determine the area of Callie's rectangle, multiply the length of 5.4 cm by the width of 3.2 cm.

Use the formula of Area = length × width to determine the area. Be sure to include the appropriate unit of measure with your answer.

$A = l \times w$

$A = 5.4 \times 3.2$

$A = 17.28$ cm²

The area of the rectangle Callie drew is 17.28 cm².

Example

The floor of a room is covered by eight square tiles. Each square tile has a side length of 4 m.

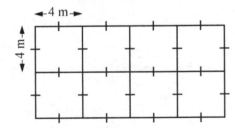

What is the total area of the tiled floor?

Solution

Step 1

Determine the length and width of the tiled floor. The length of the tiled floor is 16 m.

$4 m \times 4 = 16$ m

The width of the tiled floor is 8 m.

$4 m \times 2 = 8$ m

Step 2

Calculate the area of the tiled floor.

$A = l \times w$

$\quad = 16 \times 8$

$\quad = 128 \text{ m}^2$

The total area of the tiled floor is 128 m².

SOLVING PROBLEMS INVOLVING THE VOLUME OF A TRIANGULAR PRISM

To solve problems involving the volume of a triangular prism, use the formula

V = area of triangular base × height of prism.

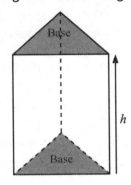

Example

A wedge of cheese has a volume of 35 cm³, and its height is 5 cm.

What is the area of the base of the wedge of cheese?

Solution

The wedge of cheese is in the shape of a triangular prism.

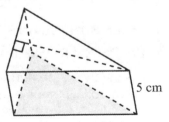

The area of the base is equal to the area of the triangle in the triangular prism.

Substitute the known values into the volume formula.

$V_{\text{triangular prism}} = A_{\text{triangle}} \times h$

$\qquad 35 = A_{\text{triangle}} \times 5$

$\qquad \dfrac{35}{5} = \dfrac{A_{\text{triangle}} \times 5}{5}$

$\quad 7 \text{ cm}^2 = A_{\text{triangle}}$

The area of the triangle is 7 cm².

SOLVING PROBLEMS INVOLVING THE SURFACE AREAS OF RECTANGULAR PRISMS

To find the surface area of a rectangular right prism, follow these steps:

1. Draw the net of the rectangular prism.
2. Calculate the area of each face.
3. Add the areas of the faces.

Example

Andrew wants to wrap a gift for a friend.
The box the gift is in has a length of 12.5 cm, a width of 11.5 cm, and a height of 4 cm.

What is the minimum amount of gift-wrapping Andrew needs to cover the box if there is no overlap?

Solution

The surface area of the box must be determined.

Step 1

Draw the net of the shape.

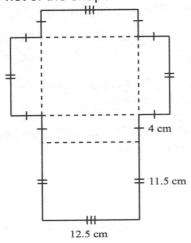

Step 2

Calculate the area of the faces.
Looking at the net, it can be seen that the following faces are the same size:

- Top and bottom
- Front and back
- Sides (left and right)

Find the surface areas of the given pairs of faces. This requires the surface area of one face to be calculated and then multiplied by 2 in order to calculate the areas of both faces.

$$A_{\text{front and back}} = 2(lw)$$
$$= 2(12.5 \times 4)$$
$$= 2(50)$$
$$= 100 \text{cm}^2$$

$$A_{\text{sides}} = 2(lw)$$
$$= 2(11.5 \times 4)$$
$$= 2(46)$$
$$= 92 \text{ cm}^2$$

$$A_{\text{top and bottom}} = 2(lw)$$
$$= 2(11.5 \times 12.5)$$
$$= 2(143.75)$$
$$= 287.5 \text{ cm}^2$$

Step 3

Calculate the surface area.
Add the areas of the faces.

$$SA_{\text{rectangular prism}}$$
$$= A_{\text{front and back}} + A_{\text{sides}} + A_{\text{top and bottom}}$$
$$= 100 \text{ cm}^2 + 92 \text{ cm}^2 + 287.5 \text{ cm}^2$$
$$= 479.5 \text{ cm}^2$$

The surface area of the box is 479.5 cm².

SOLVING PROBLEMS INVOLVING THE SURFACE AREA OF A TRIANGULAR PRISM

To solve problems involving the surface area of a right triangular prism, follow these steps:

1. Draw a net that represents the problem.
2. Calculate the areas of the faces.
3. Add the areas of all the faces.

Example

Johnathon drew a sketch of the water trough he wants to make out of sheet metal.

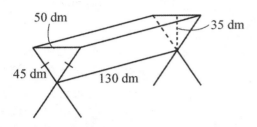

How much material is needed to make the water trough?

Solution

Step 1

Draw the net of the shape.

A triangular right prism is made up of three rectangles, that may or may not be the same size, joined to two triangular faces. In this triangular right prism, one of the faces is not shown.

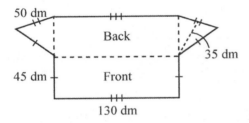

Step 2

Calculate the area of the faces.

Looking at the net, there are some faces that are the same size:

- Front and back (rectangular faces)
- Sides (triangular faces)

Find the area for one face, and multiply it by 2 because the measures of the two faces are the same.

$$A_{\text{front and back}} = 2(l \times w)$$
$$= 2(130 \times 45)$$
$$= 2(5,850)$$
$$= 11,700$$

$$A_{\text{triangles}} = 2\left(\frac{bh}{2}\right)$$
$$= 2\left(\frac{50 \times 35}{2}\right)$$
$$= 2\left(\frac{1,750}{2}\right)$$
$$= 2(875)$$
$$= 1,750$$

Step 3

Calculate the total area of the triangular right prism.

$$SA_{\text{water trough}} = A_{\text{front and back}} + A_{\text{triangles}}$$
$$= 11,700 + 1,750$$
$$= 13,450 \text{ dm}^2$$

Johnathon needs 13,450 dm^2 of sheet metal to make his water trough.

Solution

CALCULATING THE AREA OF A TRIANGLE

To calculate the area of a triangle, follow these steps:

1. Determine the given values.
2. Substitute the known values into the area formula, $A_{\text{triangle}} = \dfrac{b \times h}{2}$, and solve.

Example

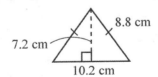

Find the area of the triangle.

Solution

Step 1

Determine the given values.

The base is the length of the horizontal line: $b = 10.2$ cm.

The height is the length of the line from the top to the base that forms a right angle with the base: $h = 7.2$ cm.

Step 2

Substitute the known values into the area formula, and solve.

$$A_{triangle} = \frac{b \times h}{2}$$
$$= \frac{10.2 \times 7.2}{2}$$
$$= \frac{73.44}{2}$$
$$= 36.72$$

The area of the triangle is 36.72 cm^2.

Example

Determine the base of the triangle.

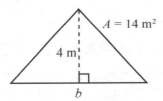

Solution

Step 1

Determine the given values.

The height is the length of the line from the top to the base that forms a right angle with the base: $h = 4$ m.

The area is 14 m^2.

Step 2

Substitute the known values into the area formula, and solve for the unknown measure.

$$A_{triangle} = \frac{b \times h}{2}$$
$$14 = \frac{b \times 4}{2}$$
$$2 \times 14 = \frac{b \times 4}{2} \times 2$$
$$28 = b \times 4$$
$$\frac{28}{4} = \frac{b \times 4}{4}$$
$$7 = b$$

The base of the triangle is 7 m.

CALCULATING THE AREA OF A PARALLELOGRAM

The area of a parallelogram can be calculated using the formula $A_{parallelogram} = b \times h$.

Follow these steps to calculate the area of a parallelogram:

1. Determine the given values.
2. Substitute the known values into the area formula, and solve.

Example

Find the area of the parallelogram.

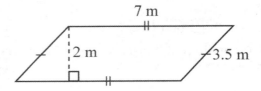

Solution

Step 1

The base or length of the parallelogram is 7 m. The height is shown on the parallelogram where the dotted line forms a square corner to the base. The height of the parallelogram is 2 m.

Step 2

Use the area formula for a rectangle (parallelogram), substituting 7 m for the base and 2 m for the height.

Area = base × height

Area = 7 × 2

Area = 14 m^2

The area of the parallelogram is 14 m^2.

Example

The base of a parallelogram is 4 cm. The height of this parallelogram is twice the base.

What is the area of the parallelogram?

Solution

Step 1

Determine the given values.

The base of the parallelogram is 4 cm, and its height is twice the base.

Therefore, the height of the parallelogram is 2 × 4 = 8cm.

Step 2

Use the area formula for a parallelogram.

$A = bh$

$= 4 × 8$

$= 32$ cm^2

Therefore, the area of the parallelogram is 32 cm^2.

Example

An image of a rhombus is given.

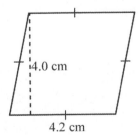

Find the area of this rhombus.

Solution

Step 1

Determine the given values.

The base of the rhombus is 4.2 cm, and its height is 4.0 cm.

Step 2

Use the area formula for a rhombus (parallelogram). Substitute 4.2 cm for the base and 4.0 cm for the height.

A_{rhombus} = base × height

$= 4.2 × 4.0$

$= 16.8$

Therefore, the area of the rhombus is 16.8 cm^2.

CALCULATING THE AREA OF A RECTANGLE

A rectangle has a length and a width. Use these measurements when calculating the area of a rectangle.

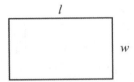

To calculate the area of a rectangle, follow these steps:

1. Determine the values of *l* and *w*.
2. Substitute the known values into the area formula for a rectangle, $A_{\text{rectangle}} = l × w$.
3. Evaluate the equation.

Example

This diagram represents the length and width of a rectangular sand pit at a school.

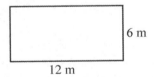

Use a formula to determine the area of the rectangular sand pit.

Solution

Step 1

Determine the values of *l* and *w*.

Looking at the diagram, *l* = 12 m and *w* = 6 m.

Step 2

Substitute the known values into the area formula for a rectangle.

$A = l × w$

$A = 12 × 6$

Step 3
Evaluate the equation.
$A = 12 \times 6$
$A = 72 \text{ m}^2$
The area of the rectangular sand pit is 72 m². It would take 72 m² to cover the surface of the rectangular sand pit.

SOLVING PROBLEMS INVOLVING VOLUME OF RECTANGULAR PRISMS

To calculate the volume of a rectangular prism, use the formula $V_{\text{rectangular prism}} = lwh$, where l represents the length, w represents the width, and h represents the height of the rectangular prism.

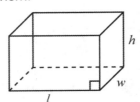

You can use this knowledge to help you solve a wide variety of real-world problems. Whenever you have a problem that involves finding the volume of rectangular prisms, follow this four-step problem-solving process:

1. Read the question carefully, and determine what is being asked.
   Pay special attention to the numbers and values that are given, and look for keywords. Sometimes you may want to draw a picture or diagram to help you understand the problem more clearly. Decide what kind of answer you will give. (Is it a money amount? A volume? A quantity?) Decide if your answer will be a big number or a small one.
2. Make a plan. Decide which operations to use and the order to use them in.
3. Solve the problem. Carry out the plan that you made.
4. Decide if your answer is reasonable.
   You can use estimation or the context of the problem to decide if an answer is reasonable. You can also think about the operation that you are using. For example, if you are multiplying, you know that your answer will be greater than the numbers you are multiplying. If your answer is less, then it is not reasonable. Once you have made sure your answer is reasonable, give your answer as a sentence.

Example

Christine uses the given measurements to calculate the volumes of a box of cereal and a box of popcorn.

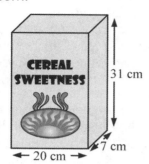

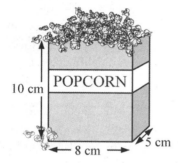

What is the difference between the volume of the box of cereal and the volume of the box of popcorn?

Solution

Step 1

Determine what is being asked.

The cereal box is 20 cm by 7 cm by 31 cm. The popcorn box is 10 cm by 8 cm by 5 cm.

You need to use this information to find the difference in volume between the two boxes.

Your answer will be given in units cubed because it will be a volume. Also, because it is the difference between the two volumes, it has to be less than the volume of the larger container.

Step 2

Make a plan.

First, find the volume of each container.
Use the formula for volume, $V = lwh$.

Next, find the difference. Subtract the volume of the smaller container from the volume of the larger container.

Step 3

Solve the problem.

Calculate the volume of each container.

$$V_{cereal} = lwh$$
$$= 20 \times 7 \times 31$$
$$= 4{,}340 \text{ cm}^3$$
$$V_{popcorn} = lwh$$
$$= 10 \times 8 \times 5$$
$$= 400 \text{ cm}^3$$

Find the difference.

$4{,}340 - 400 = 3{,}940 \text{ cm}^3$

Step 4

Decide if your answer is reasonable.

Your answer is in cubic centimeters and is smaller than the volume of the larger container, which is what you predicted in step 1.

You can also use estimation to check your answer.

For the cereal container, round 31 to 30 and then multiply by 7.
$20 \times 30 = 600$
$600 \times 7 = 4{,}200$

For the popcorn box, round 8 up to 10 and then multiply by 5.
$10 \times 10 = 100$
$100 \times 5 = 500$

The difference between the estimated volumes is $4{,}200 - 500 = 3{,}700$. This is very close to the answer you calculated, so it is a reasonable answer.

The difference between the volumes of the two containers is $3{,}940 \text{ cm}^3$.

Example

Theo is using three containers in a chemistry lab. Each container has the shape of a rectangular prism. The containers have the following dimensions:

- Container 1 has a length, width, and height of 15 in, 10 in, and 12 in, respectively.
- Container 2 has a length, width, and height of 10 in each.
- Container 3 has a length, width, and height of 20 in, 5 in, and 2 in, respectively.

When their volumes are arranged from least to greatest, what is the order of the given containers?

Solution

Step 1
Determine what is being asked.

You are given the dimensions of three containers, and you are asked to order them.

Your answer will be a list of the containers with the smallest one first and the largest one last.

Step 2
Make a plan.

First, find the volume of each container. Use the formula for finding the volume of rectangular prisms, $V = lwh$.

Next, order the containers from smallest to largest.

Step 3
Solve the problem.

Find the volume of each container.

$V_{\text{container 1}} = lwh$
$= 15 \times 10 \times 12$
$= 1{,}800 \text{ in}^3$
$V_{\text{container 2}} = lwh$
$= 10 \times 10 \times 10$
$= 1{,}000 \text{ in}^3$
$V_{\text{container 3}} = lwh$
$= 20 \times 5 \times 2$
$= 200 \text{ in}^3$

Place the containers in order.

The order is container 3 (200 in³), container 2 (1,000 in³), and container 1 (1,800 in³).

Step 4
Decide if your answer is reasonable.

Your answer is the list of containers with the smallest first and the largest last, which is what you predicted in step 1.

You can also use the dimensions of the containers to estimate the order. Container 1 has the largest dimensions and container 3 has the smallest, so it makes sense that the order is 3, 2, 1. Therefore, your answer is reasonable.

The order of the given containers is container 3, container 2, and container 1.

CALCULATING THE VOLUME OF TWO SOLID FIGURES

The volume of a prism is the amount of space the prism takes up. When you have a solid figure made up of two rectangular prisms placed together without intersecting, you can calculate the volume of each figure and then add the two volumes together.

Example

The given figure is made up of two rectangular prisms.

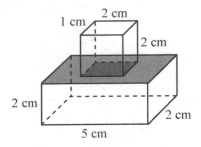

Calculate the volume of the given figure.

Solution

Substitute the known measurements into the volume formula $V = l \times w \times h$. Express your answer in cubic units.

Step 1
Calculate the volume of the larger prism.
$V = l \times w \times h$
$V = (5) \times (2) \times (2)$
$V = 20 \text{ cm}^3$

Step 2
Calculate the volume of the smaller prism.
$V = l \times w \times h$
$V = (2) \times (1) \times (2)$
$V = 4 \text{ cm}^3$

Step 3
Add the volumes.
$20 + 4 = 24$
The total volume of the given figure is 24 cm³.

SOLVING PROBLEMS INVOLVING THE SURFACE AREA OF PYRAMIDS

The surface area, SA, of a pyramid can be determined by applying the formula $SA = A_{base} + A_{lateral\ faces}$, where A_{base} is the area of the base and $A_{lateral\ faces}$ is the area of the lateral faces.

Example

A company that manufactures glass ornaments is planning to produce hollow, enclosed glass ornaments in the shape of a square-based pyramid. The company has these two possible designs in mind.

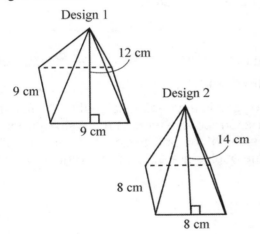

If the company plans to produce 2,000 glass ornaments and the cost to produce each ornament is $0.04/cm^2$, how much will the company save in production costs if they choose Design 2 rather than Design 1?

Solution

The surface area, SA, of a pyramid can be determined by applying the formula $SA = A_{base} + A_{lateral\ faces}$.

Step 1

Determine the area of the base of the pyramid in Design 1.

Since Design 1 has a square base, the area, A, of the base in this design can be determined by applying the formula $A = s^2$, where s is the side length of the base.

$A = s^2$

Substitute 9 for s.

$A = 9^2$

$A = 81\ cm^2$

Step 2

Determine the area of the lateral faces of the pyramid in Design 1.

Each of the four lateral faces in Design 1 is triangular. The area, A, of a triangle can be determined by applying the formula $A = \frac{1}{2}bh$, where b is the base of the triangle and h is the height of the triangle. Since Design 1 has four congruent lateral faces, the area of the lateral faces can be determined with the formula

$A = 4 \times \left(\frac{1}{2}bh \right)$.

Substitute 9 for b and 12 for h.

$A = 4 \times \left(\frac{1}{2} \times 9 \times 12 \right)$

$A = 4 \times 54$

$A = 216\ cm^2$

Step 3

Determine the surface area of the pyramid in Design 1.

In the formula $SA = A_{base} + A_{lateral\ faces}$, substitute 81 cm^2 for A_{base} and 216 cm^2 for $A_{lateral\ faces}$.

$SA = A_{base} + A_{lateral\ faces}$
$SA = 81\ cm^2 + 216\ cm^2$
$SA = 297\ cm^2$

Step 4

Determine the cost to produce 2,000 ornaments if Design 1 is chosen.

Since the surface area of one ornament is 297 cm^2 and 2,000 ornaments are to be produced at a cost of $0.04/cm^2, the cost would be 297 × 0.04 × 2,000 = $23,760 if Design 1 is chosen.

Step 5

Determine the area of the base of the pyramid in Design 2.

$A = s^2$
$A = 8^2$
$A = 64\ cm^2$

Step 6

Determine the area of the lateral faces of the pyramid in Design 2.

Substitute 8 for b and 14 for h in the formula

$A = 4 \times \left(\frac{1}{2}bh\right)$.

$A = 4 \times \left(\frac{1}{2}bh\right)$
$A = 4 \times \left(\frac{1}{2} \times 8 \times 14\right)$
$A = 4 \times 56$
$A = 224\ cm^2$

Step 7

Determine the surface area of the pyramid in Design 2.

In the formula $SA = A_{base} + A_{lateral\ faces}$, substitute 64 cm^2 for A_{base} and 224 cm^2 for $A_{lateral\ faces}$.

$SA = A_{base} + A_{lateral\ faces}$
$SA = 64\ cm^2 + 224\ cm^2$
$SA = 288\ cm^2$

Step 8

Determine the cost to produce 2,000 ornaments if Design 2 is chosen.

Since the surface area of one ornament is 288 cm^2 and 2,000 ornaments are to be produced at a cost of $0.04/cm^2, the cost would be 288 × 0.04 × 2,000 = $23,040 if Design 2 is chosen.

Step 9

Determine how much the company would save in production costs if Design 2 is chosen over Design 1.

The company would save
$23,760 – $23,040 = $720 in production costs if Design 2 is chosen.

CALCULATING THE AREA OF REGULAR POLYGONS

A **polygon** is a two-dimensional (2-D), flat shape that is formed with three or more straight lines. If all the sides of the polygon are the same length and all the angles are equal, it is a **regular polygon**.

This table gives some examples of regular polygons.

Equilateral Triangle	
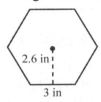	3 equal sides
	3 equal angles
Square	
	4 equal sides
	4 equal angles
Regular Pentagon	
	5 equal sides
	5 equal angles
Regular Hexagon	
	6 equal sides
	6 equal angles
Regular Octagon	
	8 equal sides
	8 equal angles

If you want to calculate the area of an equilateral triangle or a square, you can use the appropriate formula. Calculate the area of a triangle using the formula $A = \frac{1}{2}bh$. Calculate the area of a square using the formula $A = lw$.

If you want to calculate the area of any other regular polygon, use one of the following methods:

- Divide the shape into smaller shapes.
- Use the formula for the area of regular polygons.

DIVIDING THE SHAPE INTO SMALLER SHAPES

Any regular polygon can be divided into equal-sized triangles. You can calculate the area of each small triangle and then add these areas to find the area of the whole shape.

Example

A regular hexagon is given.

What is the area of the given hexagon?

Solution

Step 1

Divide the shape into small triangles. All of the sides of the hexagon are the same length, so each of the six triangles is exactly the same.

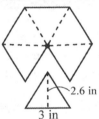

Step 2

Calculate the area of one small triangle.

Use the formula $A = \frac{1}{2}bh$. In this triangle, the base is 3 in, and the height is 2.6 in.

$$A = \frac{1}{2}bh$$

$$A = \frac{1}{2}(3)(2.6)$$

$$A = \frac{1}{2}(7.8)$$

$$A = 3.9 \text{ in}^2$$

Each small triangle has an area of 3.9 in².

Step 3

Find the area of the hexagon.

The hexagon is made up of 6 small triangles, so multiply the area of one small triangle by 6.

$A_{hexagon} = A_{triangle} \times 6$

$A_{hexagon} = 3.9 \times 6$

$A_{hexagon} = 23.4 \text{ in}^2$

The area of the hexagon is 23.4 in^2.

USING THE FORMULA FOR THE AREA OF REGULAR POLYGONS

There is a formula that can be used to find the area of any regular polygon. The formula uses a measurement called the apothem. The **apothem** of a polygon is the distance from the center of the polygon to the middle of one of its edges.

The hexagon in the previous example has an apothem of 2.6 in.

In the previous example, the hexagon was divided into 6 small triangles, and you used the formula for the area of a triangle to find the area of the regular hexagon. You can use this knowledge to develop a general formula for the area of regular polygons.

The formula for the area of a triangle is

$A_{triangle} = \frac{1}{2}bh$. The base of the triangle is equal

to the length of one of the sides of the hexagon. The height of the triangle is equal to the apothem of the hexagon. You can change the letters in the

formula to $A_{triangle} = \frac{1}{2}sa$, where s is the length of

one of the sides of the hexagon and a is the apothem.

After you found the area of the triangle, you multiplied it by the number of triangles in the complete shape. The number of triangles is always the same as the number of sides of the polygon. Let n equal the number of sides in the polygon, and rewrite the formula.

$A = \text{number of sides} \times \frac{1}{2}sa$

$A = \frac{1}{2}nsa$

The formula to find the area of the polygon is

$A = \frac{1}{2}nsa$, where n is the number of sides, s is the

length of one side, and a is the length of the apothem.

Example

A regular pentagon is given.

9 cm

13.1 cm

What is the area of the given pentagon?

Solution

Use the formula for the area of regular

polygons, $A = \frac{1}{2}nsa$.

In the given pentagon, the number of sides is 5, the side length is 13.1 cm, and the length of the apothem is 9 cm. Substitute the known values into the formula.

$A = \frac{1}{2}nsa$

$A = \frac{1}{2}(5)(13.1)(9)$

$A = \frac{1}{2}(589.5)$

$A = 294.75 \text{ cm}^2$

The given pentagon has an area of 294.75 cm^2.

Solving Problems with the Area of a Trapezoid

A **trapezoid** is a quadrilateral that has exactly two parallel sides.

For the given trapezoid, *a* and *b* are the two bases, and *h* is the height of the trapezoid.

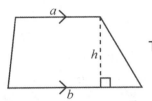

The measurements of the two bases (*a* and *b*) and the height (*h*) are used to calculate the area of a trapezoid.

The area formula for a trapezoid is

$A = \frac{1}{2}(a + b)h$. You can apply the area formula for a trapezoid to solve problems involving the area of a trapezoid.

Example

Emma planted flowers that outline the shape of a trapezoid in her backyard. She would like to lay sod in the enclosed section of dirt with the following dimensions:

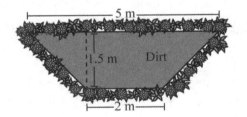

If sod costs $3.60/m², how much will it cost to cover the trapezoidal section of dirt?

Solution

To determine the cost to lay sod in the trapezoidal section of dirt, first determine the area of the trapezoidal section. You can apply the formula for the area of a trapezoid,

$A = \frac{1}{2}(a + b)h$, where *a* and *b* are the lengths of the bases, and *h* is the height of the trapezoid.

Step 1

Determine the values of *a*, *b*, and *h*.

The bases, *a* and *b*, are the two parallel sides of the trapezoid. Therefore, the values of *a* and *b* are 5 m and 2 m, respectively. The height of the trapezoid, *h*, is the perpendicular distance between the two bases. The dotted line between the parallel sides indicates the distance between the two sides and measures 1.5 m. Therefore, the value of *h* is 1.5 m.

Step 2

Determine the area of the trapezoidal section. Substitute 1.5 for *h*, 5 for *a*, and 2 for *b* into the formula $A = \frac{1}{2}(a + b)h$.

$A = \frac{1}{2}(a + b)h$

$A = \frac{1}{2}(5 + 2) \times 1.5$

$A = \frac{1}{2}(7) \times 1.5$

$A = 3.5 \times 1.5$

$A = 5.25$

The area of the trapezoid is 5.25 m².

Step 3

Determine the total cost of the sod needed to cover the trapezoidal section of dirt.

Since the area of the trapezoid is 5.25 m², and the cost of sod is $3.60/m², the total cost of sod would be 5.25 × $3.60 = $18.90.

CALCULATING MISSING SIDE LENGTHS

A composite shape is made up of two or more shapes. To calculate the perimeter or the area of composite shapes, sometimes you need to start by calculating the lengths of missing sides.

Example

This composite shape is made up of a rectangle and a square.

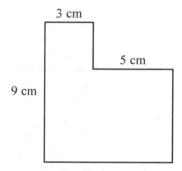

The shape has 6 sides, but only 3 side lengths are given. If you want to calculate the perimeter or area, you need to start by finding all the missing side lengths.

To calculate missing side lengths, you can use tick marks or add or subtract known sides.

USING TICK MARKS

Tick marks are small marks on the sides of shapes. Sometimes, they are also called hash marks or hatch marks. If two sides have the same kind of ticks, then those two sides have the same length.

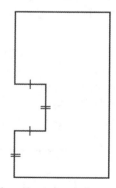

The sides that each have one tick are the same length, and the sides that each have two ticks are the same length.

Example

A shape is given.

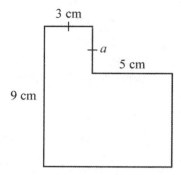

What is the length of side *a*?

Solution

Side *a* has one tick on it. The other side with one tick on it has a length of 3 cm. This means that side *a* also has a length of 3 cm.

USING ADDITION

Whenever a shape has square corners, then the opposite sides are equal. In this shape, the top and bottom sides have the same length, even though they do not have ticks to show it. Also, the sum of the three sides on the left is equal to the side on the right.

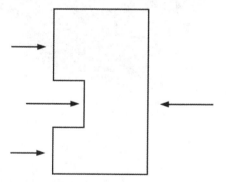

If you know the lengths of all the short sides, you can add them up to find the length of the long side.

Example

A shape is given.

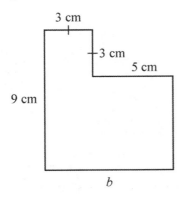

What is the length of side *b*?

Solution

The length of side *b* is the same as the total of the side lengths that are opposite.

The two opposite sides have lengths of 3 cm and 5 cm. 3 + 5 = 8

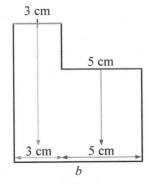

Side *b* has a length of 8 cm.

USING SUBTRACTION

You can also use the fact that opposite sides of a shape with square corners are equal to find the length of one of the short sides. If you know the length of the long side and you are missing the length of one of the short sides, you can subtract.

Example

A shape is given.

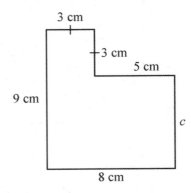

What is the length of side *c*?

Solution

The length of side *c* plus 3 cm needs to add up to 9 cm.

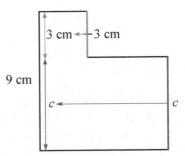

This means that you can subtract 3 from 9 to find the missing length.

9 – 3 = 6

Side *c* has a length of 6 cm.

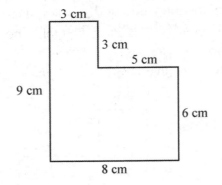

EXERCISE #1—GEOMETRY

Use the following information to answer the next question.

The given table shows how three original lengths were changed to their image lengths. It also shows the scale factor used for each change.

Original Length (cm)	Scale Factor	Image Length (cm)
8	x	16
y	$\frac{1}{8}$	56
10	0.2	z

149. What are the values for x, y, and z that correctly complete the given table?

A. $x = \frac{1}{2}$, $y = 7$, and $z = 2$

B. $x = 2$, $y = 7$, and $z = 50$

C. $x = 2$, $y = 448$, and $z = 2$

D. $x = \frac{1}{2}$, $y = 448$, and $z = 50$

Use the following information to answer the next question.

This map shows the distance between an amusement park and a school. The map scale is 1 in = 5 mi.

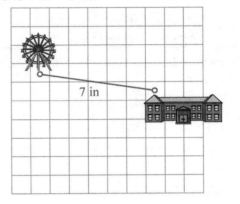

7 in

150. What is the actual distance between the amusement park and the school?

A. 25 mi   B. 30 mi

C. 35 mi   D. 40 mi

Use the following information to answer the next question.

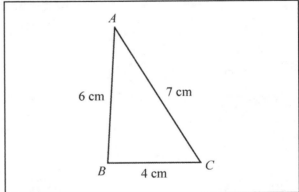

151. If triangle ABC is enlarged to make triangle XYZ, such that the shortest side measures 6 cm, then the longest side of triangle XYZ will measure

A. 14.5 cm   B. 10.5 cm

C. 9 cm   D. 8 cm

Use the following information to answer the next question.

A trapezoid with an area, A_1, of 21 m² has a scale factor of 0.82 applied to it.

152. Rounded to the nearest tenth, the area, A_2, of the new trapezoid is _____ m².

Use the following information to answer the next question.

Triangle *ABC* is an isosceles triangle, where $\angle A = \angle B$.

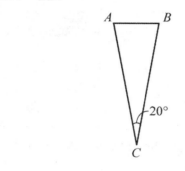

153. What is the measure of $\angle A$?
   A. 60°   B. 70°
   C. 80°   D. 90°

154. Which of the following diagrams shows a triangle with measurements that are **not** possible?

A.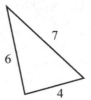

B.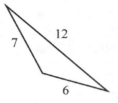

C.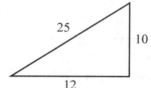

D.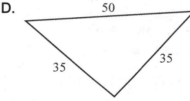

Use the following information to answer the next question.

The measures of two of the angles of triangle *ABC* are 47° and 43°. A third measurement is required in order for triangle *ABC* to be a unique triangle.

155. Which of the following statements is **true** with respect to a possible third measurement for triangle *ABC*?
   A. The measure of the third angle of triangle *ABC* must be 90°.

   B. The measure of the third angle of triangle *ABC* could be less than 90°.

   C. The length of the hypotenuse of triangle *ABC* must be the third measurement.

   D. The length of the side between the two given angles could be the third measurement.

156. Draw a triangle that has side lengths of 8 cm and 10 cm with an 84° angle between the two sides.

157. Using a ruler and a protractor, draw a triangle that has angles that measure 45° and 80° with a side length of 5.3 cm between them.

Use the following information to answer the next question.

A plane intersects a right prism as shown.

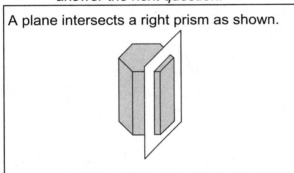

158. What is the shape of the plane section?

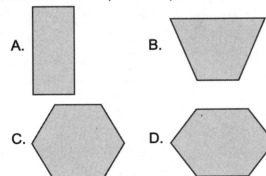

A.
B.
C.
D.

159. The circumference of a circle is πd when the diameter is d. If the radius of the same circle is cut into half, the circumference of the circle will be

A. $\dfrac{\pi d}{4}$ B. $\dfrac{\pi d}{2}$

C. $2\pi d$ D. $4\pi d$

Use the following information to answer the next question.

Benji has a wire ring that has a radius of 6 cm.

160. A good estimate of the actual area of the wire ring is

A. 18 cm^2 B. 36 cm^2

C. 108 cm^2 D. 115 cm^2

Use the following information to answer the next question.

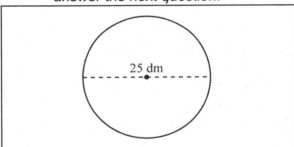

25 dm

161. Calculate the circumference.

Use the following information to answer the next question.

Vanessa is replacing all the springs in her circular trampoline. The diameter of her trampoline is 3.5 m. Around the edge of the trampoline, there are 10 springs per meter.

162. How many replacement springs does Vanessa need? _____

Use the following information to answer the next question.

Tina wants to cover three identical round end tables in her living room with fabric. The diameter of each table is 18 in. When determining how much fabric she will need, she uses 3.14 as the value for pi.

163. What is the area of fabric that she will need given to two decimal places? _____ in²

Use the following information to answer the next question.

Jason is a member of his school's running team. At his first track meet, he is told the circumference of the circular track that he will be running is 15.7 km.

164. What is the radius of the track?
    A. 1.5 km   B. 2.5 km
    C. 3 km   D. 5 km

165. If angles *x* and *x* + 30° are complementary, what is the value of *x*?
    A. 30°   B. 45°
    C. 60°   D. 75°

Use the following information to answer the next question.

Arthur's teacher shows him this image. Then, he asks him to find another angle measuring 65°.

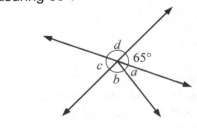

166. The angle that Arthur should say has a measure of exactly 65° is
    A. ∠*a*   B. ∠*b*
    C. ∠*c*   D. ∠*d*

Use the following information to answer the next question.

Triangle *ABC* is shown.

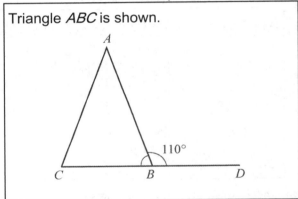

167. The measure of ∠*ABC* is _____°.

Use the following information to answer the next question.

Amy is given a diagram. She measures ∠4 and discovers that it is a right angle.

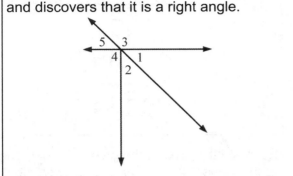

168. Which two angles are complementary?

   A. ∠1 and ∠2

   B. ∠1 and ∠4

   C. ∠3 and ∠5

   D. ∠2 and ∠3

169. Which of the following pairs of angles are supplementary angles?

   A. 63° and 17°   B. 52° and 90°

   C. 90° and 120°   D. 63° and 117°

Use the following information to answer the next question.

If this rectangular prism was divided in half diagonally, two identical right-angled triangular prisms would be created.

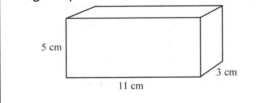

170. What would the volume be of each triangular prism?

   A. 825 cm^3

   B. 165 cm^3

   C. 82.5 cm^3

   D. 16.5 cm^3

Use the following information to answer the next question.

Ann wants to paint the walls of her bedroom, which is 3 m long, 3.5 m wide, and 2.5 m high.

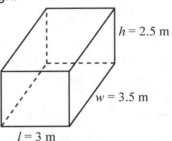

Ann wants to cover the walls of her room with two coats of paint.

Each can of paint contains 1 L of paint and covers approximately 10 m^2 of drywall.

171. Rounded to the nearest whole number, how many cans of paint does she need to buy?

Use the following information to answer the next question.

A triangular prism is given.

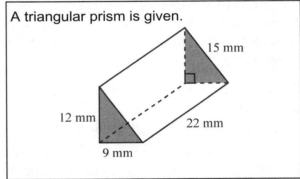

172. Determine the surface area of the given triangular prism.

Use the following information to answer the next question.

Macy owns a rectangular plot of land that measures 15 m × 6.5 m. In order to plough the land, Macy digs down and evenly removes 0.75 m of dirt from the top portion of the plot.

173. By the time she finishes, how much dirt will Macy remove, rounded to the nearest hundredth?

   A. 27.08 m³   **B.** 52.34 m³

   C. 73.13 m³   **D.** 94.25 m³

Use the following information to answer the next question.

Kelly's math teacher asked her to measure a particular triangular prism and then calculate its volume.
Kelly made these measurements:

- Height of triangular base: 6 cm
- Length of triangular base: 9 cm
- Height of triangular prism: 12 cm

174. What is the volume of the triangular prism Kelly measured?

   A. 648 cm³   **B.** 324 cm³

   C. 192 cm³   **D.** 90 cm³

Use the following information to answer the next question.

This figure is a rhombus, which is a kind of parallelogram.

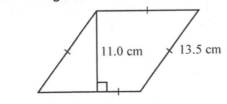

175. Which of the following measures is a reasonable estimate of the area of the given figure?

   A. 200 cm²   **B.** 154 cm²

   C. 145 cm²   **D.** 50 cm²

Use the following information to answer the next question.

A triangle is shown on the grid.

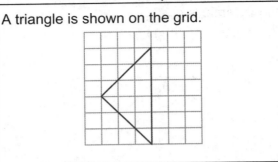

176. Estimate the area of the given triangle, and then evaluate the estimate by comparing it to the actual area of the triangle.

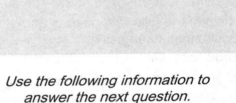

Use the following information to answer the next question.

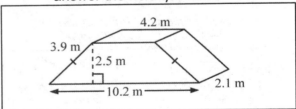

177. What is the surface area of the given trapezoidal prism?

   A. 118.62 m²   **B.** 104.04 m²

   C. 82.62 m²   **D.** 74.43 m²

A pyramid is given.

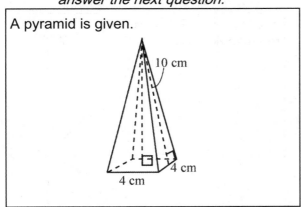

178. Calculate the surface area of this pyramid.

179. The area of a trapezoid is the same as the area of a
A. rectangle and two right triangles
B. rectangular prism
C. parallelogram
D. rhombus

The two parallel sides of the trapezoid shown have lengths of 10 cm and 16 cm.

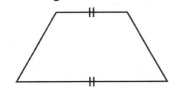

180. If the height of the trapezoid is 8 cm, what is the area of the trapezoid?
A. 80 cm^2
B. 104 cm^2
C. 128 cm^2
D. 160 cm^2

A lifeguard at a beach has 300 m of heavy cord to rope off a rectangular swimming area, with the beach forming one side of the rectangle.

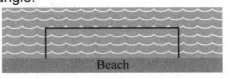

181. What is the area of the roped-off section when the side parallel to the beach has a measure of 200 m?
A. 2,500m^2
B. 5,000m^2
C. 10,000m^2
D. 20,000 m^2

The given diagram illustrates a two-man tent. This tent is in the shape of a triangular prism.

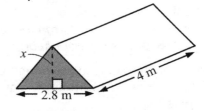

182. If the volume of the tent shown is 8.96 m^3, what is the area of the front, or shaded section, of the tent?
A. 1.6 m^2
B. 2.24 m^2
C. 3.2 m^2
D. 4.48 m^2

A flower vase is in the shape of a rectangular prism.

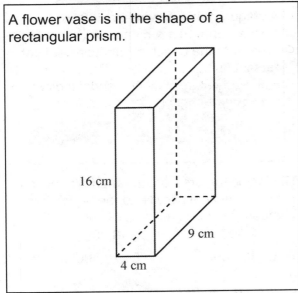

16 cm

9 cm

4 cm

183. What is the surface area of the exterior of the vase?
  A. 421 cm²
  B. 452 cm²
  C. 489 cm²
  D. 517 cm²

A wedge of cheese is in the shape of a triangular prism. The dimensions are shown in the given figure.

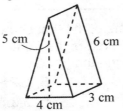

5 cm

6 cm

4 cm

3 cm

Tom would like to wrap the wedge of cheese in tinfoil.

184. Tom will need _____ cm² of tinfoil to wrap the wedge of cheese.

Jason drew a five-sided shape made up of the triangles *ABC*, *BCE*, and *CDE*.

A

8 cm   8 cm

B   *C*

8 cm

E   *D*
12 cm

185. What is the area of triangle *CDE*?
  A. 10 cm²
  B. 20 cm²
  C. 48 cm²
  D. 96 cm²

Parallelogram *WXYZ* has side *WX* with a length of 20 cm. The lengths of the heights *BX* and *AZ* are 16 cm and 14 cm, respectively.

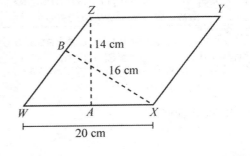

Z   *Y*

B   14 cm

16 cm

W   *A*   *X*

20 cm

186. The length of side *WZ* is
  A. 16.0 cm
  B. 17.5 cm
  C. 18.0 cm
  D. 19.5 cm

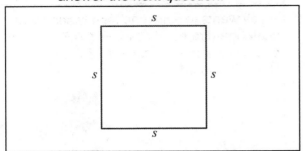

187. If the given square has an area of 169 cm², what is the length of each side?

Laura has a rectangular sandbox that is 2 ft long, 3 ft wide, and 1 ft deep. She wants to make it 2 ft longer, 1.5 ft wider, and 1 ft deeper.

188. How much larger than her old sandbox will Laura's new sandbox be?
- A. 3 ft³
- B. 9 ft³
- C. 30 ft³
- D. 36 ft³

A shape is given.

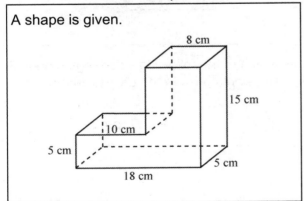

189. What is the volume of the given shape? _____ cm³

An outside light fixture is in the shape of an inverted square-based pyramid. The light fixture has a circular hole in the top where a light bulb is to be inserted. The slant height of the light fixture is 32 cm, and the diameter of the circular hole is 16 cm.

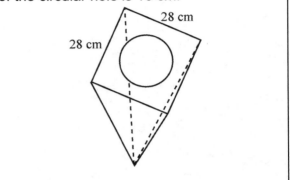

190. To the nearest whole number, the surface area of the light fixture is
- A. 1,772 cm²
- B. 1,943 cm²
- C. 2,186 cm²
- D. 2,375 cm²

191. Which of the following equations correctly shows how to use the formula $A = \frac{1}{2}nsa$ to calculate the area of the matching equilateral triangle?

A.

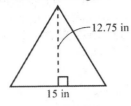

$A = \frac{1}{2}(3)(15)(12.75)$

B.

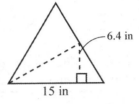

$A = \frac{1}{2}(3)(15)(6.4)$

C.

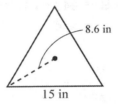

$A = \frac{1}{2}(3)(15)(8.6)$

D.

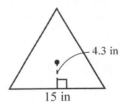

$A = \frac{1}{2}(3)(15)(4.3)$

Use the following information to answer the next question.

Haley wants to paint one side of her wooden skateboard ramp. At a local hardware store, she can purchase paint for $3.35/ m^2. Her skateboard ramp is shown.

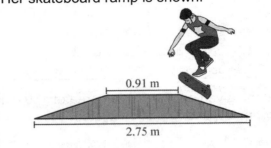

192. If the height of her skateboard ramp is 0.36 m, then how much will it cost Haley to paint the side of her ramp?
   A. $0.66
   B. $1.32
   C. $2.21
   D. $4.41

Use the following information to answer the next question.

A shape is given.

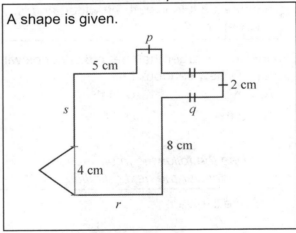

193. Which of the following side lengths **cannot** be calculated with the given information?
   A. p
   B. q
   C. r
   D. s

EXERCISE #1—GEOMETRY ANSWERS AND SOLUTIONS

149. C	161. See solution	173. C	185. C
150. C	162. 110	174. B	186. B
151. B	163. 763.02	175. B	187. See solution
152. 14.1	164. B	176. See solution	188. C
153. C	165. A	177. C	189. 850
154. C	166. C	178. See solution	190. D
155. D	167. 70	179. A	191. D
156. See solution	168. A	180. B	192. C
157. See solution	169. D	181. C	193. B
158. A	170. C	182. B	
159. B	171. 7	183. B	
160. C	172. See solution	184. 68	

149. C

Determine the missing values from the table by using the scale factor formula for the values in each row of the table. Substitute the known values into the formula, and solve for the unknown value.

Step 1
Solve for x.

$$\text{scale factor} = \frac{\text{image length}}{\text{original length}}$$
$$x = \frac{16}{8}$$
$$= 2$$

Step 2
Solve for y.

$$\text{scale factor} = \frac{\text{image length}}{\text{original length}}$$
$$\frac{1}{8} = \frac{56}{y}$$
$$y = 8(56)$$
$$= 448$$

Step 3
Solve for z.

$$\text{scale factor} = \frac{\text{image length}}{\text{original length}}$$
$$0.2 = \frac{z}{10}$$
$$0.2(10) = \left(\frac{z}{10}\right)(10)$$
$$z = 2$$

Therefore, $x = 2$, $y = 448$, and $z = 2$.

150. C

According to the map scale, 1 in = 5 mi. On the map, the distance between the amusement park and the school is 7 in. To find the actual distance, multiply by 5.

7×5 mi = 35 mi

The actual distance between the amusement park and the school is 35 mi.

151. B

The shortest side of triangle ABC is 4 cm. Since triangle XYZ is simply an enlargement of triangle ABC, the two triangles are similar. Therefore, the shortest side of triangle ABC corresponds to the shortest side of triangle XYZ.

$$\text{Enlarged triangle} = \frac{\text{shortest side of } \Delta XYZ}{\text{shortest side of } \Delta ABC} = \frac{6 \text{ cm}}{4 \text{ cm}}$$
$$= \frac{3}{2} = 1.5$$

Therefore, the length of the longest side of triangle XYZ is 1.5 × the length of the longest side of triangle ABC.
$$= 1.5 \times 7 \text{ cm}$$
$$= 10.5 \text{ cm}$$

152. 14.1

Use the formula $A_2 = A_1 \times (\text{scale factor})^2$.

Substitute 21 for A_1 and 0.82 for the scale factor.

$$A_2 = A_1 \times (\text{scale factor})^2$$
$$= 21 \times (0.82)^2$$
$$= 21 \times 0.6724$$
$$= 14.1204$$
$$\approx 14.1 \text{ m}^2$$

Rounded to the nearest tenth, the new trapezoid will have an area of 14.1 m[2].

153. C

Step 1
Determine which angle measures are given.
∠C = 20°

Step 2
Substitute the given values into the angle property for a triangle, and simplify.

Since this is an isosceles triangle, ∠A and ∠B have the same measure.

Modify the property.

$$\angle A + \angle B + \angle C = 180°$$
$$\angle A + \angle A + \angle C = 180°$$
$$2\angle A + \angle C = 180°$$
$$2\angle A + 20° = 180°$$
$$2\angle A + 20° - 20° = 180° - 20°$$
$$\frac{2\angle A}{2} = \frac{160°}{2}$$
$$\angle A = 80°$$

Therefore, ∠A and ∠B each have a measure of 80°.

154. C

The triangle inequality theorem states that any side of a triangle is less than the sum of the other two sides.

In triangle C, the side with a length of 25 is greater than the sum of the lengths of the other two sides.

25 > 12 + 10
25 > 22

A triangle with measurements of 25, 12, and 10 is not possible.

155. D

Step 1
Determine if the measure of the third angle of triangle ABC must be 90°.

The sum of the measures of the angles in a triangle must equal 180°. Since two of the angles in triangle ABC are 47° and 43°, the measure of the third angle must be 180° – (47° + 43°) = 90°.

However, there are an infinite number of triangles that can be formed when given the measurements of all three angles, so triangle ABC would not be a unique triangle.

Step 2
Determine if the measure of the third angle of triangle ABC could be less than 90°.

If the third angle of triangle ABC was less than 90°, triangle ABC would not exist because it would be impossible for the sum of the measures of the three angles of triangle ABC to equal 180°.

Step 3
Determine if the length of the hypotenuse of triangle ABC must be the third measurement.

If the length of the hypotenuse of triangle ABC is the third measurement, then the angle-side-angle (ASA) condition would be satisfied and triangle ABC would be a unique triangle. However, because of the ASA condition, if the length of a side other than the hypotenuse is given, triangle ABC would still be a unique triangle.

Therefore, the third measurement of triangle ABC does not have to be the length of the hypotenuse.

Step 4
Determine if the length of the side between the two given angles could be the third measurement.

If the length of the side between the two given angles (the included side) is the third measurement, then the angle-side-angle (ASA) condition would be satisfied and triangle ABC would be a unique triangle.

Thus, if the length of the side between the two given angles is the third measurement, then triangle ABC would be a unique triangle.

156.

Step 1
Draw and label a line that is 8 cm long.

Step 2
Draw and label an angle of 84° at the end of the 8 cm line.

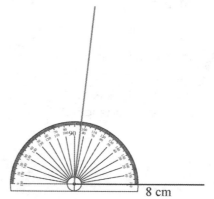

Step 3
Place a mark on the new line 10 cm away from the vertex of the angle.

8 cm

Step 4
Draw a line from the other end of the 8 cm line to the mark on the 10 cm line.

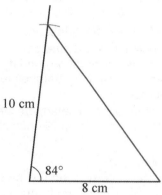

10 cm

84°

8 cm

157.

Step 1
Use a ruler to draw a line that is 5.3 cm long.

Step 2
Use a protractor to draw a 45° angle at one end of the 5.3 cm line.

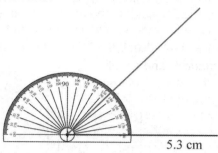

5.3 cm

Step 3
Use a protractor to draw an 80° angle at the other end of the 5.3 cm line.

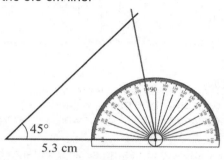

45°

5.3 cm

Since the lines already meet, they do not need to be extended.

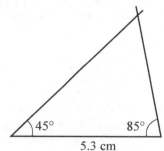

45°   85°

5.3 cm

158. A

The plane intersects the prism along four edges, so the plane section must have four sides. The plane is also perpendicular to the base of the prism, which means that the plane section forms a right angle with the base. The only shape that the plane section can be is a rectangle.

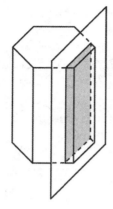

159. B

The diameter of a circle is twice as long as the radius of the same circle. In other words, $C = \pi d$ is the same as $C = 2\pi r$.

If the radius of the same circle is cut into half, then the radius must be divided by two.

Substitute $\frac{r}{2}$ for r in the circumference formula.

$$C = 2\pi r$$
$$C = 2\pi\left(\frac{r}{2}\right)$$
$$C = \frac{2\pi r}{2}$$

Since $d = 2r$, substitute d into the formula.

$$C = \frac{2\pi r}{2}$$
$$C = \frac{\pi d}{2}$$

The circumference of the new circle is represented by $C = \frac{\pi d}{2}$.

160. C

The formula used to calculate the area of a circle is $A = \pi r^2$.

The value of π is approximately 3.14.
When estimating the area inside the wire ring, multiply the square of its radius by 3.

$$A = \pi r^2$$
$$= 3 \times (6)^2$$
$$= 3 \times 36$$
$$= 108 \text{ cm}^2$$

161.

Step 1
Choose the appropriate formula using the given values.
The question is asking for circumference and gives the diameter.
$C = \pi d$

Step 2
Substitute in the known values.
In this case, the diameter d is 25 dm and the value of π is 3.14.
$C = \pi d$
$\quad = (3.14)(25)$

Step 3
Solve for the unknown.
$C = \pi d$
$\quad = (3.14)(25)$
$\quad = 78.5$
The circumference of the circle is about 78.5 dm.

162. 110

Step 1
Determine what is being asked.
The trampoline has a diameter of 3.5 m, and there are 10 springs per meter around its edge.
The distance around the trampoline is the circumference.
Use this information to determine the total number of springs around the circumference of the trampoline.

Step 2
Make a plan.
First, find the circumference of the trampoline.
Use the formula for circumference, $C = \pi d$.
Multiply your answer by 10 to find the total number of springs.

Step 3
Solve the problem.
Calculate the circumference of the trampoline.
You can use 3.14 to approximate pi.
$C = \pi d$
$C \approx 3.14 \times 3.5$
$C \approx 10.99$
The circumference is about 11 m.
Multiply the result by 10.
$11 \times 10 = 110$

Step 4
Decide if your answer is reasonable.
Round the diameter of the trampoline up to 4, and round π down to 3.

$C = \pi d$
$C \approx 3(4)$
$C \approx 1$
$12 \times 10 = 120$

This is very close to the calculated result, so the answer is reasonable.

Vanessa needs 110 springs.

163. 763.02

Step 1
Understand the problem.

Tina has three tables. Each table has a diameter of 18 in.

You need to use this information to find the amount of fabric she will need to cover all three tables.

Step 2
Make a plan.

First, find the area of one table using the formula for the area of a circle, $A = \pi r^2$. Then, find the total area of the three tables by multiplying the area of one table by 3.

Step 3
Solve the problem.

1. Find the area of one table. The radius of a table
   is $18 \div 2 = 9$ in.

$$A = \pi r^2$$
$$A = 3.14 \times 9 \times 9$$
$$A = 254.34 \text{ in}^2$$

2. Find the area of three tables.

$$A_{\text{three tables}} = A_{\text{one table}} \times 3$$
$$A_{\text{three tables}} = 254.34 \times 3$$
$$A_{\text{three tables}} = 763.02 \text{ in}^2$$

Step 4
Check your answer.

You can use estimation to see if your answer is reasonable. Round 9 to 10 and π to 3 rather than 3.14.

The area of one table is about

$3 \times 10 \times 10 = 300 \text{ in}^2$.

Next, find the area of three tables.

$300 \times 3 = 900 \text{ in}^2$

This is close to your calculation, so your answer is reasonable.

The area of fabric that she will need is 763.02 in².

164. B

Step 1
Determine the formula to use.

Manipulate the circumference formula to isolate r.

$$r = \frac{C}{2\pi}$$

Step 2
Substitute in known values.

$$r = \frac{15.7}{2 \times 3.14}$$

Step 3
Simplify.

$$r = \frac{15.7}{2 \times 3.14}$$
$$= \frac{15.7}{6.28}$$
$$= 2.5 \text{ km}$$

The radius of the track is 2.5 km.

165. A

If two angles are complementary, the sum of their measures is equal to 90°.

Angles x and $x + 30°$ are complementary. Therefore, they must equal 90°.

$$x + x + 30° = 90°$$
$$2x + 30° = 90°$$
$$2x = 60°$$
$$x = 30°$$

Therefore, the value of x is 30°.

166. C

In the given diagram, $\angle c$ is vertically opposite the angle measuring 65°.

Since vertically opposite angles have the same measure, Arthur can determine that $\angle c = 65°$ without measuring.

167. 70

Two angles on a straight line have a sum of 180°. Angles ABD and ABC make a straight line, so their sum is 180°.

The measure of $\angle ABD$ is 110°, so $\angle ABC$ is $180° - 110° = 70°$.

168. A

If two angles are complementary, the sum of their measures is 90°.

Since $\angle 4$ is a right angle, it means that $\angle 1$ and $\angle 2$ together also form a right angle. Since the sum of the measures of $\angle 1$ and $\angle 2$ is 90°, $\angle 1$ and $\angle 2$ are complementary.

169. D

Supplementary angles are angles whose measures add up to 180°.

Add each of the given pairs of angles to determine which adds up to 180.

- 63 + 17 = 80 ≠ 180
- 52 + 90 = 142 ≠ 180
- 90 + 120 = 210 ≠ 180
- 63 + 117 = 180

170. C

Step 1

Calculate the volume of the rectangular prism.

$V = l \times w \times h$
$V = 11 \times 3 \times 5$
$V = 165 \text{ cm}^3$

Step 2

Since each of the two triangular prisms is half the rectangular prism, then each triangular prism will have half the volume of the rectangular prism. Therefore, divide the volume of the rectangular prism by 2.

$V = \dfrac{l \times w \times h}{2}$

$V = \dfrac{165}{2} = 82.5 \text{ cm}^3$

The volume of each identical triangular prism is 82.5 cm³.

171. 7

Step 1

Determine the area that will be painted.

Ann is only painting the walls; therefore, the ceiling and the floor are not included in the surface area that will be painted.

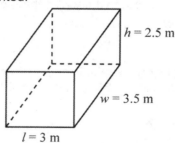

$h = 2.5$ m
$w = 3.5$ m
$l = 3$ m

$SA_{\text{walls}} = 2(lh) + 2(wh)$
$= 2(3.5 \times 2.5) + 2(3 \times 2.5)$
$= 2(8.75) + 2(7.5)$
$= 17.5 + 15$
$= 32.5 \text{ m}^2$

Step 2

Since Ann will be applying 2 coats of paint, the surface area must be doubled.
$SA = 2(32.5)$
$= 65$

Ann needs enough paint to cover 65 m².

Step 3

Determine the number of cans of paint Ann needs.

$\dfrac{65 \text{ m}^2}{10 \text{ m}^2 \text{ per can}} = 6.5 \text{ cans}$

Rounded to the nearest whole number, Ann must buy 7 cans of paint.

172.

Step 1

Determine the areas of the three rectangular faces using the formula $A = l \times w$.

Although each rectangular face has the same length, they each have a different width. One rectangular face has a width of 9 mm and a length of 22 mm. Another rectangular face has a width of 12 mm and a length of 22 mm. The final rectangular face has a width of 15 mm and a length of 22 mm.

Substitute the appropriate lengths and widths into the formula.

- $A = 9 \text{ mm} \times 22 \text{ mm} = 198 \text{ mm}^2$

- $A = 12 \text{ mm} \times 22 \text{ mm} = 264 \text{ mm}^2$

- $A = 15 \text{ mm} \times 22 \text{ mm} = 330 \text{ mm}^2$

Determine the combined area of the three rectangular faces.

$198 \text{ mm}^2 + 264 \text{ mm}^2 + 330 \text{ mm}^2 = 792 \text{ mm}^2$

Step 2

Determine the area of the triangular base using the formula $A = \dfrac{b \times h}{2}$.

Substitute the length of the triangular base (9 mm) and the height of the triangle (12 mm) into the formula.

$A = \dfrac{9 \text{ mm} \times 12 \text{ mm}}{2} = \dfrac{108 \text{ mm}^2}{2}$

$A = 54 \text{ mm}^2$

Since there are two congruent triangular bases, multiply the area by 2.

$54 \text{ mm}^2 \times 2 = 108 \text{ mm}^2$

Step 3

Determine the surface area.

Add the combined area of the three rectangular faces and the two triangular bases.

$SA = 792 \text{ mm}^2 + 108 \text{ mm}^2$
$SA = 900 \text{ mm}^2$

The surface area of the triangular prism is 900 mm^2.

173. C

The dirt that is removed from the land is in the shape of a rectangular prism.

To calculate the volume of the rectangular prism, substitute the given values into the volume formula.

$V_{\text{rectangular prism}} = A_{\text{base}} \times h$
$V_{\text{rectangular prism}} = A_{\text{rectangle}} \times h$
$\qquad = (l \times w) \times h$
$\qquad = 15 \times 6.5 \times 0.75$
$\qquad = 73.125 \text{ m}^3$

Round 73.125 to the nearest hundredth.
73.13

Macy will remove 73.13 m^3 of dirt by the time she is finished plowing the land.

174. B

Determine the volume of the triangular prism by using the formula for volume.

V = area of base × height of prism

$V = \left(\dfrac{\text{base} \times \text{height}}{2}\right) \times h$

Substitute the numbers for the length of the base (9 cm), the height of the base (6 cm), and the height of the prism (12 cm) into the formula.

$V = \left(\dfrac{9 \times 6}{2}\right) \times 12$

$V = 27 \times 12 = 324 \text{ cm}^3$

The volume of the prism Kelly measured is 324 cm^3.

175. B

Step 1

Round the length and height of the parallelogram to the nearest whole number.

- 11.0 → 11 because 0 < 5.
- 13.5 → 14 because 5 = 5.

Step 2

Use the area formula for a rectangle, substituting the rounded length and height into the formula.

A = length × height
$A = 14 \times 11 = 154 \text{ cm}^2$

A reasonable estimate of the area of the parallelogram (rhombus) is 154 cm^2.

176.

Step 1

Estimate the area by counting the number of squares and half squares.

There are 6 squares and 6 half squares.

Two half squares equal one full square.

$6 + 3 = 9$

A good estimate of the area is 9 square units.

Step 2

Count the number of squares in the base and the height.

It may help to rotate the triangle 90° to see the base and height more easily.

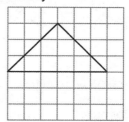

There are 6 squares in the base.
The triangle is 3 squares high.

Step 3

Use the area formula to determine the area of the triangle.

$A = \dfrac{1}{2}(\text{base} \times \text{height})$

$A = \dfrac{1}{2}(6 \times 3)$

$A = \dfrac{1}{2}(18)$

$A = 9 \text{ units}^2$

Step 4

Compare the estimated area to the calculated area.

The calculation of the area (9 units^2) is the same as the estimate (9 square units).

177. C

Step 1

Draw the net of the shape.

A trapezoidal prism is made up of four rectangular faces (both sides, bottom, and top in the diagram) that join the two trapezoidal bases (front and back).

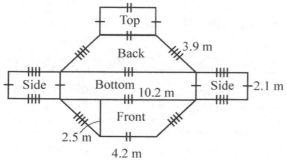

Step 2

Calculate the area of each face.

Solve for the area of each face by applying the appropriate formula.

$$A_{bottom} = lw$$
$$= (10.2)(2.1)$$
$$= 21.42 \text{ m}^2$$

$$A_{front \text{ and } back} = 2\left[\frac{h}{2}(b_1 + b_2)\right]$$
$$= h(b_1 + b_2)$$
$$= 2.5(4.2 + 10.2)$$
$$= 2.5(14.4)$$
$$= 36 \text{ m}^2$$

$$A_{2 \text{ sides}} = 2lw$$
$$= 2(3.9)(2.1)$$
$$= 16.38 \text{ m}^2$$

$$A_{top} = lw$$
$$= (4.2)(2.1)$$
$$= 8.82 \text{ m}^2$$

Step 3

Add the areas of the faces.

$$SA_{trapezoidal \text{ prism}}$$
$$= A_{bottom} + A_{front \text{ and } back} + A_{2 \text{ sides}} + A_{top}$$
$$= 21.42 + 36 + 16.38 + 8.82$$
$$= 82.62 \text{ m}^2$$

The surface area of the trapezoidal prism is 82.62 m².

178.

The formula used to calculate the surface area of a square-based pyramid is $SA = b^2 + 2(bs)$.

Substitute 4 for b and 10 for s, and then simplify.

$$SA_{square \text{ pyramid}}$$
$$= b^2 + 2(bs)$$
$$= (4)^2 + 2(4 \times 10)$$
$$= 16 + 2(40)$$
$$= 16 + 80$$
$$= 96 \text{ cm}^2$$

179. A

A trapezoid can be broken up into the following pieces:

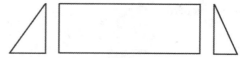

Thus, the area of a trapezoid is the same as the area of a rectangle and two right triangles.

180. B

Step 1

Determine the values of h, b_1, and b_2.

The value of h is 8 cm.

The value of b_1 is 10 cm.

The value of b_2 is 16 cm.

Step 2

Substitute the known values into the area formula for a trapezoid.

$$A_{trapezoid} = \frac{h}{2}(b_1 + b_2)$$
$$= \frac{8}{2}(10 + 16)$$

Step 3

Simplify the equation.

$$= \frac{8}{2}(26)$$
$$= 4 \times 26$$
$$= 104 \text{ cm}^2$$

The area of the trapezoid is 104 cm².

181. C

Step 1

Calculate the length and width of the roped-off section.

The length (l) is equal to the side parallel to the beach, so l = 200 m.

To find the width (w), subtract the length from the total amount of cord, and divide by 2.

$$w = \frac{300 - 200}{2}$$

$$= \frac{100}{2}$$

$$= 50 \text{ m}$$

Step 2

Determine the area of the roped-off section.

Substitute 200 for l and 50 for w.

$A = l \times w$
$\quad = 200 \times 50$
$\quad = 10,000$

The area of the roped-off swimming section is 10,000 m^2.

182. B

In order to determine the volume of the tent, which is in the shape of a triangular prism, it is necessary to consider one of the triangular faces as the base of the tent.

Step 1

Let x represent the height of one of the triangular faces, and determine an expression for the area of the base of the tent by applying the formula for the area of a triangle.

Substitute 2.8 for b and x for h in the formula

$A = \dfrac{bh}{2}$, and then simplify.

$A = \dfrac{bh}{2}$

$A = \dfrac{2.8 \times x}{2}$

$A = 1.4x \text{ m}$

Step 2

Solve for x by applying the formula for the volume of a triangular prism.

Substitute $1.4x$ for A_{base}, 4 (the given height) for h, and 8.96 (the given volume) for V in the formula $V = A_{base} \times h$. Solve for x.

$\quad V = A_{base} \times h$
$8.96 = (1.4x)(4)$
$8.96 = 5.6x$
$1.6 \text{ m} = x$

The value of x, the height of the triangular face, is 1.6 m.

Step 3

Determine the area of the front of the tent by applying the formula for the area of a triangle.

Substitute 2.8 for b and 1.6 for h in the formula

$A = \dfrac{bh}{2}$, and solve for A.

$A = \dfrac{bh}{2}$

$A = \dfrac{2.8 \times 1.6}{2}$

$A = \dfrac{4.48}{2}$

$A = 2.24 \text{ m}^2$

The area of the front of the tent is 2.24 m^2.

183. B

Step 1

Calculate the areas of the faces.

Looking at the diagram, it can be seen that the faces of the front and back are the same size. The faces of the sides (left and right) are also the same size The top and bottom have the same size, but the top will be open, so its area will not contribute to the surface area of the exterior of the vase.

Calculate the area of each face. For the pairs of matching faces, calculate the area of one face, and then multiply by 2 in order to find the areas of both faces.

$A_{front\ and\ back} = 2(lw)$
$A_{front\ and\ back} = 2(16 \times 4)$
$A_{front\ and\ back} = 2(64)$
$A_{front\ and\ back} = 128 \text{ cm}^2$

$A_{sides} = 2(lw)$
$A_{sides} = 2(16 \times 9)$
$A_{sides} = 2(144)$
$A_{sides} = 288 \text{ cm}^2$

$A_{top} = lw$
$A_{top} = 4 \times 9$
$A_{top} = 36 \text{ cm}^2$

Copyright Protected

Step 2

Calculate the surface area.

Add the areas of the faces.

$SA_{prism} = A_{front\ and\ back} + A_{sides} + A_{top}$
$= 128 + 288 + 36$
$= 452\ cm^2$

The surface area of the flower vase is 452 cm^2.

184. 68

Step 1

Draw the net of the shape.

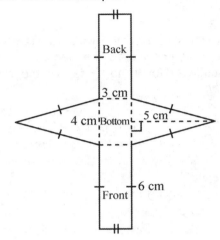

Step 2

Calculate the area of the faces.

Calculate the area of the front and back faces.

$A_{front\ and\ back} = 2(l \times w)$
$A_{front\ and\ back} = 2(3 \times 6)$
$A_{front\ and\ back} = 2(18)$
$A_{front\ and\ back} = 36$

Calculate the area of the bottom face.

$A_{bottom} = l \times w$
$A_{bottom} = 3 \times 4$
$A_{bottom} = 12$

Calculate the area of the triangular faces.

$A_{triangle} = 2\left(\dfrac{bh}{2}\right)$
$A_{triangle} = 2\left(\dfrac{4 \times 5}{2}\right)$
$A_{triangle} = 20$

Step 3

Calculate the total surface area of the triangular prism.

$SA_{cheese} = A_{front\ and\ back} + A_{bottom} + A_{triangle}$
$SA_{cheese} = 36 + 12 + 20$
$SA_{cheese} = 68 cm^2$

Tom will need 68 cm^2 of tinfoil to wrap the cheese.

185. C

Step 1

Determine the measurements of the base and the height of triangle *CDE*.

The length of the base is 12 centimeters, and the height is 8 centimeters.

Step 2

Substitute the known values into the area formula, and solve.

$A = \dfrac{bh}{2}$
$= \dfrac{12 \times 8}{2}$
$= \dfrac{96}{2}$
$= 48\ cm^2$

The area of triangle *CDE* is 48 cm^2.

186. B

Step 1

Determine the area of the parallelogram.

The length of the base *WX* of the parallelogram is 20 cm, and the corresponding height *AZ* is 14 cm. Substitute the values into the area formula for a parallelogram and solve.

$A_{parallelogram} = b \times h$
$= 20 \times 14$
$= 280$

The area of the parallelogram is 280 cm^2.

Step 2

Determine the length of side *WZ*.

Use *WZ* as the base and *BX* as the height. Substitute the known values into the formula, and solve for *WZ*.

$A_{parallelogram} = b \times h$
$280 = WZ \times BX$
$280 = WZ \times 16$
$\dfrac{280}{16} = \dfrac{WZ \times 16}{16}$
$17.5 = WZ$

The length of side *WZ* is 17.5 cm.

187.

Be sure to include the appropriate unit of measure with your answer.

Step 1

In order to solve this problem, you need to remember that a square has four congruent sides, which means all four sides will have the same length.

Use the formula for area to help you determine the side lengths of the square.

$A = l \times w$

Since the length and width of the square are the same, let the letter s (side) represent both the length and width in the area formula.

$$A = s \times s$$
$$169 \text{cm}^2 = s \times s$$

Step 2

Think of a number that when multiplied by itself has a product of 169.

If you know that $10 \times 10 = 100$ and $15 \times 15 = 225$, then you know that the letter s will represent a number between 10 and 15.

You can use a strategy of guess and check to determine the answer.

$11 \times 11 = 121$
$12 \times 12 = 144$
$13 \times 13 = 169$

The length of each side of the square is 13 cm.

188. C

Step 1

Determine what is being asked.

The sandbox is 2 ft by 3 ft by 1 ft. It will be increased by 2 ft, 1.5 ft, and 1 ft.

This information needs to be used to find the difference in volume between the new measurements and the old measurements.

Your answer will be given in units cubed because it will be a volume. Also, because it is the difference between the two volumes, it has to be less than the volume of the new sandbox.

Step 2

Make a plan.

First, find the volume of the original sandbox using the formula $V = lwh$.

Then, find the dimensions of the new sandbox by adding the increases to the original measurements.

Next, use the new measurements to find the volume of the expanded sandbox.

Finally, find the difference in volume by subtracting the old sandbox volume from the new sandbox volume.

Step 3

Solve the problem.

Find the volume of the original sandbox.

$V_{\text{old}} = lwh$
$\quad\quad = 2 \times 3 \times 1$
$\quad\quad = 6 \text{ ft}^3$

Calculate the measurements of the new sandbox.

$l = 2 + 2 = 4$ ft
$w = 3 + 1.5 = 4.5$ ft
$h = 1 + 1 = 2$ ft

Find the volume of the expanded sandbox.

$V_{\text{new}} = lwh$
$\quad\quad = 4 \times 4.5 \times 2$
$\quad\quad = 36 \text{ ft}^3$

Find the difference.

$36 - 6 = 30 \text{ ft}^3$

Step 4

Decide if your answer is reasonable.

Your answer is in cubic feet and is smaller than the volume of the expanded sandbox, which is what you predicted in step 1. Therefore, your answer is reasonable.

Laura's new sandbox is 30 ft³ larger than her original sandbox.

189. 850

$V_{\text{composite figure}} = V_{\text{small rectangular prism}}$
$+ V_{\text{large rectangular prism}}$

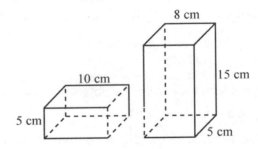

Step 1

Calculate the volume of the larger prism.

$V = l \times w \times h$
$V = (8) \times (5) \times (15)$
$V = 600 \text{ cm}^3$

Step 2

Calculate the volume of the smaller prism.

$V = l \times w \times h$
$V = (10) \times (5) \times (5)$
$V = 250 \text{ cm}^3$

Step 3

Add the volumes.

$600 + 250 = 850$

The total volume of the given figure is 850 cm³.

190. D

The surface area, SA, of a pyramid can be determined by applying the formula $SA = A_{base} + A_{lateral\ faces}$, where A_{base} is the area of the base and $A_{lateral\ faces}$ is the area of the lateral faces.

Step 1

Determine the area of the base (top) of the light fixture.

If the base of the light fixture did not have a circular hole cut into it, the area of the base would be $28 \times 28 = 784$ cm².

However, since there is a circular hole in the base, the actual area of the base is 784 cm² minus the area of the circular hole.

The formula $A = \pi r^2$ can be used to determine the area of the circular hole. Substitute $16 \div 2 = 8$ for r, and then solve for A.

$A = \pi(8)^2$
$A = 64\pi$
$A \approx 201.06$ cm²

Thus, the area of the base is approximately 784 cm² $- 201.06$ cm² $= 582.94$ cm².

Step 2

Determine the area of the lateral faces of the light fixture.

Each of the four lateral faces in the light fixture is triangular in shape. The area, A, of each triangle can be determined by applying the formula $A = \frac{1}{2}bh$, where b is the length of the base of the triangle and h is the height.

Since the lateral faces are congruent, the total area of the lateral faces can be determined by using the formula $A = 4 \times \left(\frac{1}{2}bh\right)$.

Substitute 28 for b and 32 for h, and then solve for A.

$A = 4 \times \left(\frac{1}{2} \times 28 \times 32\right)$
$A = 4 \times 448$
$A = 1{,}792$ cm²

Step 3

Determine the surface area of the light fixture. Apply the surface area formula for a pyramid.

$SA = A_{base} + A_{lateral\ faces}$

Substitute 582.94 cm² for A_{base} and 1,792 cm² for $A_{lateral\ faces}$.

$SA = 582.94$ cm² $+ 1{,}792$ cm²
$SA = 2{,}374.94$ cm²

To the nearest whole number, the surface area of the light fixture is 2,375 cm².

191. D

In the formula $A = \frac{1}{2}nsa$, n is the number of sides in a polygon, s is the length of one of the sides, and a is the apothem. The apothem is the distance from the center of a polygon to the middle of one of its edges. The diagram in alternative D is the only diagram that correctly shows the apothem, so the equation in D is the only correct use of the formula $A = \frac{1}{2}nsa$.

192. C

The side of the skateboard ramp has the shape of a trapezoid. You can find the area using the area formula $A = \frac{1}{2}(a + b)h$, where a and b are parallel sides and h is the height between a and b. Then, using the area, you can find the cost of the paint needed to paint the trapezoidal side.

Step 1

Determine the values of a, b, and h.

The dimensions on the skateboard ramp show that the parallel sides, a and b, are 0.91 m and 2.75 m, respectively. As well, it is given that the height, h, is 0.36 m.

Step 2

Determine the area of the trapezoidal side.

Substitute 0.91 for a, 2.75 for b, and 0.36 for h into the area formula, $A = \frac{1}{2}(a + b)h$.

$A = \frac{1}{2}(a + b)h$

$A = \frac{1}{2}(0.91 + 2.75) \times 0.36$

$A = \frac{1}{2}(3.66) \times 0.36$

$A = 1.83 \times 0.36$
$A = 0.6588$

Step 3

Find the cost of the paint required to paint the side of the ramp.

The cost of the paint is $3.35/m^2$, and the paint must cover 0.6588 m^2.

0.6588 m$^2 \times \$3.35/\text{m}^2 \approx \$2.21$

Therefore, Haley will have to pay $2.21 to paint the side of her skateboard ramp.

193. B

Look at each of the missing sides, and see if the length can be calculated with the given information.

Step 1

Look at side p.

Side p has one tick on it. The other side with one tick on it has a length of 2 cm. This means that side p also has a length of 2 cm.

Step 2

Look at side r.

The length of side r is equal to the sum of the lengths of the opposite sides. Both of the opposite side lengths are given, so it is possible to calculate the length of r.

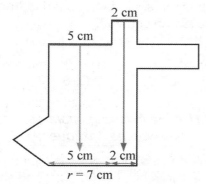

Step 3

Look at side s.

The sum of side s and 4 cm is equal to the sum of 2 cm and 8 cm. It is possible to calculate the length of s by adding 2 and 8 and subtracting 4.

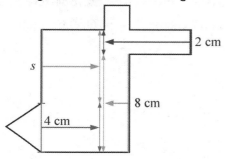

Step 4

Look at side q.

Side q has two ticks on it. The length of the other side with two ticks on it is not given, so it is impossible to calculate the length of side q.

EXERCISE #2—GEOMETRY

194. A tomato plant is 75 cm tall in real life. What is the height of the tomato plant in a diagram that has a scale factor of 1:25?

Use the following information to answer the next question.

Dave and Vance wanted to make a scale drawing of their bedroom. They decided on a scale that would work and used grid paper to make the drawing, as shown.

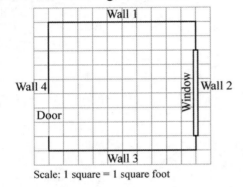

Scale: 1 square = 1 square foot

195. Based on the given scale drawing, the length measurement of the window in the boys' room is

A. 6 in   B. 6 ft

C. 6 cm   D. 6 m

Use the following information to answer the next question.

The given diagram shows circle C, with center $(-3, 2)$, and circle D, with center $(1, 2)$.

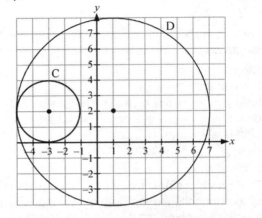

196. What is the scale factor used to transform circle C into circle D?

A. $\dfrac{1}{6}$ B. $\dfrac{1}{3}$

C. 3   D. 6

Use the following information to answer the next question.

Vickie has a sketch of an irregular polygon with an area, A_1, of 260 cm^2, and she wants to apply a scale factor of 2.2 to it.

197. Rounded to the nearest whole number, what is the area, A_2, of the new irregular polygon?

A. 572 cm^2 B. 834 cm^2

C. 1,258 cm^2 D. 1,646 cm^2

Use the following information to answer the next question.

A triangle is given.

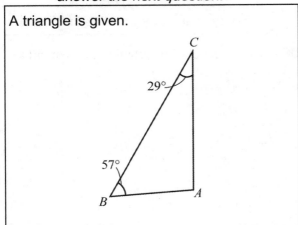

198. What is the measure of ∠A?

A. 84 °   B. 94 °

C. 104 °   D. 114 °

Use the following information to answer the next question.

Triangle *ABC* has side lengths of 5, 9, and *x*.

199. Which of the following side lengths could **not** be the length of *x*?

A. 5   B. 8

C. 13   D. 16

Use the following information to answer the next question.

Two side lengths of a particular triangle are 7 cm and 10 cm.

200. Which of the following values could be the length of the third side of the triangle?

A. 2 cm   B. 11 cm

C. 17 cm   D. 19 cm

Use the following information to answer the next question.

A triangle has side lengths of 12 cm and 7 cm. The angle between the sides measures 115°.

201. Draw the given triangle.

202. Using a protractor and a ruler, draw a triangle that has angles that measure 25° and 100° with a side length of 5.8 cm between them.

203. Which of the following plane sections is a triangle?

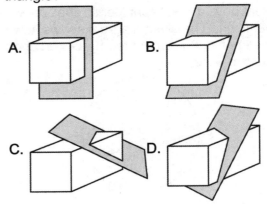

A.   B.

C.   D.

Use the following information to answer the next question.

A piece of wire with a length of L forms a circle with a radius of R. The wire is then cut into two pieces whose lengths are L_1 and L_2. These pieces form two new circles whose radii are R_1 and R_2, as shown in the diagram.

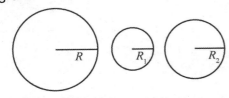

204. Which of the following equations represents the relationship between the radii R, R_1, and R_2?
   A. $R = R_1 \times R_2$
   B. $R = R_1 + R_2$
   C. $R = R_1 - R_2$
   D. $R = \dfrac{R_1}{R_2}$

Use the following information to answer the next question.

Hera buys a small sprinkler so she can water her lawn. The given diagram shows how far the sprinkler, represented by O, can shoot out the water.

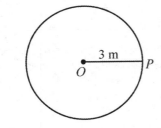

205. The approximate area of grass that Hera's sprinkler can cover is
   A. 9 m²
   B. 18 m²
   C. 22 m²
   D. 27 m²

Use the following information to answer the next question.

A motorcycle tire has a radius of 25 cm.

206. How far will the tire travel in one revolution?

207. The circumference of a bicycle wheel is 219 cm. To the nearest centimeter, what is the radius of the wheel?
   A. 30 cm
   B. 35 cm
   C. 40 cm
   D. 45 cm

Use the following information to answer the next question.

The diameter of a motorcycle's rear wheel is 60 cm.

208. To the nearest ten, what is its area?
   A. 90 cm²
   B. 190 cm²
   C. 2,830 cm²
   D. 11,300 cm²

Use the following information to answer the next question.

The diagram shows a circular running track with a diameter of 42 m.

Circular track

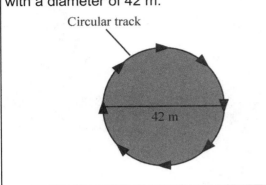

42 m

209. If Lyle runs around the track twice, what distance, rounded to the nearest meter, will he have traveled?

A. 66 m

B. 84 m

C. 132 m

D. 264 m

Use the following information to answer the next question.

Two angles are complementary. One angle is 35°.

210. What is the value of the other angle?

A. 55°

B. 65°

C. 155°

D. 165°

Use the following information to answer the next question.

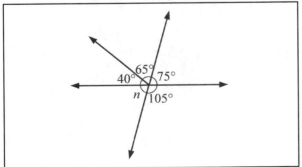

211. The measure of ∠n is

A. 105°

B. 75°

C. 65°

D. 40°

Use the following information to answer the next question.

A pair of angles is given.

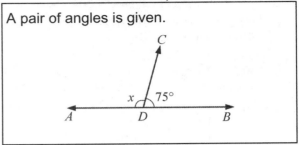

212. What is the size of the missing angle? _____°

213. Which of the following pairs of angles are complementary angles?

A. 45° and 35°

B. 50° and 40°

C. 60° and 20°

D. 65° and 35°

Use the following information to answer the next question.

This diagram shows five angles.

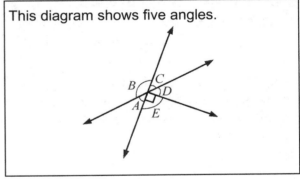

214. Which of the following angles are supplementary angles?

A. ∠A and ∠B

B. ∠C and ∠D

C. ∠A and ∠E

D. ∠C and ∠A

Use the following information to answer the next question.

Two cubes, each having side lengths of 10 cm, are joined side to side.

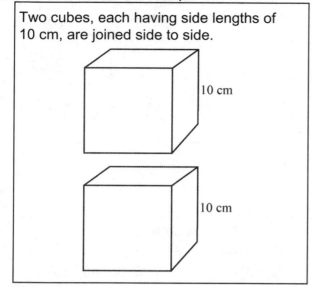

215. What is the surface area of the resulting shape?

A. 100 cm²

B. 600 cm²

C. 800 cm²

D. 1,000 cm²

Use the following information to answer the next question.

A triangular prism is given.

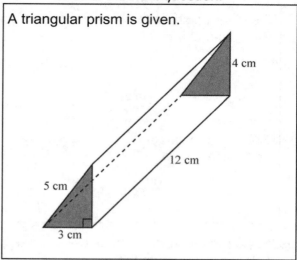

216. Determine the surface area of the given triangular prism.

Use the following information to answer the next question.

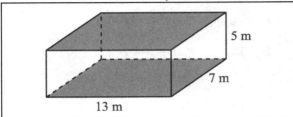

217. Calculate the volume of the rectangular prism.

Use the following information to answer the next question.

A triangular prism is shown.

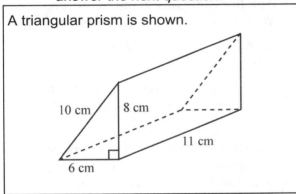

218. The volume of the given triangular prism is

A. 528 cm³

B. 264 cm³

C. 132 cm³

D. 55 cm³

Use the following information to answer the next question.

A triangular prism is shown.

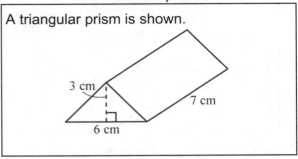

219. What is the volume of the given triangular prism?

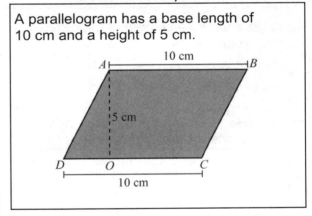

Use the following information to answer the next question.

A parallelogram has a base length of 10 cm and a height of 5 cm.

220. What is the area of the parallelogram?

A. 30 cm²

B. 40 cm²

C. 45 cm²

D. 50 cm²

Use the following information to answer the next question.

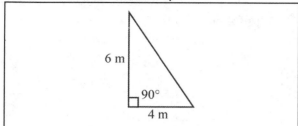

221. What is the area of the given triangle?
    A. 4 m²   B. 10 m²
    C. 12 m²   D. 24 m²

Use the following information to answer the next question.

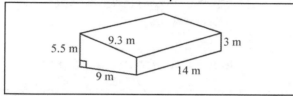

222. What is the surface area of the given trapezoidal prism?
    A. 455.9 m²   B. 451.7 m²
    C. 447.5 m²   D. 413.4 m²

Use the following information to answer the next question.

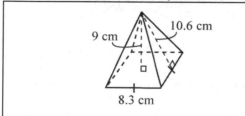

223. Find the surface area of the given shape to the tenths place.

224. Which of the following formulas can be used to calculate the area of a trapezoid?

A. $A_{trapezoid} = h\frac{b+a}{2}$

B. $A_{trapezoid} = h \times a \times b$

C. $A_{trapezoid} = \left(\frac{a}{2}\right)(h+a)$

D. $A_{trapezoid} = \frac{h}{2}(b+a)$

Use the following information to answer the next question.

The given diagram illustrates one of the ramps in a skateboard park.

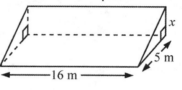

225. If the volume of the ramp shown is 136 m³, then the value of *x* to the nearest tenth is
    A. 3.4 m   B. 3.8 m
    C. 4.2 m   D. 4.5 m

Use the following information to answer the next question.

Jason is having a birthday party, and his parents bought him a birthday cake. An overhead view of the birthday cake with its dimensions are shown in the given diagram.

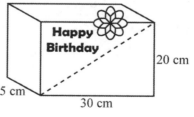

226. What is the surface area of Jason's birthday cake?
    A. 1,700 cm²   B. 1,800 cm²
    C. 1,900 cm²   D. 2,000 cm²

Use the following information to answer the next question.

Leigh Ann would like to replace the lining of her tent. In order to determine how much lining she will need, she draws a sketch of the tent, which is in the shape of a triangular prism.

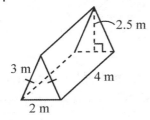

227. How much lining will Leigh Ann need to cover the outside of the tent? _____ m²

Use the following information to answer the next question.

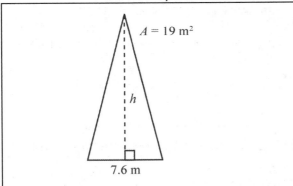

228. Find the length of *h* of the given triangle.

Use the following information to answer the next question.

A rhombus is given.

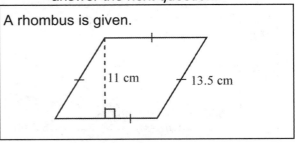

229. What is the area of the rhombus?
A. 24.5 cm²   B. 54 cm²
C. 121 cm²   D. 148.5 cm²

230. The area of a rectangle is 108 m². If the length of the rectangle is 15 m, what is the width of the rectangle?

Use the following information to answer the next question.

Richard needs to fill a rectangular fish tank that is 35 cm long, 25 cm wide, and 32 cm tall. The jug he is using to carry the water from the sink holds 4,000 cm³.

231. How many trips to the sink will Richard have to make in order to fill the fish tank? _____

Use the following information to answer the next question.

A rectangular prism is stacked on top of a cube.

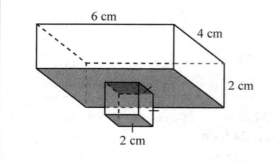

232. What is the total volume of the given figure?

A. 48 cm³

B. 56 cm³

C. 51 in³

D. 62 in³

Use the following information to answer the next question.

A Christmas tree ornament is in the shape of an enclosed rectangular-based pyramid, as shown.

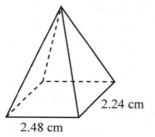

Each face with a 2.48 cm base has a slant height of 3.96 cm, and each face with a 2.24 cm base has a slant height of 4 cm.

233. To the nearest whole number, the surface area of the Christmas tree ornament is

A. 44 cm²

B. 43 cm²

C. 24 cm²

D. 23 cm²

Use the following information to answer the next question.

A regular octagon is given.

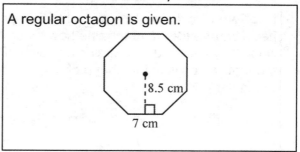

234. What is the area of this octagon?

A. 29.75 cm²

B. 59.5 cm²

C. 238 cm²

D. 476 cm²

Use the following information to answer the next question.

Jenny wants to renovate her office by covering her desk with a slab of marble. Her desk is composed of 3 identical parts, as shown in the given diagram.

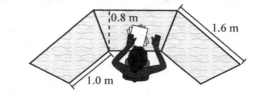

235. How much marble, to the nearest hundredth, will Jenny have to purchase in order to cover her entire desk? _____ m²

Use the following information to answer the next question.

A shape is given.

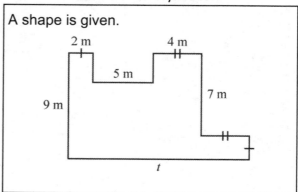

236. What is the length of side t? _____ m

The floor of a room contains 8 square tiles. Each square tile has a side length of 4 m.

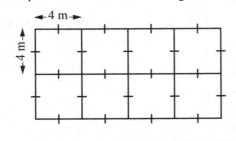

237. What is the total area of the tiled floor?

    A. 128 m^2 B. 130 m^2

    C. 132 m^2 D. 140 m^2

EXERCISE #2—GEOMETRY ANSWERS AND SOLUTIONS

194. 3	205. D	216. See solution	227. 29
195. B	206. See solution	217. See solution	228. See solution
196. C	207. B	218. B	229. D
197. C	208. C	219. See solution	230. See solution
198. B	209. D	220. D	231. 7
199. D	210. A	221. C	232. B
200. B	211. B	222. B	233. C
201. See solution	212. 105	223. See solution	234. C
202. See solution	213. B	224. D	235. 3.12
203. C	214. A	225. A	236. 15
204. B	215. D	226. A	237. A

194. 3

Step 1
Determine the height of the original shape.
The tomato plant is 75 cm tall.

Step 2
Use the formula for scale factor to find the height of the image.

The scale factor can be written as a fraction of $\frac{1}{25}$.

Set up a proportion.

scale factor = $\frac{\text{image length}}{\text{original length}}$

$$\frac{1}{25} = \frac{x}{75}$$
$$25x = 75$$
$$\frac{25x}{25} = \frac{75}{25}$$
$$x = 3$$

The tomato plant in the diagram is 3 cm high.

195. B

The scale the boys used for their drawing says that 1 square equals 1 ft², which means that each side of a square is equal to 1 ft.

Since the window in the scale drawing is 6 squares long, the length of the window is 6 ft.

196. C

From the diagram the radius of circle C is 2 units, and the radius of circle D is 6 units.

The scale factor can be determined by finding the ratio of the corresponding radii. Because the transformation from circle C to circle D is an enlargement, the scale factor is greater than one.

Scale factor = $\frac{\text{image length}}{\text{original length}}$
$$= \frac{6}{2}$$
$$= 3$$

197. C

Use the formula $A_2 = A_1 \times (\text{scale factor})^2$.

Substitute 260 for A_1 and 2.2 for the scale factor.

$$A_2 = A_1 \times (\text{scale factor})^2$$
$$A_2 = 260 \times (2.2)^2$$
$$A_2 = 260 \times 4.84$$
$$A_2 = 1,258.4$$
$$A_2 \approx 1,258 \text{ cm}^2$$

Rounded to the nearest whole number, Vickie's new irregular polygon will have an area of 1,258 cm².

198. B

Step 1
Determine what angle measures are given.
In the given triangle, $\angle B = 57°$ and $\angle C = 29°$.

Step 2

Substitute the given values into the formula for the angle property for a triangle, and simplify.

$\angle A + \angle B + \angle C = 180°$
$\angle A + 57° + 29° = 180°$
$\angle A + 86° = 180°$
$\angle A + 86° - 86° = 180° - 86°$
$\angle A = 94°$

The measure of $\angle A = 94°$.

199. D

Step 1

Calculate the minimum length by finding the difference between the lengths of the two known sides.

Subtract 5 from 9.

$8 - 5 = 4$

This means that x has to be greater than 4.

Step 2

Calculate the maximum length by finding the sum of the lengths of the two known sides.

Add 5 and 9.

$5 + 9 = 14$

This means that x has to be less than 14.

The length of x has to be between 4 and 14.

The length cannot be 16.

200. B

Remember that the length of each side of a triangle must be less than the sum of the lengths of the other two sides of the triangle.

Step 1

Determine if 2 cm is a possible side length for the third side of the given triangle.

Since 10 cm is greater than the sum of 2 cm and 7 cm, 2 cm is not a possible side length for the third side of the triangle.

Step 2

Determine if 11 cm is a possible side length for the third side of the given triangle.

Since 7 cm is less than the sum of 10 cm and 11 cm, 10 cm is less than the sum of 7 cm and 11 cm, and 11 cm is less than the sum of 7 cm and 10 cm, 11 cm is a possible side length for the third side of the given triangle.

Step 3

Determine if 17 cm is a possible side length for the third side of the given triangle.

Since 17 cm is equal to, but not less than, the sum of 7 cm and 10 cm, 17 cm is not a possible side length for the third side of the given triangle.

Step 4

Determine if 19 cm is a possible side length for the third side of the given triangle.

Since 19 cm is greater than the sum of 7 cm and 10 cm, 19 cm is not a possible side length for the third side of the given triangle.

Therefore, from the given choices, only 11 cm is a possible side length for the third side of the given triangle.

201.

Step 1

Draw and label a line that is 12 cm long.

Step 2

Draw and label an angle of 115° at the end of the 12 cm line.

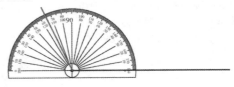

Step 3

Place a mark on the new line 7 cm away from the vertex of the angle.

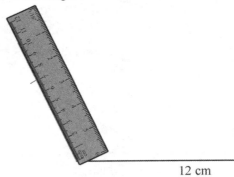

12 cm

Step 4

Draw a line from the right end of the 12 cm line to the mark on the 7 cm line.

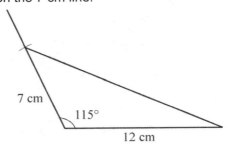

7 cm

115°

12 cm

202.

Step 1

Use a ruler to draw a line that is 5.8 cm long.

Step 2

Use a protractor to draw a 25° angle at one end of the 5.8 cm line.

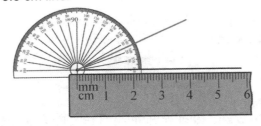

Step 3

Use a protractor to draw a 100° angle at the other end of the 5.8 cm line.

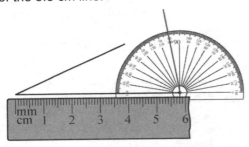

If the lines do not meet, extend them until they cross to complete the triangle.

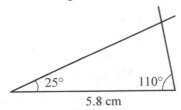

25°   110°

5.8 cm

203. C

A triangle has three sides. You need to find the plane section that intersects the prism along three edges.

Plane sections A, B, and D all intersect four edges of the prism. Only plane section C intersects the prism along three edges.

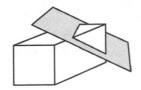

204. B

Step 1

Use the formula describing the relationship between the radius and the circumference of a circle to determine the radii of the three circles.

The circumference of a circle, C, with a radius of r is given by the formula $C = 2\pi r$.

Rearrange the formula to solve for r.

$$r = \frac{C}{2\pi}$$

Use the formula to determine the relationship between R, R_1, R_2 and L, L_1, L_2.

$$R = \frac{L}{2\pi}$$

$$R_1 = \frac{L_1}{2\pi}$$

$$R_2 = \frac{L_2}{2\pi}$$

Step 2

The circumference of the largest circle is equal to the sum of the circumferences of the other two circles.

$$L = L_1 + L_2$$

Divide both sides of the equation by 2π.

$$L = L_1 + L_2$$
$$\frac{L}{2\pi} = \frac{L_1 + L_2}{2\pi}$$
$$= \frac{L_1}{2\pi} + \frac{L_2}{2\pi}$$
$$R = R_1 + R_2$$

Therefore, the equation that represents the relationship between R, R_1, and R_2 is $R = R_1 + R_2$.

205. D

The formula used to calculate the area of a circle is $A = \pi r^2$.

The value of π is approximately 3.14. When estimating the area of grass the sprinkler covers, multiply the square of the radius by 3.

$$A = \pi \times r^2$$
$$= 3 \times (3)^2$$
$$= 3 \times 9$$
$$= 27 \text{ m}^2$$

Hera's sprinkler can cover approximately 27 m² of grass.

206.

Step 1

Choose the appropriate formula using the given values.

The question is asking for circumference and gives the radius.

$C = 2\pi r$

Step 2

Substitute in the known values.

In this case, the radius r is 25 cm and the value of π is 3.14.

$C = 2\pi r$
$\quad = 2(3.14)(25)$

Step 3

Solve for the unknown.

$C = 2\pi r$
$\quad = 2(3.14)(25)$
$\quad = 157$

The tire travels about 157 cm in one revolution.

207. B

Step 1

Use the formula for the circumference of a circle. The circumference (C) of a circle is given by the formula $C = 2\pi r$, where r is the radius of the circle. Substitute 219 for C and 3.14 for π.

$\quad C = 2\pi r$
$219 \approx 2 \times 3.14 \times r$

Step 2

Simplify.
$219 \approx 2 \times 3.14 \times r$
$219 \approx 6.28 \times r$
Divide each side by 6.28.
$\dfrac{219}{6.28} \approx r$
$\quad r \approx 34.8726 \ldots$

Step 3

Round to the nearest centimeter.

The digit at the tenths place is 8, which is greater than 5. Therefore, round up.

$34.8726 \ldots \rightarrow 35$

To the nearest centimeter, the radius of the wheel is 35 cm.

208. C

Step 1

Determine the radius.

If the diameter of the motorcycle's rear wheel is 60 cm, then the radius is
$60 \div 2 = 30$

Step 2

Use the area formula for a circle, substitute the known value for r, and solve.

$A_{circle} = \pi r^2$
$\quad\quad = 3.14(30)^2$
$\quad\quad = 2{,}826 \text{ cm}^2$

The area of the motorcycle's rear wheel, to the nearest ten, is 2,830 cm².

209. D

To calculate the distance that Lyle ran around the circular track, use the circumference formula for a circle, substitute in the known value for d, and solve.

$C = \pi d$
$C = \pi(42)$
$C = 131.88$

$C = 132$, rounded to the nearest meter. To calculate the distance covered in two laps, multiply the circumference by 2.

$2 \times 132 = 264$

Thus, Lyle will have traveled a distance of 264 m.

210. A

The sum of two complementary angles is equal to 90°.

To find the other angle, subtract the first angle (35°) from 90°.

$90° - 35° = 55°$

The value of the second angle is 55°.

211. B

In the given diagram, $\angle n$ is vertically opposite the angle measuring 75°.

Since vertically opposite angles have the same measure, $\angle n = 75°$.

212. 105

Two angles on a straight line have a sum of 180°. Angles ADC and CDB make a straight line, so their sum is 180°.

The measure of $\angle CDB$ is 75°, so $\angle ADC$ is
$180° - 75° = 105°$.

The measure of the missing angle is 105°.

213. B

Complementary angles are two angles whose measures have a sum of 90°.

Add each of the pairs of angles to determine which pair is complementary.

- $45 + 35 = 80 \neq 90$
- $50 + 40 = 90$
- $60 + 20 = 80 \neq 90$
- $65 + 35 = 100 \neq 90$

Therefore, 50° and 40° form a pair of complementary angles.

214. A

Angles C and D are complementary angles, not supplementary angles, because they add up to 90°. Angle E is a right angle and could only be supplementary to another right angle and not angle A.

Angles A and C are opposite angles; these would be supplementary only if they were both right angles. Angles A and B are supplementary to each other because they add up to 180° and form a straight line.

215. D

Step 1
Join the two cubes.

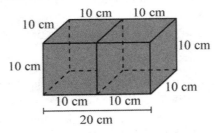

The resulting shape is a rectangular prism.

Step 2
From the figure, determine the measurements of the prism.
The length is 20 cm, the width is 10 cm, and the height is 10 cm.

Step 3
Calculate the area of the faces.
Find the area for one face, and multiply it by 2 because the measures of the two faces are the same.

$A_{\text{top and bottom}} = 2(20 \times 10)$
$= 400$

$A_{\text{front and back}} = 2(10 \times 20)$
$= 400$

$A_{\text{sides}} = 2(10 \times 10)$
$= 200$

Step 4
Add the areas of the faces.
$SA = A_{\text{top and bottom}} + A_{\text{front and back}} + A_{\text{sides}}$
$= 400 + 400 + 200$
$= 1{,}000$
The surface area of the resulting shape is 1,000 cm^2.

216.

Step 1
Determine the areas of the three rectangular faces using the formula $A = l \times w$. Substitute the numbers for the appropriate lengths and widths into the formula.

- $12 \text{ cm} \times 3 \text{ cm} = 36 \text{ cm}^2$
- $12 \text{ cm} \times 4 \text{ cm} = 48 \text{ cm}^2$
- $12 \text{ cm} \times 5 \text{ cm} = 60 \text{ cm}^2$

Determine the combined area of the three rectangular faces.
$36 \text{ cm}^2 + 48 \text{ cm}^2 + 60 \text{ cm}^2 = 144 \text{ cm}^2$

Step 2
Determine the area of the triangular base using the formula $A = \frac{1}{2}(b \times h)$. Substitute the numbers for the base (3 cm) and the height (4 cm) of the triangular prism into the formula.

$A = \frac{1}{2}(3 \text{ cm} \times 4 \text{ cm}) = 6 \text{ cm}^2$

Since there are two triangular bases, multiply the area by 2.
$6 \text{ cm}^2 \times 2 = 12 \text{ cm}^2$

Step 3
Determine the surface area by adding the combined areas of the three rectangular faces and two triangular bases.
$144 \text{ cm}^2 + 12 \text{ cm}^2 = 156 \text{ cm}^2$

217.

The shape of the base is a rectangle. The height is the distance between two parallel base faces.

$V_{\text{rectangular base}} = A_{\text{base}} \times h$
$V_{\text{rectangular base}} = A_{\text{rectangle}} \times h$
$\qquad = (l \times w) \times h$
$\qquad = 13 \times 7 \times 5$
$\qquad = 455 \text{ m}^3$

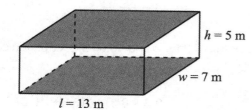

$h = 5 \text{ m}$
$w = 7 \text{ m}$
$l = 13 \text{ m}$

218. B

To determine the volume of the triangular prism, use the formula $V = A \times h$. In this formula, A refers to the area of the triangular base and h refers to the height of the triangular prism (11 cm).

Step 1
Determine the area of the triangular base.

Use the formula $A = \dfrac{\text{base} \times \text{height}}{2}$.

Substitute the numbers for the length of the triangular base (6 cm) and the height of the triangular base (8 cm) into the formula.

$A = \dfrac{6 \times 8}{2} = \dfrac{48}{2} = 24 \text{ cm}^2$

The area of the triangular base is 24 cm².

Step 2
Determine the volume of the triangular prism.
Use the formula V = area of base × height of prism.
Substitute the area of the base (24 cm²) and the height of the prism (11 cm) into the formula.

$V = 24 \text{ cm}^2 \times 11 \text{ cm} = 264 \text{ cm}^3$

The volume of the triangular prism is 264 cm³.

219.

You can find the volume of the triangular prism by using one of two methods.

Method 1
Find the area of the rectangular prism with the same dimensions, and divide by 2.

$V = \dfrac{lwh}{2}$

$V = \dfrac{6 \times 7 \times 3}{2}$

$V = \dfrac{126}{2}$

$V = 63 \text{ cm}^3$

Method 2
Find the area of the triangular base, and multiply that area by the height of the prism.

$V = Bh$

$V = \dfrac{6 \times 3}{2} \times 7$

$V = \dfrac{18}{2} \times 7$

$V = 9 \times 7$

$V = 63 \text{ cm}^3$

220. D

If triangle ADO was translated to the right side of the parallelogram, the parallelogram would be transformed into a rectangle.

Therefore, you can use a formula for the area of a rectangle to determine the area of the parallelogram.

One formula for determining the area of a rectangle or parallelogram is $A = b \times h$.

Substitute the appropriate numbers for the base and the height.

$A = 10 \text{ cm} \times 5 \text{ cm} = 50 \text{ cm}^2$

The area of the parallelogram is 50 cm².

221. C

Base of the triangle = 4 m
Height of the triangle = 6 m

The area of a triangle = $\dfrac{1}{2}$ × base × height

$A = \dfrac{1}{2} \times 4 \text{ m} \times 6 \text{ m}$

$A = \dfrac{1}{2} \times 24 \text{ m}^2$

$A = 12 \text{ m}^2$

222. B

Step 1

Draw the net of the shape.

A right trapezoidal prism is made up of four rectangular faces (front, bottom, back, and top in the diagram) that join the two trapezoidal bases (sides).

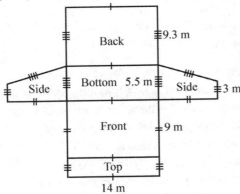

Step 2

Calculate the area of each face.

Solve for the area of each face by applying the appropriate formula.

$$A_{sides} = h(b_1 + b_2)$$
$$= 9(3 + 5.5)$$
$$= 9(8.5)$$
$$= 76.5 \text{ m}^2$$

$$A_{front} = lw$$
$$= (14)(3)$$
$$= 42 \text{ m}^2$$

$$A_{bottom} = lw$$
$$= (14)(9)$$
$$= 126 \text{ m}^2$$

$$A_{back} = lw$$
$$= (14)(5.5)$$
$$= 77 \text{ m}^2$$

$$A_{top} = lw$$
$$= (14)(9.3)$$
$$= 130.2 \text{ m}^2$$

Step 3

Add the areas of the faces.

$$SA_{trapezoidal \ prism}$$
$$= A_{sides} + A_{front} + A_{bottom} + A_{back} + A_{top}$$
$$= 76.5 + 42 + 126 + 77 + 130.2$$
$$= 451.7 \text{ m}^2$$

The surface area of the trapezoidal prism is 451.7 m².

223.

The formula used to calculate the surface area of a square-based pyramid is $SA = b^2 + 2(bs)$.

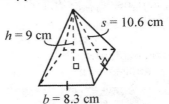

Substitute 8.3 for b and 10.6 for s, and then simplify.

$$SA_{square \ prism} = b^2 + 2(bs)$$
$$= (8.3)^2 + 2(8.3 \times 10.6)$$
$$= (8.3 \times 8.3) + 2(8.3 \times 10.6)$$
$$= (68.89) + 2(87.98)$$
$$= 68.89 + 175.96$$
$$= 244.85$$
$$\approx 244.9 \text{cm}^2$$

224. D

$$A_{trapezoid} = A_{triangle} + A_{rectangle}$$

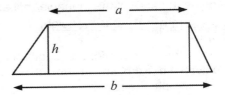

The base of the triangle is equal to $b - a$, and the height of the triangle is equal to h. The base of the rectangle is equal to a, and the height of the rectangle is equal to h. Add together and simplify the formula for the area of a triangle and the formula for area of a rectangle to find the formula for the area of a trapezoid.

$$A_{trapezoid} = \frac{(b-a)h}{2} + ah$$
$$= \frac{(b-a)h}{2} + \frac{2ah}{2}$$
$$= \frac{(b-a)h + 2ah}{2}$$
$$= \frac{1}{2}[(b-a)h + 2ah]$$
$$= \frac{1}{2}h(b - a + 2a)$$
$$= \frac{1}{2}h(b + a)$$
$$= \frac{h}{2}(b + a)$$

225. A

The skateboard ramp is in the shape of a triangular prism. In order to determine its volume, it is necessary to consider one of the triangular faces as the base of the ramp.

Step 1

Determine an expression for the area of the base of the ramp by applying the formula for the area of a triangle, $A = \dfrac{bh}{2}$.

Substitute 5 for b and x for h, and then simplify as follows:

$A = \dfrac{bh}{2}$

$A = \dfrac{5 \times x}{2}$

$A = 2.5x$

Step 2

Solve for x by applying the formula for the volume of a triangular prism, $V = A_{base} \times h$.

Substitute $2.5x$ for A_{base}, 16 for h, and 136 for V, and then solve for x as follows:

$V = A_{base} \times h$

$136 = (2.5x)(16)$

$136 = 40x$

$3.4 = x$

The value of x is 3.4 m.

226. A

Step 1

Calculate the area of each face.

In the diagram, the following faces are the same size: the top and the bottom, the front and the back, and the two sides.

Therefore, the area of each of these pairs of faces can be found by calculating the area of one face and multiplying by 2.

$A_{front\ and\ back} = 2(lw)$
$= 2(30 \times 5)$
$= 2(150)$
$= 300\ cm^2$

$A_{sides} = 2(lw)$
$= 2(5 \times 20)$
$= 2(100)$
$= 200\ cm^2$

$A_{top\ and\ bottom} = 2(lw)$
$= 2(30 \times 20)$
$= 2(600)$
$= 1,200\ cm^2$

Step 2

Calculate the total surface area.

Add the areas of the faces.

$SA_{rectangular\ prism}$
$= A_{top\ and\ bottom} + A_{sides} + A_{front\ and\ back}$
$= 1,200 + 200 + 300$
$= 1,700\ cm^2$

The surface area of Jason's cake is 1,700 cm².

227. 29

The lining must cover the total surface area of the tent, excluding the bottom rectangular face.

Step 1

Draw the net of the triangular prism.

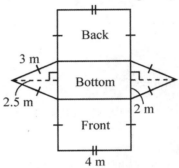

Step 2

Calculate the area of the faces of the tent.

The front and back rectangular faces of the net are the same size. The two triangular sides are the same size as well.

Find the area for one of each face shape and multiply by 2.

$A_{front\ and\ back} = 2(l \times w)$
$= 2(4 \times 3)$
$= 2(12)$
$= 24$

$A_{triangles} = 2\left(\dfrac{bh}{2}\right)$
$= (2)\left(\dfrac{2 \times 2.5}{2}\right)$
$= 2(2.5)$
$= 5$

Step 3

Calculate the total surface area.

$SA_{tent} = A_{front\ and\ back} + A_{triangles}$
$= 24 + 5$
$= 29\ m^2$

The amount of lining needed to cover the outside of the tent is 29 m².

228.

Step 1

Determine the given values.

The base is the length of the horizontal line:
$b = 7.6$ m

The area is 19 m².

Step 2

Substitute the known values into the area formula, and solve for the unknown measure.

$$A_{\text{triangle}} = \frac{b \times h}{2}$$

$$19 = \frac{7.6 \times h}{2}$$

$$2 \times 19 = \frac{7.6 \times h}{2} \times 2$$

$$38 = 7.6 \times h$$

$$\frac{38}{7.6} = \frac{7.6 \times h}{7.6}$$

$$5 = h$$

The height of the triangle is 5 m.

229. D

Step 1

Determine the given values.

All four sides of the rhombus are congruent. Therefore, the base, or length, of the parallelogram is 13.5 cm.

The height is shown on the rhombus where the dotted line forms a square corner to the base. Therefore, the height of the rhombus is 11 cm.

Step 2

Use the area formula for a rhombus.

Substitute 13.5 cm for the base and 11 cm for the height.

$$A = b \times h$$
$$= 13.5 \times 11$$
$$= 148.5$$

Therefore, the area of the rhombus is 148.5 cm².

230.

To determine the width of the rectangle, use the formula for area, substituting the appropriate numbers for the area (108 m²) and for the length (15 m).

$$A = l \times w$$
$$108 \text{ cm}^2 = 15 \times w$$
$$108 \div 15 = w$$
$$7.2 = w$$

Be sure to include the appropriate unit of measure with your answer.

The width of the rectangle is 7.2 m.

231. 7

Step 1

Determine what is being asked.

The question is asking how many times 4,000 cm³ of water will need to go into the fish tank in order to fill it.

Step 2

Make a plan.

First, find the volume of the fish tank.

Next, find out how many jugs of water are needed by dividing the volume of the fish tank by the volume of the jug.

Step 3

Solve the problem.

Calculate the volume of the fish tank.

$$V = l \times w \times h$$
$$= 35 \times 25 \times 32$$
$$= 28,000$$

The fish tank holds 28,000 cm³ of water.

Calculate the number of jugs of water needed to fill the tank by dividing the volume of the fish tank by the volume of the jug.

$$\text{jugs needed} = \frac{V_{\text{fish tank}}}{V_{\text{jug}}}$$
$$= \frac{28,000}{4,000}$$
$$= 7$$

Step 4

Decide if your answer is reasonable.

Use estimation to check the answer.

Estimate the volume of the fish tank that is 35 cm long, 25 cm wide, and 32 cm tall.

Since both the numbers 35 and 25 have digits that are in the middle for rounding, one number will be rounded up and the other number will be rounded down to make the estimation more balanced.

Thus, 35 will be rounded up to 40, and 25 will be rounded down to 20. Round 32 down to 30.

The estimated volume of the fish tank will be $40 \times 20 \times 30 = 24,000$.

The division of the estimated fish tank volume by the jug of water volume is $\frac{24,000}{4,000} = 6$. This is very close to the original calculation, so the answer is reasonable.

Since 7 jugs of water are needed to fill the tank, Richard will need to make 7 trips to the sink.

232. B

Step 1
Calculate the volume of each prism.

$V = l \times w \times h$

Volume of the cube:

$2 \times 2 \times 2 = 8$ cm^3

Volume of the rectangular prism:

$6 \times 4 \times 2 = 48$ cm^3

Step 2
Add the two volumes.

$48 + 8 = 56$

The total volume of the given figure is 56 cm^3.

233. C

The surface area, SA, of a pyramid can be determined by applying the formula

$SA = A_{base} + A_{lateral\ faces}$, where A_{base} is the area of the base and $A_{lateral\ faces}$ is the area of the lateral faces.

Step 1
Determine the area of the base of the Christmas tree ornament.

Since the base of the ornament is in the shape of a rectangle, the area, A, of the base can be determined by applying the formula $A = lw$, where l is the length and w is the width of the rectangle.

$A = lw$

Substitute 2.48 for l and 2.24 for w, and then solve for A.

$A = 2.48 \times 2.24$

$A = 5.5552$ cm^2

Step 2
Determine the area of the lateral faces of the Christmas tree ornament.

Two of the lateral faces are triangular in shape, have bases that are 2.48 cm long, and have slant heights of 3.96 cm.

The other two lateral faces are triangular in shape, have bases that are 2.24 cm long, and have slant heights of 4 cm.

The area of each triangle can be determined by applying the formula $A = \frac{1}{2}bh$, where b is the length of the base and h is the slant height.

If A_1 is the area of the two lateral faces that have 2.48 cm bases and A_2 is the area of the two lateral faces that have 2.24 cm bases, then the area, A, of the lateral faces of the Christmas tree ornament can be determined as follows:

$A = A_1 + A_2$

$A = 2\left(\frac{1}{2}bh\right) + 2\left(\frac{1}{2}bh\right)$

$A = \left(\begin{array}{l} 2\left(\frac{1}{2} \times 2.48 \times 3.96\right) \\ + 2\left(\frac{1}{2} \times 2.24 \times 4\right) \end{array}\right)$

$A = 2(4.9104) + 2(4.48)$

$A = 9.8208 + 8.96$

$A = 18.7808$ cm^2

Step 3
Determine the surface area of the Christmas tree ornament.

Apply the formula $SA = A_{base} + A_{lateral\ faces}$.

Substitute 5.5552 for A_{base} and 18.7808 for $A_{lateral\ faces}$.

$SA = 5.5552 + 18.7808$

$SA = 24.336$

To the nearest whole number, the surface area of the Christmas tree ornament is 24 cm^2.

Copyright Protected

234. C

Method 1

Break the octagon into smaller shapes.

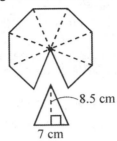

8.5 cm

7 cm

Use the formula for area to find the area of one triangle.

$$A = \frac{1}{2}bh$$
$$= \frac{1}{2}(7 \text{ cm})(8.5 \text{ cm})$$
$$= 29.75 \text{ cm}^2$$

Multiply the area by 8 because there are eight small triangles.

$29.75 \text{ cm}^2 \times 8 = 238 \text{ cm}^2$

Method 2

Use the formula for finding the area of regular shapes $A = \frac{1}{2}nsa$, where n is the number of sides, s is the side length, and a is the apothem.

The number of sides is 8, the side length is 7, and the apothem is 8.5.

$$A = \frac{1}{2}nsa$$
$$= \frac{1}{2}(8)(7 \text{ cm})(8.5 \text{ cm})$$
$$= 238 \text{ cm}^2$$

235. 3.12

To find the amount of marble required, first find the area of each part of the desk. Since each part is shaped like a trapezoid, you can use the area formula for a trapezoid, $A = \frac{1}{2}(a+b)h$, where a and b represent parallel sides, and h represents the height between the a and b. The area of one part of the desk can then be multiplied by 3 to find the area of the entire desk.

Step 1

Determine the values of a, b, and h.

Since the three parts of the desk are identical, the dimensions for each part will be the same.
Therefore, the values of a and b are 1.0 m and 1.6 m, respectively, and the value of h is 0.8 m.

Step 2

Determine the area of one trapezoidal part of the desk.

Substitute 1.0 for a, 1.6 for b, and 0.8 for h into the area formula, $A = \frac{1}{2}(a+b)h$.

$$A = \frac{1}{2}(a+b)h$$
$$A = \frac{1}{2}(1.0 + 1.6) \times 0.8$$
$$A = \frac{1}{2}(2.6) \times 0.8$$
$$A = 1.3 \times 0.8$$
$$A = 1.04$$

The area of one part of the desk is 1.04 m².

Step 3

Find the amount of marble needed for the entire desk.

Multiply the area of one part by 3.
$1.04 \times 3 = 3.12$
The total amount of marble that Jenny needs to purchase in order to cover the entire desk is 3.12 m².

236. 15

Step 1

Look at the diagram.
The length of the long side on the bottom is equal to the sum of all the shorter opposite sides.

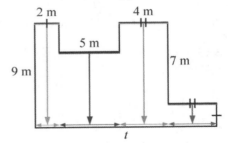

2 m   4 m

5 m

9 m   7 m

t

Step 2

Find the missing side length along the top of the shape.

The side with the missing length has two ticks on it. The other side with two ticks on it has a length of 4 m. This means that the missing side length is 4 m.

Step 3

Find the length of side t.

The sides that are opposite m have lengths of 2 m, 5 m, 4 m, and 4 m.
$2 + 5 + 4 + 4 = 15$
Side t has a length of 15 m.

237. A

Step 1

Determine the length and width of the tiled floor.
The length of the tiled floor is 16 m.
$4 \text{ m} \times 4 = 16 \text{ m}$
The width of the tiled floor is 8 m.
$4 \text{ m} \times 2 = 8 \text{ m}$

Step 2

Calculate the area of the tiled floor.
$A = l \times w$

$A = 16 \times 8 = 128 \text{ m}^2$

The total area of the floor covered by the tiles is 128 m^2.

NOTES

Statistics and Probability

STATISTICS AND PROBABILITY

Table of Correlations

Standard		Concepts	Exercise #1	Exercise #2
7.SP	Statistics and Probability			
7.SP.1	*Understand that statistics can be used to gain information about a population by examining a sample of the population; generalizations about a population from a sample are valid only if the sample is representative of that population. Understand that random sampling tends to produce representative samples and support valid inferences.*	Using Populations in Investigations	238	255
		Determining if a Sample Accurately Represents the Population	239	257
		Significance of Sample Size in Interpreting Data	240	256
7.SP.2	*Use data from a random sample to draw inferences about a population with an unknown characteristic of interest. Generate multiple samples (or simulated samples) of the same size to gauge the variation in estimates or predictions.*	Significance of Sample Size in Interpreting Data	240	256
		Making Inferences	241	
7.SP.3	*Informally assess the degree of visual overlap of two numerical data distributions with similar variabilities, measuring the difference between the centers by expressing it as a multiple of a measure of variability.*	Comparing Two Sets of Data Using a Box-and-Whisker Plot	242	258
7.SP.4	*Use measures of center and measures of variability for numerical data from random samples to draw informal comparative inferences about two populations.*	Calculating Mean	243	259
		Calculating Median	244	260
		Calculating Mode	245	261
		Calculating Range	246	262
		Compare Two Related Sets of Data	247	263
7.SP.5	*Understand that the probability of a chance event is a number between 0 and 1 that expresses the likelihood of the event occurring. Larger numbers indicate greater likelihood. A probability near 0 indicates an unlikely event, a probability around 1/2 indicates an event that is neither unlikely nor likely, and a probability near 1 indicates a likely event.*	Understanding Probability as a Number between 0 and 1	248	264
7.SP.6	*Approximate the probability of a chance event by collecting data on the chance process that produces it and observing its long–run relative frequency, and predict the approximate relative frequency given the probability.*	Experimental Probability	249	265
		Predict the Frequency of an Outcome	250	266

7.SP. 7A	Develop a probability model and use it to find probabilities of events. Compare probabilities from a model to observed frequencies; if the agreement is not good, explain possible sources of the discrepancy. Develop a uniform probability model by assigning equal probability to all outcomes, and use the model to determine probabilities of events.	Comparing Theoretical Probability with Experimental Probability	249, 251	267
7.SP. 7B	Develop a probability model and use it to find probabilities of events. Compare probabilities from a model to observed frequencies; if the agreement is not good, explain possible sources of the discrepancy. Develop a probability model (which may not be uniform) by observing frequencies in data generated from a chance process.	Experimental Probability	249	265
		Comparing Theoretical Probability with Experimental Probability	249, 251	267
7.SP. 8A	Find probabilities of compound events using organized lists, tables, tree diagrams, and simulation. Understand that, just as with simple events, the probability of a compound event is the fraction of outcomes in the sample space for which the compound event occurs.	Identifying Sample Space for Two Independent Events	252	268
		Calculating the Probability of Two Independent Events	253	269
7.SP. 8B	Find probabilities of compound events using organized lists, tables, tree diagrams, and simulation. Represent sample spaces for compound events using methods such as organized lists, tables and tree diagrams. For an event described in everyday language, identify the outcomes in the sample space which compose the event.	Identifying Sample Space for Two Independent Events	252	268
7.SP. 8C	Find probabilities of compound events using organized lists, tables, tree diagrams, and simulation. Design and use a simulation to generate frequencies for compound events.	Using Different Models to Simulate an Event	254	270

7.SP.1 Understand that statistics can be used to gain information about a population by examining a sample of the population; generalizations about a population from a sample are valid only if the sample is representative of that population. Understand that random sampling tends to produce representative samples and support valid inferences.

USING POPULATIONS IN INVESTIGATIONS

A **population** can be defined as all the items, objects, or people being considered in an investigation. For example, all the parents in a school district are asked their opinion on a year-round schooling policy. All the parents in the school district make up the population for the investigation.

Surveying an entire population will produce more accurate results because everyone in the population has the opportunity to contribute his or her opinions.

However, depending on the nature of the investigation, surveying the entire population may take up too much time and cost too much money.

Example

A coffee shop owner would like to know if customers would use pre-paid coffee cards to make coffee purchases instead of counting change every time they purchase a coffee. The owner decides to give a complimentary ten-dollar gift card to every customer for a one-week period. Then, he will record how often they use the coffee card.

Is is reasonable to use a population in this investigation?

Solution

The population for this investigation could be enormous, seeing that many people drink coffee each day, sometimes several cups of coffee a day. If people found out that a coffee shop was giving away complimentary gift cards, they would probably frequent that coffee shop numerous times in hopes of receiving a complimentary gift card. This would cause the collected data to contain a bias because a gift is being used to promote the collection of data and would end up costing the coffee shop owner more money than he may have anticipated.

It would not be reasonable to use a population in this investigation because the population would be limited only to the people who visit that coffee shop.

Example

The manager of a software company wants to build a workout facility in the office building. He wants to find out what percentage of his 150 employees would be interested in using this service. He sends out an interoffice email survey to ask his employees for their opinions.

Is it reasonable to use a population in this investigation?

Solution

Since the manager is considering building an expensive addition in the office building, he should make sure that a majority of his employees will use the facility. In order to do this, it makes sense to ask every employee their opinion since there are not too many to survey. By using an interoffice email survey, the cost of conducting the investigation will be relatively low and the time it takes to conduct the survey will be low as well.

In this investigation, using a population would be a suitable option.

DETERMINING IF A SAMPLE ACCURATELY REPRESENTS THE POPULATION

A **sample** is a smaller portion of an entire **population**. Surveying a population can be very costly, impractical, and time consuming. Surveying a sample of a population is an easier way to collect data.

A good sample is taken using a sampling method that is appropriate to the investigation. A good sample will also be proportionate to the population, meaning that a large sample should be taken if the population is large, and a smaller sample is sufficient if the population is small. A sample should also be free of **bias**, as bias will lead to inaccurate results.

Example

A high school counselor is organizing a volunteer fair. She surveys students to see what their interests are regarding volunteering for local non-profit organizations. There are 100 students in each of the grades 10, 11, and 12. The counselor decides to survey 33 students from each grade using systematic sampling. The results of her survey indicate that 68% of the students surveyed would like to volunteer for an organization that helps animals. Based on these results, the counselor decides to dedicate most of the volunteer fair to animal-welfare organizations.

Explain whether or not the sample represents the views of the population accurately.

Solution

In the counselor's survey, each of the grades is represented fairly, with 33% of the students in each grade being surveyed. This sample represents the views of the population accurately because each grade is being represented equally and fairly.

Sometimes, the data collected from a sample does not accurately reflect the population. In these cases, the data collected is considered not to be valid.

Example

A camp counselor is deciding what movie to play for movie night. There are 300 campers ranging in age from 9 to 15 years old. The camp counselor decides to ask the first 20 campers who walk into the dining hall that night what movie they would like to watch.

Explain whether or not the sample represents the views of the population accurately.

Solution

The sample is not representative of the population because the campers' ages range from 9 to 15 years old. The first 20 campers who walk into the dining hall will not necessarily provide an accurate representation of all the age groups. If the first 20 campers are all between the ages of 13 and 15, then the preferences of the 9-, 10-, 11-, and 12-year olds will not be represented in the survey.

SIGNIFICANCE OF SAMPLE SIZE IN INTERPRETING DATA

Sample size refers to the number of people, objects, or items used in an investigation.

Determining the sample size to use in an investigation is an important aspect of data collection. The sample size chosen should be representative of the population. If the population is relatively small, the sample size can be smaller. If the population is large, the sample size should be larger as well.

The main goal of determining a sample size is to represent the population fairly and accurately. If the sample size is large, the collected data will be more accurate because it takes into account many more opinions. The more opinions you have, the more accurate the conclusions will be. If the sample size is too small, the data collected may lead to misleading or inaccurate results. A small sample does not guarantee that all views are represented. The sample must be large enough to ensure that the sample data does not differ significantly from the corresponding population data.

Example

Portia and Aneesh attend a junior high school for students in grades 7, 8, and 9.

Portia surveys the students in her seventh grade math class and finds that 76% of them use text messaging as a form of communication. She concludes that 76% of the students in the school use text messaging as a form of communication.

Aneesh surveys 30% of the students in each of the grades 7, 8, and 9 and finds that 63% of them use text messaging as a form of communication. He concludes that 63% of the students in the school use text messaging as a form of communication.

Whose conclusion is more accurate?

Solution

Both Portia and Aneesh are using samples of the population in their investigations.

Portia is only sampling the students in her math class and making conclusions about the entire student population. Her sample size is much smaller than Aneesh's.

Aneesh surveys a sample that is representative of all the grades. His sample size is much larger. His conclusions about using text messaging as a form of communication are more accurate because his sample size is larger and covers a broader range of ages than Portia's. He can take into account many more opinions regarding the use of text messaging.

7.SP.2 Use data from a random sample to draw inferences about a population with an unknown characteristic of interest. Generate multiple samples (or simulated samples) of the same size to gauge the variation in estimates or predictions.

MAKING INFERENCES

After sampling has been completed and the gathered information has been organized, the information can be used to make inferences, or predictions, about characteristics of a certain population.

Example

A sample of families was surveyed regarding the number of pets each family owns.

Number of Pets	Percentage of Families (%)
0	20
1	23
2	22
3	15
4	12
5+	8

Explain whether or not it can be inferred that the majority of families surveyed have pets at home.

Solution

Of the families surveyed, 80% have one or more pets. This is clearly a majority.

Explain whether or not it can be inferred that 20% of families surveyed do not like animals.

Solution

Just because a family does not have a pet does not mean that they dislike animals. There may be other reasons a family does not have pets, such as allergies, lack of space, etc.

Explain whether or not it can be inferred that not very many of the families surveyed have five or more pets because they do not have enough space at home.

Solution

A lack of space at home is not necessarily the reason that not very many families have five or more pets. Other factors could prevent families from owning more pets, such as the cost of owning and caring for many pets.

7.SP.3 Informally assess the degree of visual overlap of two numerical data distributions with similar variabilities, measuring the difference between the centers by expressing it as a multiple of a measure of variability.

COMPARING TWO SETS OF DATA USING A BOX-AND-WHISKER PLOT

A box-and-whisker plot can be used to compare two sets of data. Plot each set of data in a box-and-whisker plot, and draw both plots above or below one number line to make the comparison easier.

Example

Two sets of data were plotted on a double box-and-whisker plot, as shown.

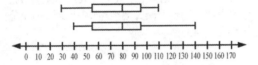

What values are the same between the two sets of data? What values are different?

Solution

From the double box-and-whisker plot, it can be seen that each box is the same size and shape, and each box is at exactly the same place along the number line. This means that each set of data has the same median (which is 80), lower quartile (which is 55), and upper quartile (which is 95).

The whiskers of each plot are different lengths. This means that the least value and the greatest value of each set of data are different.

7.SP.4 Use measures of center and measures of variability for numerical data from random samples to draw informal comparative inferences about two populations.

CALCULATING MEAN

When given a set of data, statistical analysis can be performed to determine important information from the data. The mean, median, and mode are three measures of central tendency for a set of data. A set of data is an unordered collection of values. The set is usually within curly brackets { }.

The mean is often referred to as the average of a set of data.

To calculate the mean of a set of numbers, follow these steps:

1. Find the sum of the values.
2. Divide the sum of the values by the number of values.

Example

{12, 10, 14, 8, 16}

Calculate the mean of the given data set.

Solution

Step 1
Find the sum of the values.
12 + 10 + 14 + 8 + 16 = 60

Step 2
Divide the sum of the values by the number of values.
There are five values, so divide the sum by 5.
60 ÷ 5 = 12
The mean of the data set is 12.

CALCULATING MEDIAN

When given a set of data, statistical analysis can be performed to determine important information from the data. Central tendency is the tendency of data to merge around certain points near the middle of a set of data. The mean, median, and mode are three measures of central tendency for a set of data. A set of data is an unordered collection of values. The set is usually within curly brackets { }.

The median is the middle value in a set of data when the data is arranged in ascending order. It divides the data so that 50% of the data is above the median and 50% is below the median.

There are two possible results for median:

- Odd number of values—the number located exactly in the middle.
- Even number of values—the average of the two middle numbers.

To determine the median of a set of numbers, follow these steps:

1. Place the values in order from least to greatest.
2. Determine the middle number(s).

Example

{14, 18, 16, 12, 13, 17, 15}

Determine the median of the given data set.

Solution

Step 1
Place the values in order from least to greatest.
12, 13, 14, 15, 16, 17, 18

Step 2
Determine the middle number.
There is an odd number of values, so only one number is in the middle.
12, 13, 14, **15**, 16, 17, 18
The median is 15.

Example

{20, 12, 16, 26, 15, 24}

Determine the median of the given data set.

Solution

Step 1
Place the values in order from least to greatest.
12, 15, 16, 20, 24, 26

Step 2
Determine the middle numbers.
There is an even number of values.

12 15 | 16 20 | 24 26

Calculate the average of the two middle numbers.
16 + 20 = 36
36 ÷ 2 = 18
The median is 18.

Calculating Mode

When given a set of data, statistical analysis can be performed to determine important information from the data. **Central tendency** is the tendency of data to merge around certain points near the middle of a set of data. The mean, median, and mode are three measures of central tendency for a set of data. A set of data is an unordered collection of values. The set is usually within curly brackets { }.

The mode of a set of data is the value in the set that occurs most often.

There are three possible results for mode:

- One mode—one number occurs more often than the other numbers.
- More than one mode—more than one number occurs the same number of times.
- No mode—all the numbers occur the same number of times.

To determine the mode of a set of numbers, follow these steps:

1. Place the values in order from least to greatest.
2. Determine which numbers occur most often, if any.

Example

{4, 9, 12, 7, 9, 2, 12, 8, 9, 4, 11, 3}

Determine the mode of the data set.

Solution

Step 1
Place the values in order from least to greatest.
2, 3, 4, 4, 7, 8, 9, 9, 9, 11, 12, 12

Step 2
Determine which numbers occur most frequently.
The numbers 4 and 12 occur twice and 9 occurs three times. The rest of the numbers occur once.
The mode is 9 because it occurs more often than any other number.

Example
{7, 3, 4, 8, 5, 4, 6, 3}
Determine the mode of the data set.

Solution
Step 1
Place the values in order from least to greatest.
3, 3, 4, 4, 5, 6, 7, and 8
Step 2
Determine which numbers occur most often.
The 3 and 4 occur twice, and the other numbers occur once.
The modes are 3 and 4.

Example
{5, 4, 2, 8, 6, 9, 7, 0}
Determine the mode of the data set.

Solution
Step 1
Place the values in order from least to greatest.
0, 2, 4, 5, 6, 7, 8, and 9
Step 2
Determine which numbers occur most often, if any.
Each number occurs once in the data set.
Since no number occurs more than any of the others, there is no mode.

CALCULATING RANGE

Data is organized in increasing order to calculate range. **Range** is the difference between the highest and lowest values that make up the data set. A **data set** is an unordered collection of values. The set is usually within curly brackets { }.

To find the range of a set of data, follow these steps:

1. Place the values in order from the least to the greatest.
2. Subtract the least value from the greatest value.

Example
{18, 32, 12, 45, 23, 54, 33, 31, 35, 45, 30, 21}.
Calculate the range of the data set using the highest and lowest values.

Solution
Step 1
Place the numbers in order from least to greatest.
12, 18, 21, 23, 30, 31, 32, 33, 35, 45, 45, 54
Step 2
Subtract the lowest value from the highest value in the set.
The lowest value is 12, and the highest value is 54.
Range = highest value – lowest value
= 54 – 12
= 42
The range is 42.

COMPARE TWO RELATED SETS OF DATA

Two related sets of data can be presented together in tally charts, stem-and-leaf plots, double-bar graphs, and broken-line graphs. When the two sets of data are presented side by side, it is easier to see their similarities and differences.

Example

The date in the given double-bar graph compares the number of students who drank white milk and the number of students who drank chocolate milk over a three-month period. When the two sets of data are presented in this way, it is easy to compare them. For example, you can see at a glance that for the month of May, four times more students drank white milk than chocolate milk.

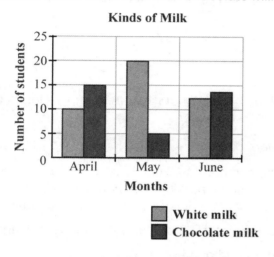

Kinds of Milk

Months

■ **White milk**
■ **Chocolate milk**

Two related sets of data can be compared by using the **shape** of each set of data.

Example

Both data sets begin and end at a mid range (10 to 15). For white milk, the data set is at the highest point (20) for the month of May, but for chocolate milk, the data set is at its lowest point (5) for the month of May.

You can compare two sets of related data by comparing their **means**, **medians**, and **modes**. The given chart provides a quick review of the difference between a mean, a median, and a mode.

Mean	An average of the values; the sum of all the values divided by the number of values
Median	The middle number of an ordered group of values
Mode	The value that occurs the most often

Example

Gary used a chart to record the number of points that he and his friend David scored in nine consecutive basketball games.

	Game								
	1	2	3	4	5	6	7	8	9
Gary	8	9	5	2	10	7	5	7	1
David	7	4	8	5	1	3	9	6	2

Calculate and compare the mean number of points for each boy. Explain your answer.

Solution

Example explanation:

First, I calculated the means for each set of data. I did this by finding the sum of the values and then dividing the sum by the number of values.

Gary:
8 + 9 + 5 + 2 + 10 + 7 + 5 + 7 + 1 = 54
54 ÷ 9 = 6

David:
7 + 4 + 8 + 5 + 1 + 3 + 9 + 6 + 2 = 45
45 ÷ 9 = 5

Gary has a mean of 6, which means that he scored an average of 6 points per game. David has a mean of 5, which is lower than Gary's mean, but is close to it. Gary scored an average of 5 points per game.

7.SP.5 Understand that the probability of a chance event is a number between 0 and 1 that expresses the likelihood of the event occurring. Larger numbers indicate greater likelihood. A probability near 0 indicates an unlikely event, a probability around 1/2 indicates an event that is neither unlikely nor likely, and a probability near 1 indicates a likely event.

UNDERSTANDING PROBABILITY AS A NUMBER BETWEEN 0 AND 1

Probability is a measure of how likely it is that an event will occur. Probability can be expressed using words or numbers.

- A probability of 1 means that an event is certain to happen. The probability that the sun will rise in the morning is 1.
- A probability of 0 means that an event is impossible. The probability that a dog will have kittens is 0.
- A probability of $\frac{1}{2}$ means that an event has an equal chance of happening or not happening. The probability that you flip a coin and it will land on heads is $\frac{1}{2}$.

The following diagram shows how the words used to describe probabilities are connected to the numbers.

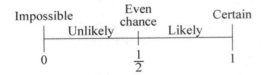

Probabilities can be written as any number between 0 and 1. The more likely it is that an event will happen, the closer the probability is to 1. For example, if a meteorologist says that there is a good chance it will rain tomorrow, the probability is close to 1. However, it is not certain that it will rain, so the probability is not exactly 1.

Example

Hazel has a spinner with 6 sections on it. She spins the arrow, and it lands on a number.

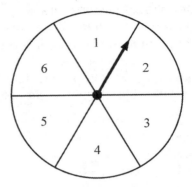

What is the probability that the arrow lands on an odd number?

Solution

The spinner has 3 sections with odd numbers and 3 sections with even numbers. There is an even chance of landing on an odd number.

Therefore, the probability that the arrow lands on an odd number is $\frac{1}{2}$.

What is the probability that the arrow lands on 8?

Solution

The number 8 does not appear on the spinner, so landing on it is impossible.

Therefore, the probability that the arrow lands on 8 is 0.

Estimate the probability that the arrow lands on a number less than 5.

Solution

The numbers on the spinner less than 5 include 1, 2, 3, and 4. This is more than half of the spinner, but it is not all of it. Therefore, the event is likely to happen.

The probability that the arrow lands on a number less than 5 is between $\frac{1}{2}$ and 1.

Approximate the probability of a chance event by collecting data on the chance process that produces it and observing its long–run relative frequency, and predict the approximate relative frequency given the probability.

EXPERIMENTAL PROBABILITY

Experimental probability is determined by actually conducting an experiment. The results of the experiment are the experimental probability. Experimental probability is used to predict the results of future experiments. For example, when a coin is tossed, it is equally likely to obtain either heads or tails. The theoretical probability of obtaining heads is $\frac{1}{2}$. When the experiment is actually performed, heads might be obtained 3 times out of 4. The experimental probability of obtaining heads is $\frac{3}{4}$. As the number of coin tosses increases, the experimental probability will get closer and closer to the theoretical probability.

To determine experimental probability, follow these steps:

1. Record the results in a table of values.
2. Determine the number of favorable outcomes.
3. Determine the total possible outcomes.
4. Calculate the experimental probability of the desired event using the probability formula. Reduce if possible.

Example

A die was rolled 25 times, and the outcomes were recorded in the table shown.

Number rolled	1	2	3	4	5	6
Number of times rolled	4	5	6	2	4	4

Based on the data, what is the experimental probability of rolling a 3?

Solution

Step 1
Determine the number of favorable outcomes.
The favorable outcomes of rolling a 3 occurred 6 times in the experiment.

Step 2
Determine the total possible outcomes.
The number of times the experiment is conducted is the total possible outcomes. The total number of times the die was rolled was 25 ($4 + 5 + 6 + 2 + 4 + 4 = 25$).

Step 3
Calculate the experimental probability of the desired event.
Substitute the values into the probability formula. Reduce if possible.

$$P_{(\text{favorable outcome})} = \frac{\text{number of favorable outcomes}}{\text{total possible outcomes}}$$

$$P_{(3)} = \frac{6}{25}$$

To use experimental probability to make predictions, follow these steps:

1. Calculate the experimental probability of the desired event.
2. Calculate the prediction.

Example

A die was rolled 25 times, and the outcomes were recorded in the table shown.

Number rolled	1	2	3	4	5	6
Number of times rolled	4	5	6	2	4	4

If the same die were rolled 150 times, predict how many times a 4 will be rolled.

Solution

Step 1
Calculate the experimental probability of the desired event.
Substitute the values into the probability formula. Reduce if possible.

$$P_{(\text{favorable outcome})} = \frac{\text{number of favorable outcomes}}{\text{total possible outcomes}}$$

$$P_{(4)} = \frac{2}{25}$$

Step 2

Calculate the prediction.

Multiply the resulting probability by the number of die rolls of the predicted event.

$$\frac{2}{25} \times \frac{150}{1} = \frac{300}{25} = 12$$

When the die is rolled 150 times, the expected number of times that a 4 will be rolled is 12.

Experimental probabilities are often different than theoretical probabilities. The larger the number of trials in a probability experiment, the closer the probability will be to the theoretical probability. The results from rolling a die 1,000 times will be closer to the theoretical probability than the results from rolling a die 50 times.

A larger data set reduces the statistical significance of random results that do not fit the theoretical probability. One unusual result in 50 trials will affect the experimental probability more than one unusual result in 1,000 trials.

PREDICT THE FREQUENCY OF AN OUTCOME

You can use what you now know about theoretical probability to determine the probability of real-life events.

You must know how many possible outcomes exist and how many favorable outcomes exist in a given circumstance.

The experiment must be fair, meaning that each outcome has an equal chance of occurring.

To predict the frequency of an event in a probability experiment, you must calculate the theoretical probability of the outcome occurring once and then multiply the probability by the number of trials.

Example

The probability of tossing a coin and it landing on heads is $\frac{1}{2}$ or 0.5.

How many times will a coin land on heads in 20 tosses?

Solution

Step 1

Multiply the probability of landing on heads by the number of tosses.

20 × 0.5 = 10

Step 2

Determine the probability.

Since 20 × 0.5 = 10. The number of times you could expect heads to be the result in 20 coin tosses is 10.

Example

If a color wheel with four equal-sized areas with different colors is spun 100 times, predict how often the spinner will land on the same color.

Solution

Step 1

Determine the theoretical probability of spinning the wheel and landing on any color.

The spinner is made up of four equal sized areas that each have a different color.

The probability of spinning the wheel and landing on any color is $\frac{1}{4}$ or 0.25.

Step 2

Predict how often the spinner will land on the same color if the wheel is spun 100 times.

multiply 0.25 by 100.

0.25 × 100 = 25

The spinner will land on the same color 25 times when spun 100 times.

7.SP.7A Develop a probability model and use it to find probabilities of events. Compare probabilities from a model to observed frequencies; if the agreement is not good, explain possible sources of the discrepancy. Develop a uniform probability model by assigning equal probability to all outcomes, and use the model to determine probabilities of events.

COMPARING THEORETICAL PROBABILITY WITH EXPERIMENTAL PROBABILITY

When you conduct an experiment, you start off with a prediction, then conduct the actual experiment. Sometimes your results will match your prediction and sometimes they will not.

The same concept applies to probability experiments. When conducting a probability experiment, your predicted outcome is referred to as the theoretical probability, and your actual outcome is the experimental probability.

Theoretical probability uses a formula to determine the outcome of an event, whereas experimental probability uses the results of an actual experiment to determine the outcome of an event.

Theoretical probability is based on the reasoning that each outcome has an equal chance of occurring.

The probability formula is

$$P_{\left(\substack{favorable \\ outcome}\right)} = \frac{\text{\# of favorable outcomes}}{\text{\# of possible outcomes}}$$

This formula is used to calculate theoretical probability. The favorable outcomes are determined using logical reasoning and are placed over the total number of possible outcomes.

Example

What is the theoretical probability of tossing heads on a coin?

Solution

Substitute the known values into the probability formula and simplify.

The favorable outcome is heads, and there is only 1 head on a coin.

The total possible outcomes are tossing heads or tails, which means there are 2 total possible outcomes.

$$P_{(heads)} = \frac{\text{favorable outcomes}}{\text{total possible outcomes}}$$
$$= \frac{1}{2}$$
$$= 0.5$$

The same formula is used to express experimental probability. The favorable outcomes are the outcomes that have happened, and they are placed over the total number of times the experiment was conducted.

Example

Perform a simulation by tossing a coin 20 times and record the results of each toss.

You may get the following results: 14 heads and 6 tails.

The experimental probability of tossing heads in this simulation is as follows:

$$P_{(heads)} = \frac{\text{number of favorable outcomes}}{\text{total number of possible outcomes}}$$
$$= \frac{14}{20}$$
$$= 0.7$$

How do the results from calculating the theoretical probability compare to conducting a probability experiment?

Experimental probabilities are often different than theoretical probabilities. This is because theoretical probability is based on results that are calculated as if the variables in the experiment were perfect and there were no outside influences. When you are calculating theoretical probability, you are making a prediction, and not all the results of an experiment will match the prediction.

Example

A coin is flipped and a number cube is rolled 16 separate times. The combination of tossing heads and rolling a number greater than 4 was obtained on 4 of the 16 trials.

Determine the theoretical probability of obtaining heads and a number greater than 4, and compare this to the experimental probability of obtaining the same combination.

Solution

There are 12 possible outcomes, as shown in the following table.

Coin Toss	Number Rolled on Number Cube	Possible Outcomes
H	1	H, 1
H	2	H, 2
H	3	H, 3
H	4	H, 4
H	5	H, 5
H	6	H, 6
T	1	T, 1
T	2	T, 2
T	3	T, 3
T	4	T, 4
T	5	T, 5
T	6	T, 6

There are two favorable outcomes in the table: (H, 5) and (H, 6).

$$P(H, 5 \text{ or } 6) = \frac{2}{12}$$
$$= \frac{1}{6}$$
$$= 0.167$$
$$= 16.7\%$$

The experimental probability of obtaining the same combination is as follows:

$$\frac{4}{16} = 0.25 = 25\%$$

Therefore, the experimental probability is greater than the theoretical probability.

7.SP.8A Find probabilities of compound events using organized lists, tables, tree diagrams, and simulation. Understand that, just as with simple events, the probability of a compound event is the fraction of outcomes in the sample space for which the compound event occurs.

IDENTIFYING SAMPLE SPACE FOR TWO INDEPENDENT EVENTS

Independent events are events in which one outcome has no effect on the next outcome. An example of independent events would be the tossing of two coins. The first coin could have the outcomes of heads or tails, and the second coin could have the same two outcomes of heads or tails. The outcome of the first event has no effect on the second event.

Sample space is a data set that contains all possible outcomes of an experiment.

To identify sample space, follow these steps:

1. Identify the two events.
2. Display outcomes of each event.
3. Add up all the outcomes.

Sample space can be displayed using tables or tree diagrams.

Example

Glynn has a four-sided die and a spinner with the colors red, blue, green, and yellow on it.

Use a table to determine the sample space for the outcomes of the two independent events.

Solution

Step 1
Identify the two events.
Event 1: The result of rolling a die.
Event 2: The result of spinning the spinner.

Step 2

Display outcomes of each event.

The table headers are the objects being used in the experiment. Combine the side outcomes with the top outcomes.

		Spinner			
		Red (R)	Blue (B)	Green (G)	Yellow (Y)
Die	1	1R	1B	1G	1Y
	2	2R	2B	2G	2Y
	3	3R	3B	3G	3Y
	4	4R	4B	4G	4Y

Step 3

Add up all the outcomes.

Write each outcome only once.

The sample space according to the table is {1R, 1B, 1G, 1Y, 2R, 2B, 2G, 2Y, 3R, 3B, 3G, 3Y, 4R, 4B, 4G, 4Y}.

Example

Glynn has a four-sided die and a spinner with the colors red, blue, green, and yellow on it.

Use a tree diagram to determine the sample space for the outcomes of the two independent events.

Solution

Step 1

Identify the two events.

Event 1: The result of rolling a die.
Event 2: The result of spinning the spinner.

Step 2

Display outcomes of each event.

Start with one of the objects being used (die), and list the outcomes (1, 2, 3, 4). Draw a branch from each of these outcomes for each of the next outcomes (red, blue, green, yellow) of the second object.

Roll	Spin	Possible outcomes
1	Red	1R
	Blue	1B
	Green	1G
	Yellow	1Y
2	Red	2R
	Blue	2B
	Green	2G
	Yellow	2Y
3	Red	3R
	Blue	3B
	Green	3G
	Yellow	3Y
4	Red	4R
	Blue	4B
	Green	4G
	Yellow	4Y

Step 3

Add up all the outcomes.

Write each outcome only once.

The sample space according to the tree diagram is {1R, 1B, 1G, 1Y, 2R, 2B, 2G, 2Y, 3R, 3B, 3G, 3Y, 4R, 4B, 4G, 4Y}.

CALCULATING THE PROBABILITY OF TWO INDEPENDENT EVENTS

Independent events are events in which one outcome has no effect on the next. Consider the event of tossing two coins. The first coin toss could be either heads or tails. The second coin toss has the same two possible outcomes: heads or tails. The outcome of the first event has no effect on the outcome of the second event.

Reflection

Two events are **dependent** if the outcome of one event affects the outcome of the next event. Imagine a bag with four marbles, each with a different color: blue, red, yellow, and orange. If you pull out two marbles without replacing them, then the events are dependent. Think about the probability of pulling out a red marble on the second draw. After the first draw, there are only three marbles in the bag. If you drew a blue, yellow, or orange marble first, then the probability of drawing a red marble on the second pull is $\frac{1}{3}$.

If you drew a red marble on the first pull, the red marble would be already gone from the bag, and the probability of drawing a red marble on the second pull would be $\frac{0}{3}$, or 0.

Imagine what would happen if you replaced the marble after each draw. Then, no matter what color you pulled out the first time, you would put it back into the bag, and the probability of pulling out a red marble on the second pull would be $\frac{1}{4}$.

These events would be **independent** because the probability of the second event stays the same no matter what happens in the first event.

There are two methods that can be used to find the probability of two or more independent events occurring.

The first method involves the following steps:

1. Determine the possible outcomes for each independent event.
2. Determine the sample space.
   The **sample space** is the set of all the possible outcomes of an event. The number of different ways you can choose something from the sample space is the total number of possible outcomes.
3. Calculate the probability of the desired event.

Example

When two coins are tossed, what is the probability of obtaining two heads?

Solution

Step 1

Determine the possible outcomes for each independent event.

Each coin has a possible outcome of heads (H) or tails (T).

Step 2

Determine the sample space.

List each of the possible combinations of outcomes for the event.

A tree diagram is often useful for calculating the probability of an experiment involving independent events.

Coin 1	Coin 2	Outcomes
H	H	HH
	T	HT
T	H	HT
	T	TT

Step 3

Calculate the probability of the desired event. There are four different possible outcomes. Only one outcome has both coins being heads. Substitute the values 1 and 4 appropriately into the probability formula.

$P_{(favorable\ outcome)}$

$= \dfrac{\text{number of favorable outcomes}}{\text{total number of possible outcomes}}$

$P_{(HH)} = \dfrac{1}{4}$

The probability of obtaining two heads is $\dfrac{1}{4}$.

The second method for finding the probability of two or more independent events occurring involves the following steps:

1. Determine the probability of each separate outcome.
2. Calculate the probability of the event happening by multiplying each separate probability together.

Example

Find the probability of rolling a die and getting a 4 followed by tossing a coin and obtaining heads.

Solution

Step 1

Determine the probability of each separate outcome.

The probability of rolling a 4 is $P_{(4)} = \dfrac{1}{6}$.

The probability of obtaining heads is

$P_{(heads)} = \dfrac{1}{2}$.

Step 2

Calculate the probability of the desired event. Multiply the separate probabilities together.

$P_{(AB)} = P_A \times P_B$

$P_{(4,\ heads)} = \dfrac{1}{6} \times \dfrac{1}{2}$

$= \dfrac{1}{12}$

The probability of rolling a 4 and obtaining heads is $\dfrac{1}{12}$.

7.SP.8C Find probabilities of compound events using organized lists, tables, tree diagrams, and simulation. Design and use a simulation to generate frequencies for compound events.

USING DIFFERENT MODELS TO SIMULATE AN EVENT

Real-life situations can be simulated by using models. You can use different models to represent the chance of an event occurring. These models can include coins, dice, spinners, and computer-generated data systems. It is important to select a model that has the same number of outcomes as the real-life situation.

The more times a simulation is done, the higher the chance the results will be closer to the expected probability. If a simulation representing the probability of an event is done only a few times, it is likely to be misleading.

Example

John is planning on having four children. He wants to simulate the chance of the children being male or female. He decides to use a coin to simulate the event of a baby being born because the coin has two possible outcomes: heads or tails. If the coin lands on heads, it will count as a girl, and if it lands on tails, it will count as a boy. The chance of a baby being a boy is $\frac{1}{2}$, which is equal to the chance of a coin being tails, and the chance of a baby being a girl is also $\frac{1}{2}$, which is equal to the chance of a coin being heads. He runs a simulation to find out a possible outcome for the four children. He flips a coin four times and uses a tally chart to record the outcomes.

Heads	Tails

According to the chart, the chance of a baby being a boy is $\frac{1}{4}$ and the chance of it being a girl is $\frac{3}{4}$.

From the results in the tally chart, a possible outcome is that John will have 3 girls and 1 boy.

In the above example, John only simulated the event of having four children. This is why the probability represented by this experiment is so far off the expected probability of $\frac{1}{2}$. If John had decided he wanted eight children, the results would be closer to the real-world probability.

Example

Sam has a history that for every 4 free throws he attempts during a basketball game, he makes 1.

Design and apply a simulation that could be used to determine the number of free throws Sam would make in 24 attempts.

Solution

Select a model that has the same number of outcomes as the problem.

Sam makes $\frac{1}{4}$ of his attempts. A spinner with 4 equal sides labeled 1 to 4 could be used, with section 1 shaded to represent successful free throws.

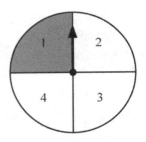

Spin the spinner 24 times, and record the data in a tally chart.

Every time the spinner lands on the number 1, it counts as a successful attempt, and every time it lands on the numbers 2 to 4, it counts as a failed attempt.

A possible outcome is shown here.

Failed Attempts	Successful Attempts

The number of successful attempts is equal to $\frac{8}{24}$, which is equivalent to $\frac{1}{3}$, $0.\overline{33}$, or $33.\overline{3}\%$.

Design and apply a simulation that could be used to determine the number of free throws Sam would make in 48 attempts.

Solution

Select a model that has the same number of outcomes as the problem.

Sam makes $\frac{1}{4}$ of his attempts. A spinner with 4 equal sides labeled 1 to 4 could be used, with section 1 shaded to represent successful free throws.

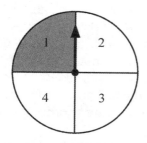

Spin the spinner 48 times, and record the data in a tally chart.

Every time the spinner lands on the number 1, it counts as a successful attempt, and every time it lands on the numbers 2 to 4, it counts as a failed attempt.

A possible outcome is shown here.

Failed Attempts	Successful Attempts
HHH HHH HHH I I HHH HHH HHH HHH	HHH HHH I

The number of successful attempts is equal to $\frac{11}{48}$, which is approximately 0.229, or 22.9 %.

From the examples above, if the simulations are done again, different results can occur. Also, the more times the spinner is spun in the experiment, the closer the probability will be to the expected probability. When the spinner was spun 24 times, it had Sam sinking 33.3% of his baskets. When it was spun 48 times, it had Sam sinking 22.9%, which is closer to the expected $\frac{1}{4}$, or 25%.

This holds true for any case. The more times a simulation representing the probability of an event is done, the higher the chance the results will be closer to the expected probability.

EXERCISE #1—STATISTICS AND PROBABILITY

Use the following information to answer the next question.

Shaylah and Trevor are conducting a survey to find out which color the students at their school would prefer on their school T-shirt. They are not sure if they should survey the whole population of the school or just a sample. They have only one week to find the answer, and they do not have much money to conduct the survey. The total population of the school is 1,500 students.

238. The **best** way for Shaylah and Trevor to determine which color to use for the school T-shirt would be to survey
   A. a sample of the population because this method would cost the greatest amount of money
   B. a sample of the population because this method would take up the least amount of time
   C. the whole population because this method would take the greatest amount of time
   D. the whole population because this method would cost the least amount of money

Use the following information to answer the next question.

A community league volunteer is in charge of ordering soccer jerseys for this year's outdoor soccer season. He wants to know what color the members of each team would prefer to wear. The colors available are black, silver, turquoise, and red. There are four divisions in the community league, and there are 28 players in each of the divisions. The volunteer decides to survey 25% of the players from each division to get their opinions. The results indicate that 75% of the players surveyed would like to wear silver jerseys. The community league volunteer decides to order the silver jerseys.

239. The sample represents the views of the population accurately because
   A. the population is too large to survey
   B. each division is being represented equally and fairly
   C. to survey the population would cost too much money
   D. each division has a biased opinion in terms of the colors of the jerseys

Use the following information to answer the next question.

Three students are arguing over what they think is the most popular food among the seventh grade students at their school. Freddy argues it is pizza, Norman thinks it is burgers, and Maria says it is ice cream. They decide to conduct a survey of the seventh grade students in order to resolve their disagreement. There are 75 students in seventh grade at their school.

240. What sample size should they use?
   A. 5 students   B. 10 students
   C. 25 students   D. 60 students

The *Student Tribune* is a school newspaper that caters to its 200 student population. The *Student Tribune* wrote an article about the school band. The newspaper asked a random sampling of 10 band students to complete a survey about how much they practice their instruments at home. The results were recorded in the following table.

Student	Hours Practiced/Week
1	9
2	5
3	11
4	15
5	8
6	5
7	0
8	12
9	3
10	2

241. Make inferences based on the data in the table.

Dean's class and Marcie's class both sold magazine subscriptions as a fund-raiser for their end-of-the-year class trip. When they finished, they drew a box-and-whisker plot to show how many subscriptions the students in each class sold. Dean and Marcie both said that their class did the best job at selling the subscriptions.

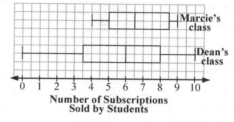

242. Which of the following arguments **cannot** be made based on the information given in the graph?
    A. Dean's class did the best because the person who sold the most subscriptions was in his class.
    B. Marcie's class did the best because everyone in the class sold at least 4 subscriptions.
    C. Marcie's class did the best because they had the highest median and quartiles.
    D. Dean's class did the best because they sold the most subscriptions.

243. Calculate the mean of the data set {125, 300, 150, 175, 50, 450, 150}.

The sets of data show the final scores for the last five games played by two basketball teams.

- Team *A*: 64, 79, 61, 86, 77
- Team *B*: 72, 89, 86, 75, 82

244. What is the difference between the median scores of the two teams?

A. 4   B. 5

C. 6   D. 7

Stem	Leaf
5	0, 0, 3, 4, 5, 5, 8
6	1, 2, 2, 4, 6, 9, 9, 9
7	0, 0, 1, 1, 3, 5, 5, 8, 9, 9

245. Which of the following statements about the mode and frequency of the data displayed in the stem and leaf plot is **true**?

A. The mode is 9, and the frequency is 3.

B. The mode is 69, and the frequency is 5.

C. The mode is 69, and the frequency is 3.

D. The mode is 79, and the frequency is 2.

246. Find the range of the data set {135, 114, 249, 187, 196}.

247. Adding the value 72 to the data set 58, 60, 61, 63, 69, 69 has the **least** effect on the

A. mean   B. mode

C. range   D. median

Andres is doing a probability experiment with some cards.

He turns the cards over, mixes them up, and draws one card.

248. The event with a probability that is closest to 1 is drawing a card with

A. the number 2

B. the number 8

C. an odd number

D. a two-digit number

249. Which of the following statements does **not** provide an example of theoretical probability?

A. The probability of a coin landing on heads after 50 tosses is $\frac{28}{50}$.

B. The probability of rolling the number 2 on a six-sided number cube is $\frac{1}{6}$.

C. The probability of getting 2 tails when two coins are tossed at the same time is $\frac{1}{4}$.

D. The probability of picking the number 6 card in a stack of cards numbered 1–10 is $\frac{1}{10}$.

Use the following information to answer the next question.

> At an airport, the probability of a plane arriving early is $\frac{1}{15}$. The probability of a plane arriving late is $\frac{1}{10}$.

250. If 180 planes are scheduled to land at the airport on a given day, how many planes are likely to arrive early?

  A. 10   B. 12

  C. 15   D. 18

Use the following information to answer the next question.

> A tetrahedral die has four triangular sides numbered 1, 2, 3, and 4. The die was rolled 50 times, and the results were recorded in this table.

Outcome	1	2	3	4
Frequency	15	20	10	5

251. Which numbers on the tetrahedral die had an experimental probability less than the theoretical probability?

  A. 1 and 2   B. 3 and 4

  C. 1 and 3   D. 2 and 4

Use the following information to answer the next question.

> Jack and Selma play a game in which a coin is tossed and a six-sided number cube is rolled. The player who gets a tail on the coin and a four on the number cube is the winner.

252. How many outcomes are there in Jack and Selma's game?

  A. 6   B. 8

  C. 12   D. 24

Use the following information to answer the next question.

> Arthur draws a card from a 52-card deck. He replaces it and then draws a second card.

253. What is the probability that Arthur draws first a king and then an even number?

  A. $\frac{1}{13}$ B. $\frac{5}{13}$

  C. $\frac{5}{169}$ D. $\frac{80}{52}$

Use the following information to answer the next question.

The given tally chart shows the results from a model that was used to simulate an event in a probability experiment.

Success	Failure
ЖН ЖН I	ЖН ЖН ЖН ЖН ЖН ЖН ЖН I I I I

Four possible events are described as follows:

1. The number of times a traffic light is green when a motorist approaches it, given that 50 different approaches are made and the light is green for 80 s, red for 80 s, and yellow for 10 s
2. The number of times a red card is drawn from a standard deck of 52 cards, given that a card is randomly drawn from the deck 50 times and put back each time
3. The number of times a particular basketball player will make a three-point shot in his next 50 attempts, given that he has a history of making 1 out of every 5 three-point attempts
4. The number of times an airplane from a particular airline arrives on-time at a city's airport in the next 50 arrivals from that airline, given that 80 % of the airline's airplanes arrive on time at this airport

For event 1, a success is defined as the light showing green and a failure is defined as the light showing yellow or red. For event 2, a success is defined as drawing a red card (heart or diamond) and a failure is defined as drawing a black card (spade or club). For event 3, a success is defined by making a three-point shot and a failure is defined as not making a three-point shot. For event 4, a success is defined as an on-time arrival and a failure is defined as an arrival that was not on time.

254. The tally chart **most likely** shows the success rate and failure rate of which of the given events?

A. 1   B. 2

C. 3   D. 4

EXERCISE #1—STATISTICS AND PROBABILITY ANSWERS AND SOLUTIONS

238. B	243. See solution	248. D	253. C
239. B	244. B	249. A	254. C
240. C	245. C	250. B	
241. See solution	246. See solution	251. B	
242. D	247. B	252. C	

238. B

Since the color chosen will be for a school T-shirt, all the students in the school should be considered. However, since the population of the school is large, it would take a lot of time and money to survey every student. It would be more practical and efficient to survey a sample population. If the sample population represents all grade levels equally, it should be a fair representation of the total school population.

Shaylah and Trevor should survey a sample of the population because this method would take the least amount of time and money.

239. B

The community league volunteer used players from each of the divisions for the survey. All players are being represented fairly, with 25% of the players in each division being asked to participate in the survey. This sample represents the views of the population accurately because each division is being represented equally and fairly.

240. C

A sample size of 25 students would be reasonable because it divides into 75 evenly and represents 33% of the student population. The smaller sample sizes of 5 and 10 students would be too small to represent the population. Using a sample size of 60 would be too large and would be very close to surveying the entire population. Surveying a sample of that size would take a lot of time.

241.

You can see by looking at the table, that 3 out of 10, or 30% of students practice more than 10 hours a week.

You can then infer that the remaining 70% of students practice less than 10 hours a week.

There is only one student who does not practice at all during the week, so you can infer that the majority of students do practice their instruments at home for some amount of time.

242. D

The graph does not show how many subscriptions were sold in total. The information is based on the median and quartile values of the data and does not show, for example, how many people were in each class. There is no way of knowing how many subscriptions were sold based on the graphs.

It is true that everyone in Marcie's class sold at least 4 subscriptions. The lowest value for Marcie's class is 4.

It is true that Marcie's class had the higher median and quartiles. The median for Marcie's class is 6.5 compared to Dean's class of 6. The lower quartile for Marcie's class is 5 compared to 3.5 for Dean's class. Finally, the upper quartile for Marcie's class is 8.5 compared to Dean's class with a value of 8.

It is true that the person who sold the most subscriptions was in Dean's class. The highest value for Dean's class is 10 compared with 9 for Marcie's class.

243.

Step 1
The mean of a set of data is defined as the ratio of the sum of the values to the number of values in the data set (in other words, taking the average of the data set).
Determine the sum of the given values.
$$\left(\begin{matrix} 125 + 300 + 150 + 175 \\ +50 + 450 + 150 \end{matrix}\right) = 1,400$$
Step 2
Divide the total sum by the number of values.
Since there are 7 values, divide by 7.
1,400 ÷ 7 = 200
Therefore, the mean of the data set is 200.

244. B

Step 1

Reorder the scores for the two teams from lowest score to highest score.

- Team *A*: 61, 64, 77, 79, 86
- Team *B*: 72, 75, 82, 86, 89

Step 2

Find the median.

The median of a data set is the value in the middle.

Since there is an odd number of scores (5), the value in the middle will be the third number in the list, with two lower scores to the left and two higher scores to the right.

- Team *A*: 61, 64, **77**, 79, 86
- Team *B*: 72, 75, **82**, 86, 89

The median score for team *A* is 77, and the median score for team *B* is 82.

Step 3

Find the difference.

Find the difference between the two medians by subtracting 77 from 82.

82 − 77 = 5

The difference between the median scores of the two teams is 5.

245. C

Step 1

Identify the mode.

The mode is the number that appears the most often.

Look at the numbers in the leaves. The number 9 in stem 6 appears three times, which is more than any other leaf.

The three 9s in stem 6 represent the number 69 three times.

The mode of the given set of data is 69.

Step 2

Identify the frequency.

The frequency is the number of times that the mode appears.

The number 69 appears three times. Therefore, the frequency of the mode (69) is 3.

The data displayed in the given stem and leaf plot has a mode of 69 and a frequency of 3.

246.

Step 1

Place the numbers in order from the lowest to the highest.

114, 135, 187, 196, 249

Step 2

Subtract the lowest value from the greatest value.

249 − 114 = 135

The range is 135.

247. B

Step 1

Calculate the mean, mode, median and range of the data set without the 72:

- The mean is about 63.3.
- The mode is 69.
- The median is 62.
- The range is 11.

Step 2

Calculate the mean, mode, median, and range of the data set with the 72:

- The mean is about 64.5.
- The mode is 69.
- The median is 63.
- The range is 14.

Step 3

Find which value changed the least.

The mode is 69 in both data sets. Each of the other values changes by at least 1. Adding 72 to the data set has the least effect on the mode.

248. D

The event with a probability that is closest to 1 is the event that is most likely. To find out which event is most likely, count how many chances Andres has to draw each kind of card:

- The cards 28, 20, 22, 12, and 12 all have the number 2. There are 5 chances of drawing a card with the number 2.
- The cards 28, 8, 8, and 18 all have the number 8. There are 4 chances of drawing a card with the number 8.
- There are no cards with odd numbers. There is 0 chance of drawing a card with an odd number.
- The cards 28, 20, 22, 18, 12, and 12 all have two-digit numbers. There are 6 chances of drawing a card with a two-digit number.

Andres is most likely to draw a card with a two-digit number. Drawing a card with a two-digit number has a probability that is closest to 1.

249. A

Step 1
Recall the definition of experimental and theoretical probability.

Experimental probability is determined by actually conducting an experiment. The results of the experiment are the experimental probability. Experimental probability is used to predict the results of future experiments.

Theoretical probability is the probability (or chance) of an outcome occurring under ideal circumstances. Theoretical probability is determined by dividing the number of favorable outcomes by the total number of possible outcomes.

Step 2
Determine whether each alternative is an example of theoretical probability.

The theoretical probability of rolling the number 2 on a six-sided number cube is 1 out of 6, or $\frac{1}{6}$.

The theoretical probability of a coin landing on heads is 1 out of 2, $\frac{1}{2}$, or $\frac{25}{50}$ for fifty tosses. Therefore, the statement that the probability of a coin landing on heads after 50 tosses is $\frac{28}{50}$ is not an example of theoretical probability.

The theoretical probability of picking the number 6 card from a stack of 10 cards is 1 out of 10, or $\frac{1}{10}$.

The possible outcomes for 2 coins are HH, HT, TH, TT. The theoretical probability of 2 coins landing tails is $\frac{1}{4}$.

250. B

Step 1
Determine the theoretical probability of the favorable outcome.

The favorable outcome is the plane arriving early.

There is a $\frac{1}{15}$ chance of a favorable outcome.

Step 2
Calculate the prediction.

Take the probability, and multiply it by 180.

$$180 \times \frac{1}{15} = 12$$

If 180 planes are scheduled to land, then 12 planes are likely to arrive early.

251. B

Step 1
Determine the theoretical probability.

The number of favorable outcomes for each number is 1, as each number occurs once.

There are 4 possible outcomes, since the numbers on the die are 1, 2, 3, and 4.

$$P(\text{theoretical}) = \frac{\text{favorable outcomes}}{\text{possible outcomes}}$$
$$= \frac{1}{4}$$
$$= 0.25$$

Step 2
Determine the experimental probability for each number on the tetrahedral die using the results recorded in the table for the 50 rolls.

Determine the experimental probability of rolling a 1.

- Number of favorable outcomes: 15
- Total possible outcomes: 50

$$P(\text{experimental 1}) = \frac{15}{50}$$
$$= \frac{3}{10}$$
$$= 0.30$$

Step 3
Determine the experimental probability of rolling a 2.

- Number of favorable outcomes: 20
- Total possible outcomes: 50

$$P(\text{experimental 2}) = \frac{20}{50}$$
$$= \frac{2}{5}$$
$$= 0.40$$

Step 4
Determine the experimental probability of rolling a 3.

- Number of favorable outcomes: 10
- Total possible outcomes: 50

$$P(\text{experimental 3}) = \frac{10}{50}$$
$$= \frac{1}{5}$$
$$= 0.20$$

Copyright Protected

Step 5
Determine the experimental probability of rolling a 4.

- Number of favorable outcomes: 5
- Total possible outcomes: 50

$$P(\text{experimental } 4) = \frac{5}{50}$$
$$= \frac{1}{10}$$
$$= 0.10$$

Step 6
Compare the theoretical probability with the experimental probabilities.
The theoretical probability for each number is 0.25.
The experimental probability of 3 and 4 is less than the theoretical probability of 0.25.

252. C

Tossing a coin has two outcomes: head and tails. Rolling a number cube has six outcomes: 1, 2, 3, 4, 5, and 6. You can use a tree diagram or a table to find out how many different outcomes there are.

Using a tree diagram:

There are 12 outcomes for flipping a coin and rolling a six-sided number cube.

- Make a tree with the outcomes for flipping a coin on the left side. Make a branch for each of the outcomes for rolling a number cube.

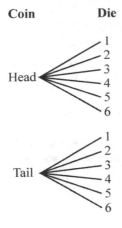

- Write all of the outcomes on the right side of the tree. The letter H means *heads* and the letter T means *tails*.

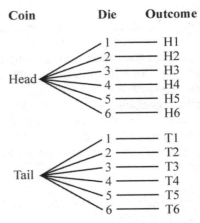

- There are 12 outcomes for flipping a coin and rolling a six-sided number cube.

Making a table:

- Write the outcomes for flipping a coin on the left side of the table and the outcomes for rolling a number cube across the top. There are 12 outcomes for flipping a coin and rolling a six-sided number cube.

		Die					
		1	2	3	4	5	6
Coin	H						
	T						

- Combine the outcomes from the top and side to fill in the table. The letter H means *heads* and the letter T means *tails*. There are 12 outcomes for flipping a coin and rolling a six-sided number cube.

		Die					
		1	2	3	4	5	6
Coin	H	1H	2H	3H	4H	5H	6H
	T	1T	2T	3T	4T	5T	6T

- There are 12 outcomes for flipping a coin and rolling a six-sided number cube.

Exercise #1 Answers and Solutions   284   Castle Rock Research

253. C

Since the first card is replaced before drawing the second card, the two events are independent.

Step 1
Determine the possible outcomes for each event.

The probability of drawing a king is $P_{(king)} = \dfrac{4}{52}$.

The even numbered cards are 2, 4, 6, 8, and 10. There are four suits, so there is a total of $5 \times 4 = 20$ even cards in the deck. The probability of drawing a card with an even number is $P_{(even)} = \dfrac{20}{52}$.

Step 2
Calculate the probability of the desired event. Multiply the separate probabilities together.

$$\begin{aligned} P_{(AB)} &= P_A \times P_B \\ &= P_{(king)} \times P_{(even)} \\ &= \frac{4}{52} \times \frac{20}{52} \\ &= \frac{1}{13} \times \frac{5}{13} \\ &= \frac{5}{169} \end{aligned}$$

The probability of drawing first a king and then a card with an even number is $\dfrac{5}{169}$.

254. C

According to the tally chart, a total of 50 tally marks are shown, of which 11 are in the success column. It follows that the event being simulated should have about a 20 % chance of occurring (11 out of 50 is a 22 % success rate). Event 3 is the only one that would be successful 20 % of the time.

Event 1 would be successful approximately 47% of the time (80 out of 170). Event 2 would be successful 50% of the time (1 out of 2). Event 4 would be successful 80% of the time (40 out of 50).

EXERCISE #2—STATISTICS AND PROBABILITY

Use the following information to answer the next question.

Rita and Miguel want to start a lawn-mowing business to help out the many senior citizens living in their neighborhood. Before they start, they want to know how many senior citizens would be interested in having their lawns mowed. Rita and Miguel are not sure if they should survey the entire population or just a sample to collect this data.

255. Rita and Miguel should survey the
  A. population because it would cost the least amount of money
  B. population because it would provide the most accurate data
  C. sample because it would provide the most accurate data
  D. sample because it would take a greater amount of time

Use the following information to answer the next question.

There are five radio stations in a city with a population of 60,000. Peter was hired to determine the approximate number of listeners each station had. He decides to survey a portion of the total population that would accurately represent the listening habits of the entire population.

256. If Peter surveys 20 listeners, would his data lead to accurate conclusions?
  A. Yes, because the sample size is proportionate to the population.
  B. Yes, because the sample represents the views of the population.
  C. No, because the sample size is not proportionate to the population.
  D. No, because the sample does not represent the views of the population.

Use the following information to answer the next question.

A survey is being conducted to test people's reactions to a new smoothie store that is being put in the mall food court. People are offered a taste of a selection of smoothies. Then, they are asked to fill out a short questionnaire about the sample beverage and the location of the new store in the food court.

257. Which of the following groups of people would **most likely** represent the population targeted by the survey?
  A. Employees of the other food vendors
  B. People in the health food store
  C. People in the food court
  D. Shoppers on the street

Use the following information to answer the next question.

The number of points scored by each team was recorded following every football game between two rival schools. After 10 years, the median score for each team was the same. A box-and-whisker plot was drawn in order to look at the data more closely.

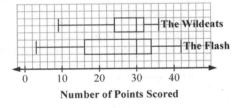

Number of Points Scored

258. Based on the box-and-whisker plot, which of the following statements is **true**?
  A. The Wildcats' highest score was 8 points higher than the Flash's highest score.
  B. The Flash's lowest score was 7 points higher than the Wildcats' lowest score.
  C. The Flash's lower quartile is 8 points higher than the Wildcats' lower quartile.
  D. The Flash's upper quartile is 2 points higher than the Wildcats' upper quartile.

259. Calculate the mean of the data set {6, 13, 40, 23, 35, 27, 31}.

Use the following information to answer the next question.

The weights of 5 apples are recorded in the table.	
	230 g
	170 g
	190 g
	220 g
	190 g

260. What is the median for the weights of the apples?

   A. 170 g   **B.** 190 g

   C. 220 g   **D.** 230 g

Use the following information to answer the next question.

This table shows the frequency of values used in a set of data.

Value	Frequency
2	4
8	3
5	1
3	1
6	1

261. The mode of the data in the given table is

   A. 1   **B.** 2

   C. 4   **D.** 8

Use the following information to answer the next question.

A data set is given.
   { 76, 45, 63, 91, 87, 73, 78, 81}

262. Calculate the range of the data set.

Use the following information to answer the next question.

Two sets of data are shown.

Set A: 17, 25, 13, 23, 29, 32, 15, 33

Set B: 31, 32, 16, 21, 22, 16, 26, 33

263. Which of the following statements **best** compares the median of set A to the median of set B?

   A. Median A is 2 less than median B.

   B. Median A is the same as median B.

   C. Median A is 2 greater than median B.

   D. Median A is 4 greater than median B.

Use the following information to answer the next question.

Eva is doing a probability experiment with a six-sided number cube.

264. The probability that the cube will land on a 4 is

A. 0

B. 1

C. closer to 0 than 1

D. closer to 1 than 0

Use the following information to answer the next question.

In an experiment, a number cube was rolled 120 times. The results are recorded in this table.

Outcome	1	2	3	4	5	6
Frequency	12	18	25	20	25	20

265. What is the probability of rolling a 5?

Use the following information to answer the next question.

A bag contains 7 green balls, 1 purple ball, 11 yellow balls, 5 red balls, and 10 white balls.

Mali picked a ball out of the bag without looking, recorded the color, and returned the ball to the bag.

She did this 20 times.

266. Which of the following tallies represents the **most likely** number of times that Mali picked a red ball?

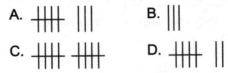

A. ||||| ||| B. |||

C. ||||| ||||| D. ||||| ||

Use the following information to answer the next question.

A spinner is divided into six equal parts. Two parts of the spinner are red, two parts are green, and two parts are blue, as shown in the diagram. The spinner is spun 30 times, and it stops on red 12 times.

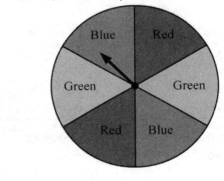

267. Based on the results of the 30 spins and 12 stops on red, the

A. experimental probability is less than the theoretical probability

B. theoretical probability is greater than the experimental probability

C. theoretical probability is the same as the experimental probability

D. experimental probability is greater than the theoretical probability

Use the following information to answer the next question.

Shea and Dana are planning a probability experiment with the spinner shown and a four-sided number cube.

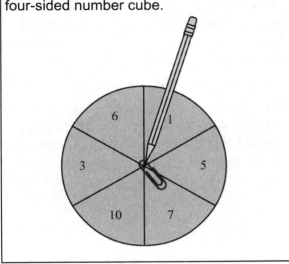

268. Which of the following tables could be used to show the possible outcomes?

A.

	1	2	3	4
1				
2				
3				
4				
5				
6				

B.

	1	5	7	10
1				
2				
3				
4				
5				
6				

C.

	1	2	3	4
1				
3				
5				
6				
7				
10				

D.

	1	5	7	10
1				
3				
5				
6				
7				
10				

269. When three coins are tossed, what is the probability of obtaining three heads?

Use the following information to answer the next question.

Four models are available to simulate a particular event:

1. Flipping a coin, and recording the respective number of times a head is obtained and a tail is obtained
2. Rolling a six-sided die, and recording the respective number of times the die shows a 1, 2, 3, 4, 5, or 6
3. Spinning a spinner with four equal sides labeled 1 to 4, and recording the respective number of times the spinner lands on a 1, 2, 3, or 4
4. Drawing a card from a standard deck of 52 cards, putting it back, and recording the respective number of times a red card is drawn and a black card is drawn

Based on past experience, a particular hockey player scores a goal 25% of the time he is involved in a shootout to decide the winner of a hockey game.

270. Which of the four given models would **best** simulate the number of times the hockey player will be successful in his next 32 attempts at scoring a goal in a shootout?

   A. 1   B. 2

   C. 3   D. 4

EXERCISE #2—STATISTICS AND PROBABILITY ANSWERS AND SOLUTIONS

255. B	259. See solution	263. B	267. D
256. C	260. B	264. C	268. C
257. C	261. B	265. See solution	269. See solution
258. C	262. See solution	266. B	270. C

255. B

If Rita and Miguel want to find out how many senior citizens would be interested in having their lawns mowed, they have to ask every senior citizen in their neighborhood. Finding out which houses belong to a senior citizen and which houses do not would take a lot of time and research. The way to gather the most accurate data for their neighborhood business is to survey the entire population of the neighborhood. Upon doing this, they may discover people other than senior citizens who would be interested in using their lawn-mowing services.

256. C

In a sample, only some people in the population are surveyed. Since Peter surveys only 20 listeners out of the population of 60,000, this group of people is referred to as a sample. The main reasons for using a sample is that time and money can be saved when conducting the survey. A sample is meant to represent the views of the entire population.

In this case, if 20 listeners are surveyed from 60,000, the sample represents only $\frac{20}{60,000} \times 100 = 0.03\%$ of the population of listeners. This percentage is far too low and will not be representative of the listening habits of the entire population.

Therefore, the results will not lead to accurate conclusions.

257. C

When you target a group of people to participate in a particular survey, you are trying to match the group of people questioned to the type of information you are trying to collect.

Since the new smoothie store will be put in the mall food court, the data about the smoothies and the location of the new store will probably be most meaningful if it is collected from people who use that particular food court and shop at that particular mall.

258. C

Evaluate each of the statements.

- The most points the Wildcats scored was 42, and the most the Flash scored was 36. The difference between the highest scores of the two teams is 6 points, not 8.
- The fewest points the Wildcats scored was 3, and the fewest the Flash scored was 9. The Flash's lowest score was 6 points higher than the Wildcats', not 7.
- The Wildcats' lower quartile is 16, and the Flash's lower quartile is 24. This is a difference of 8.
- The Wildcats's upper quartile is 34, and the Flash's upper quartile is 32. This is a difference of 2, but the Flash's upper quartile was lower than the Wildcats'.

The correct statement is "The Flash's lower quartile is 8 points higher than the Wildcats' lower quartile."

259.

Step 1
The mean of a set of data is defined as the ratio of the sum of the values to the number of values in the data set.
Determine the sum of the given values.
6 + 13 + 40 + 23 + 35+27 + 31 = 175

Step 2
Divide the total sum by the number of values.
Since there are 7 values, divide by 7.
175 ÷ 7 = 25
Therefore, the mean of the data set is 25.

260. B

Step 1
Place the values in order from least to greatest.
170, 190, 190, 220, 230

Step 2
Determine the middle number.
There is an odd number of values, so only one number is in the middle.
170, 190, 190, 220, 230
The median weight of the apples is 190 g.

261. B

The mode is the value that occurs most often.

The number in the frequency column of the table tells how many times the particular value appears in the set of data.

Since 4 is the number with the greatest value in the frequency column (4 > 3 > 1), that means the number value of 2 is used four times, which is more than any other number in this set of data.

Therefore, the mode of the data in the given table is 2.

262.

Step 1
Place the numbers in order from least to greatest.
45, 63, 73, 76, 78, 81, 87, 91

Step 2
Subtract the lowest value from the highest value in the set.

The lowest value is 45, and the highest value is 91.
91 − 45 = 46

The range is 46.

263. B

Choice B is correct. Median A is the same as median B.

To solve this problem, you first need to order the numbers in each set. Next, find the median for each set. Then, compare the two medians.

Set A: 13, 15, 17, 23, 25, 29, 32, 33

The middle numbers are 23 and 25, so the median is 24.

Set B: 16, 16, 21, 22, 26, 31, 32, 33

The middle numbers are 22 and 26, so the median is 24.

264. C

The number cube could land on a 1, 2, 3, 4, 5, or 6. It is not impossible to roll a 4, but it is not very likely.

Therefore, the probability that Eva will roll a 4 is closer to 0 than 1.

Impossible		Even chance		Certain
	Unlikely		Likely	
0		$\frac{1}{2}$		1

265.

Step 1
Determine the number of favorable outcomes.

The favorable outcome is rolling a 5, and a 5 was rolled 25 times in the experiment.

Step 2
Determine the total possible outcomes.

The number of times the experiment is conducted is the total possible outcomes: 120.

Step 3
Calculate the probability of the desired event.

Substitute the values into the probability formula. Reduce if possible.

$$P(\text{favorable outcome})$$
$$= \frac{\text{number of favorable outcomes}}{\text{total possible outcomes}}$$
$$P(5) = \frac{25}{120}$$
$$= \frac{25 \div 5}{120 \div 5}$$
$$= \frac{5}{24}$$

266. B

Of the results given, the tally representing the number 3 is the **most likely**. ||||

There are a total of 34 balls in the bag. Since there are only 5 red balls, the chance of picking a red ball is $\frac{5}{34}$.

A 3 in 20 chance is closest to the 5 in 34 chance.

267. D

Step 1
Determine the theoretical probability.

Since there are 6 parts in all, there are 6 possible outcomes.

Since there are 2 red parts, there are 2 favorable outcomes.

The theoretical probability is 2 out of 6 or $\frac{2}{6} = \frac{1}{3}$.

Step 2
Determine the experimental probability.

Since there are 30 spins in all, the number of tests is 30.

Since the spinner stops on red 12 times, the favorable outcome occurs 12 times.

The experimental probability is 12 out of 30 or $\frac{12}{30} = \frac{2}{5}$.

Step 3

Compare the two probability fractions by first making them equivalent fractions.

$\frac{1}{3} = \frac{5}{15}$ and $\frac{2}{5} = \frac{6}{15}$

The experimental probability $\left(\frac{6}{15}\right)$ is greater than the

theoretical probability $\left(\frac{5}{15}\right)$.

268. C

In a table, put the four numbers from the number cube in the row across the top and the six numbers from the spinner in the column on the left.

	1	2	3	4
1				
3				
5				
6				
7				
10				

If you want to list the outcomes, you can fill in the table. In each square, write one number from the spinner and one number from the number cube.

	1	2	3	4
1	1, 1	1, 2	1, 3	1, 4
3	3, 1	3, 2	3, 3	3, 4
5	5, 1	5, 2	5, 3	5, 4
6	6, 1	6, 2	6, 3	6, 4
7	7, 1	7, 2	7, 3	7, 4
10	10, 1	10, 2	10, 3	10, 4

269.

Step 1

Determine the possible outcomes for each independent event.

Each coin has a possible outcome of heads (H) or tails (T).

Step 2

Determine the sample space.

List each of the possible combinations of outcomes for the event.

A tree diagram is often useful for calculating the probability of an experiment involving two independent events.

Step 3

Calculate the probability of the desired event.

There are eight different possible outcomes.

Only one outcome has all three coins being heads.

Substitute the values 1 and 8 appropriately into the probability formula.

$P_{\text{(favorable outcome)}}$

$= \dfrac{\text{number of favorable outcomes}}{\text{total number of possible outcomes}}$

$P_{\text{(HHH)}} = \dfrac{1}{8}$

The probability of obtaining three heads is $\dfrac{1}{8}$.

270. C

Of the given models, the only model that could be used to simulate an event that has a 1 in 4 (25%) chance of occurring is model 3.

Theoretically, if the number 1 represents the hockey player scoring a goal in a shootout, then the spinner should stop 8 times on the 1 in 32 spins (although, in reality, the spinner may not land on the 1 exactly 8 times out of 32 spins when the experiment is conducted several times).

Model 1 or model 4 could be used to simulate the probability of an event that has a 1 in 2 (50%) chance of occurring. Model 2 could be used to simulate an event that has a 1 in $6\left(16\frac{2}{3}\%\right)$ chance of occurring.

NOTES

SOLARO Study Guides
Ordering Information

Every SOLARO Study Guide unpacks the curriculum standards and provides an overview of all curriculum concepts, practice questions with full solutions, and assignment questions for students to fully test their knowledge.

Visit www.solaro.com/orders to buy books and learn how SOLARO can offer you an even more complete studying solution.

SOLARO
Study Guide

SOLARO Study Guide—$29.95 each plus applicable sales tax

SOLARO Common Core State Standard Titles	
Mathematics 3	Algebra I
Mathematics 4	Algebra II
Mathematics 5	Geometry
Mathematics 6	English Language Arts 3
Mathematics 7	English Language Arts 4
Accelerated Mathematics 7 (Int.)	English Language Arts 5
Accelerated Mathematics 7 (Trad.)	English Language Arts 6
Mathematics 8	English Language Arts 7
Accelerated Mathematics I	English Language Arts 8
Mathematics I	English Language Arts 9
Mathematics II	English Language Arts 10
Mathematics III	English Language Arts 11
Accelerated Algebra I	English Language Arts 12

To order books, please visit
www.solaro.com/orders

Volume pricing is available. Contact us a
orderbooks@solaro.com